DIVINE REBELS

American Christian Activists for Social Justice

✝

Deena Guzder

Foreword by Shane Claiborne
Afterword by Roger S. Gottlieb

Lawrence Hill Books

Library of Congress Cataloging-in-Publication Data

Guzder, Deena.
 Divine rebels : American Christian activists for social justice / Deena Guzder ;
foreword by Shane Claiborne ; afterword by Roger S. Gottlieb.
    p. cm.
 Includes bibliographical references (p.   ) and index.
 ISBN 978-1-56976-264-6 (pbk.)
 1. Christian biography—United States. 2. Social reformers—United States—
Biography. 3. Christianity and justice—United States—History. I. Title.
 BR569.G83 2011
 261.8092'273—dc22
 [B]

                                    2010053898

Cover images from left to right: J. Zwerg © Bettmann/Corbis; D. Berrigan
    © Getty Images; S. Claiborne © Chase Snyder/The Goshen Library Record;
    R. Bourgeois courtesy of Roy Bourgeois
Interior design: Sarah Olson

© 2011 by Deena Guzder
Foreword © 2011 by Shane Claiborne
Afterword © 2011 by Roger S. Gottlieb
All rights reserved
Published by Lawrence Hill Books
An imprint of Chicago Review Press, Incorporated
814 North Franklin Street
Chicago, Illinois 60610
ISBN 978-1-56976-264-6
Printed in the United States of America
5 4 3 2 1

For Mom and Daddo

CONTENTS

FOREWORD

Shane Claiborne

I remember hearing about a study done with elderly folks. Researchers asked the seniors what they would do differently if they had a chance to do life over. The number one answer was "I would risk more."

We live in a security-obsessed culture that is held hostage by fear. Too often we come to die and find out that we have not really lived. As the old saying goes, unless you have found something worth dying for . . . you haven't lived. The pages of this book are filled with people who are alive—they have found something worth dying for, something worth going to jail for, something worth marching in the streets for. They are daredevils for love.

I grew up thinking that being a good Christian was synonymous with being a good, churchgoing, middle-class, well-behaved American. But as you take a closer look at church history, you can't miss the fact that some of the greatest saints and prophets have been holy troublemakers, instigators and agitators, prophetic pranksters and grace-filled revolu-tionaries—folks that disturb the status quo because they do not accept the world as it is but insist that another world is possible and devote their lives to seeing that world come to be . . . on earth as it is in heaven.

This book (at least the first nine chapters of it) tells the stories of some of the most beautiful holy rebels alive today. If Saint Francis is right and we preach the Gospel not just with our words, but also with our lives, then these are some good sermons.

Deena has been careful not to homogenize these stories, but to har-monize them. There is a web of subversive friendships here that invites you to join God's little conspiracy of grace spreading across the globe. Each of these chapters is about someone who has encountered suffering and injustice so deeply that it lit a fire in their bones. Their lives expose injustice, making it so uncomfortable that all of us must do something. They are provocateurs of imagination. They invite you to make your life sing, to hold the Bible in one hand and the newspaper in the other and do something beautiful for God with your life—find something worth dying for, or at least worth living for.

For some, the justice stuff is old news, but to see justice folks who love Jesus is a new idea. For others, Jesus is an old friend but connecting our faith in the God of heaven to the real stuff of earth is new. All of us are on a journey. And these folks may be a few steps further down the path of Jesus and justice . . . but they can keep us all moving. Deena doesn't argue you into stale political ideologies, old camps, and dead rhetoric— she tells stories, and it's hard to argue with the story of someone's life. Ideologies are hard things to love. In the end the Gospel revolution is not so much taught as it is caught. The "Good News" spreads best not through force but through fascination. And there is something fascinating about the lives of folks in this book—they do not just have good ideas; they also have beautiful lives. Here are some contagious lovers of God and neighbor.

One of my favorite quotes comes from the late activist Ammon Hennacy, who said: "Love without courage and wisdom is sentimentality, as with the ordinary church member. Courage without love and wisdom is foolhardiness, as with the ordinary soldier. Wisdom without love and courage is cowardice, as with the ordinary intellectual. But the one who has love, courage, and wisdom moves the world." Like Ammon and Dorothy Day and the Catholic Workers and so many others who have gone before, this little choir of holy mischief makers are seeking to live a life that is integrated and whole. And the people in the book are careful to say with Dorothy Day: "Don't call us saints; we don't want to be dismissed that easily." After all, the tendency is to celebrate heroes and martyrs who we don't have the courage to follow. But these are ordinary folks who have been set on fire with love.

Finally, one of the things I admire about the folks in this book, many of whom are dear friends, is that they are humble. Humility is in danger of extinction these days. But every wannabe radical must cling to humility like a lover. Otherwise, pride will rot away our souls. Pride is like the "yeast of the Pharisees"—it infects us like a disease. Liberal and conservative . . . self-righteousness has many different forms. Just as important as it is to be right, it is also important to be nice. To love folks who disagree with us and see our critics as our best teachers—I admire those qualities in the folks in this book. Otherwise, in fighting the beast we become the beast. So just as you learn from the courage of these stories, also learn from their humility. Many so-called rebels and revolutionaries can be pretentious, judgmental, and self-absorbed—their greatest passions and gifts become their greatest liabilities and often end in their implosion. But, as a close friend of many of the "rebels" of this book, I can say that even though they are some of the sassiest people I've ever met, they are also some of the most gentle. Part of their charm is that you don't see them coming. They remind us that if we want the revolution of Jesus, we must have the humility of Jesus . . . to come like a lamb rather than an eagle (a little imperial humor there). These "rebels" are grandmothers and promising young professionals who have been drafted into the revolution—drafted by love. They remind us that God's table is open to tax collector and zealot alike—God's revolution is big enough to set both the oppressed and the oppressors free. These folks have not always been rebels, but the Spirit of God chased them down. The love of Jesus wooed them. Injustice drafted them for a revolution. They have been set on fire by something bigger than themselves. Let their lives inspire you—not to become them, but to become you.

Shane Claiborne is an author, activist, and self-proclaimed recovering sinner. His books include Jesus for President, The Irresistible Revolution, *and a compilation of prayers called* Common Prayer. *Shane has been featured on CNN, Fox News, NPR, and in the* Wall Street Journal. *Most of all, he's a freelance troublemaker for God and is one of the divine rebels featured in this book. Visit his web site at www.thesimpleway.org.*

PREFACE

This book chronicles the extraordinary efforts of our country's radical souls, renegade angels, and divine rebels who agitate for a world free of racism, patriarchy, bigotry, retribution, ecocide, torture, poverty, and militarism.

Although this book's scope is limited to the last half century (1960–2010), it easily could be thrice its size, since there are countless stories not featured here of religiously inspired, politically progressive mass movements for social justice, ecological wisdom, and world peace. The book's geographic restriction to the United States, a country largely built on a Judeo-Christian foundation, has created inherent asymmetries in which Eastern and indigenous traditions are sidelined. I have little doubt that the theology behind any mass social movement in coming decades will reflect the diversifying religious landscape of immigrant America, providing fodder for more comprehensive books written in a similar spirit.

Though I have organized the book chronologically, readers should note there are overlaps among chapters. Newer social movements draw inspiration from older ones; activists devoted to progressive politics are often committed to multiple struggles simultaneously; and religious responses to myriad injustices cross-fertilize one another. Readers may peruse the book thematically by culling chapters that pique their interest or follow chronologically through history by reading it cover to cover.

ACKNOWLEDGMENTS

My greatest joy in finishing this book is finally having the opportunity to formally thank the people who offered their assistance throughout the laborious writing process. I must begin by thanking Three Wise Men whose advice, support, and encouragement has been more valuable than all the frankincense, myrrh, and gold in the world: Samuel G. Freedman, William Clark, and Yuval Taylor. Sam, plain and simple, this book exists because you exist; my gratitude to you is beyond Biblical proportions. William, thank you for responding favorably to a twenty-three-year-old first-time author's blind query and patiently shepherding her through the daunting publishing world. Yuval, I deeply appreciate your help editing and publishing this book.

I interviewed dozens of people over the last two years, and I am indebted to all of them, especially Jim Zwerg, Daniel Berrigan, Roy Bourgeois, John Dear, Robin Harper, Joseph Land, SueZann Bosler, Charlotte Keys, Shane Claiborne, Peter Goldberger, Karl Meyer, Molly Rush, John Schuchardt, Donna Schaper, and Carl Kabat. I also greatly benefited from correspondences with Azim Khamisa, Michael Croland, Ann Bausum, Melissa De Long, Beth Wood, Sharon Erickson Nepstad, Tom Fewel, Charlene Sinclair, Colleen Wessel-McCoy, Wayne Proudfoot, and Gadadhara Pandit Das. I am very thankful to the research librarians at Columbia University and Union Theological Seminary, as well as the congenial staff at Birch Coffee, which is the best coffeehouse in New York City.

In the world of journalism and academia, I'm deeply grateful to my mentors and muses: Dale Maharidge, Ari Goldman, Dennis Dalton, Peter Spielmann, Andrea Gurwitt, Justin Mazzola, Ling Liu, Krista Mahr, Gillian Johns, Amy Alipio, Kay Knight, Robert Amdur, Kristina Mani, and Sylvia Nasar. Thanks also to Baron Pineda and Stephen Crowley at Oberlin College for supervising my independent major in Peace and Conflict Studies, which allowed me to study social justice movements.

I must give special thanks to a precocious Columbia undergraduate, Elizabeth Kipp-Giusti, who provided brilliant feedback on the entire manuscript. I was also very fortunate to have Mitzi Steiner and Erin O'Brien help edit large chunks of this book. The Chicago Review Press staff did a phenomenal job of polishing this manuscript, and I am thankful to everyone who contributed. I am also grateful to Paul J. Patrick for his input on the cover and to Trudi Gershenov for designing the final version.

My deepest thanks to my two closest friends, who have truly multiplied every joy and divided every sorrow for as long as I've known them: Akash Nikolas and Tom Brilliant Grundy. I am also appreciative of my wider global family for providing not only intellectual, but also emotional support while I wrote this book. I regret not having the space to acknowledge everyone here, but I would like to single out Lillian Vincenza Udell, Anna Szymanski, Navrooz Irani, Laura Kwan, Ashleigh Andrews, Emily Rauhala, Rebecca Kaufman, Devon Haynie, Emily Holness, Rachel Winston, Stephanie Chang, Samina Ali, Leslie Dowell, Julia Grønnevet, Caroline Preston, Sufna Gheyara, Alicia Greene, Chisom Maduike, Jane Lee, Darshin Van Parijs, Don Duncan, Yojhanny Arce Vindas, Jennifer Lai, Farheen Malik, Kiel Telesford, James Barnard, Joanna Richards, and Veera Sidhwa. Thank you also to Roger S. Gottlieb and Robert Ellsberg for their votes of confidence.

Finally, I give not simply an acknowledgment, but all my gratitude to my parents and my sister, Karmin Guzder, for their divine gift of unconditional love.

INTRODUCTION

The Universe Bends
Toward Justice

Translate what I say in my language into your language. When I talk of God, translate, perhaps, by "nature," "evolution," what you will. If you feel in you the desire to use the qualities you have, if you think selfishness is narrow and choking, if you hunger for truth, justice, and love, you can and should go with us.

—Archbishop Dom Hélder Pessoa Câmara [1]

In January 1917, Alice Stokes Paul led mass demonstrations outside the White House demanding women's suffrage. She was imprisoned thrice in the United States and thrice in England. She responded by waging hunger strikes so severe she required hospitalization. On May 4, 1961, James Zwerg participated in Freedom Rides to the segregated South and was greeted with chants of "Kill the nigger-loving son of a bitch!" as a mob of two hundred beat the young white man nearly to death. On January 21, 1998, Roy Bourgeois was sentenced to six months in prison and fined $3,000 for illegally entering, disrupting, and attempting to close down the U.S. Army base Fort Benning, which trained notorious Latin American dictators such as Bolivia's Hugo Banzer.

The common thread connecting Paul, Zwerg, and Bourgeois is not leftist politics or anarchist leanings, but Christian convictions. Paul, a Quaker, believed all people are created with an indistinguishable "Inner

1

Light" regardless of gender. Zwerg, a minister in the United Church of Christ, regards his contribution to the civil rights movement as "an incredible religious experience" because he was doing "God's work" by protesting segregation. Bourgeois, an ordained Catholic priest, denounces America's support of dictatorships in Latin America and founded School of the Americas Watch in an effort to "live according to the justice and charity of Christ."

Divine Rebels is an examination of recent American Christian movements for social justice, an examination of faith-based radicalism far removed from the most bombastic—and often least representative—voices of the Religious Right. This is the story of divinely inspired Americans resisting colonialism, militarism, and ecocide at great personal risk. *Divine Rebels* is not a comprehensive account of the "Christian Left," but a partial chronicle of the lifelong struggles of Christian activists who stand in direct opposition to the Religious Right. By amplifying unheard voices advocating sustainable political and socioeconomic justice, *Divine Rebels* seeks to elevate the discussion of what it means—and can mean—to be Christian in twenty-first-century America.

The social justice activists profiled in this book do not pursue political power or public approval but the integrity of their own souls. They fear moral suicide over physical death and regard moral autonomy as more liberating than physical freedom. While pundits speak of the Religious Right, this book tells the underreported story of Americans who are progressive *because* they are religious. They don't see themselves as simply performing good work; they see themselves as performing *Godly* work. These activists would agree with Fannie Lou Hamer, a black civil rights leader from rural Mississippi, who said, "You can pray until you faint, but unless you get up and try to do something, God is not going to put it in your lap."[2] Although these rabble-rousers are small in number and their efficacy is best measured on the margins, they are the vanguard of American Christianity.

▪ ▪ ▪

Part of my reason for wanting to write this book is that religion has been a source of constant confusion and intense fascination in my life. What convinces a person to believe in the unknown? How does a person's faith inform her life decisions? Why is religion capable of not only breeding hatred but also fostering empathy? Why are some religious adherents fearmongers who proclaim a divine monopoly on truth while others are self-sacrificial in promoting the common good? And, if the notion of heaven and hell is true, how can "good" people ever be happy living eternally in heaven knowing that others are suffering in hell?

The daughter of Zoroastrians, I spent my childhood in a Christian boarding school in a predominantly Hindu country and grew up with very conflicted feelings toward Christianity. The missionaries I met in India preached a Gospel of a compassionate God one moment and a wrathful one the next. They claimed the same God who said "love your enemy" and "turn the other cheek" also reserved the fieriest corner of hell for nonbelievers. In fourth grade, I asked my headmistress— a buxom woman who wore her thick hair pulled back so tightly that her temples must have hurt—if God had allowed Mahatma Gandhi to enter heaven although he wasn't a Christian. When she firmly shook her head in the negative, I decided that I could never appreciate such a theology. As I grew older, I dismissed the missionaries as condescending and hypocritical, an unwanted residue of British colonialism in India. Christians, it seemed to me, wished to proselytize to darker-skinned natives in hopes of furthering their own chances of entering an illusory castle in the sky. Years later, while attending high school in the Texas Bible Belt, my image of Christians further deteriorated. I prematurely concluded that the word "Christian" was a euphemism for registered Republicans who waved flags, attended megachurches, and pontificated about a cliquish God.

On March 20, 2003, I listened to George W. Bush claim that God blessed his decision to fly U.S. missiles through Baghdad and declare war on Iraq. Soon afterward, I watched televised images of ground troops invading Iraq from the south. I immediately agreed with my left-leaning secular friends in the antiwar movement that Bush's messianic vision was terrifying, and I parroted the reigning opinion that the world would be better off without religion. However, around the same time, I met members of the historic peace churches—Mennonites, Quakers, and members of the Church of the Brethren—on the frontlines of the anti-war movement. They told me that dozens of Christian peace activists were traveling to Baghdad to stand in solidarity with Iraqis, document the civilian cost of war, and forge human connections with alleged enemies. One of the groups arranging such peace delegations was Christian

Peacemaker Teams (CPT), a spiritually centered peacemaking initiative emphasizing creative public witness, nonviolent direct action, and protection of human rights.[3] I was skeptical about CPT and erroneously assumed its volunteers were interested in preaching and converting. However, I later learned of an Iraqi Muslim named Sami Rasouli who met CPT volunteers in his homeland and so admired their firm resolution against proselytizing and selfless dedication to peacemaking that he requested they train Muslim Iraqis to work alongside CPT volunteers. Years later Rasouli founded the Muslim Peacemaker Teams in the same humanitarian spirit as CPT.[4]

The idea of CPT flew in the face of everything I had assumed about Christianity. The words of one CPT volunteer in Iraq, twenty-two-year-old Jonathan Wilson-Hartgrove, awakened me to a side of Christianity that I did not know existed. "We're followers of Jesus who were trying to demonstrate that the cross is mightier than the sword," he told *Salon.com*. "We would rather suffer with those who were suffering than to see them suffer in our names. We think that's what it means to follow Jesus."[5] My assumptions about Christianity were further shattered when I read the words of Shane Claiborne, a twenty-seven-year-old peace activist who also traveled to Iraq in opposition to the war:

> Peacemaking between Christians and Muslims will not happen through either party denying the political and public expressions of their faith (nor would that likely happen), but through continually seeking the true depths, meaning, and practice of their own faith. It is easy to forget where most problems stem from in religious conflict: it is not when each side too greatly believes their faith, but it is when people forget and confuse their faith, zealously combining it with another faith (patriotism, nationalism, global-capitalism) and violence. The befuddling mystery of our day is not the presence of sincere Muslims but violent Christians.[6]

When I later spoke with Claiborne, he recounted touring the United States with his fellow peacemakers to present a critical perspective on the Iraq War based on their interviews with their Iraqi friends. Claiborne said he reminded his coreligionists that Jesus told his disciples that he sent them out as "sheep among wolves" and never once told them to turn into wolves when they encountered other scarier wolves. Claiborne said he asked his audience how different the world would have looked if, instead of seeking vengeance after 9/11, we stood together in our human pain, looking honestly at the shared sin and sadness we suffered.

Claiborne, I discovered, was not alone in practicing a type of Christianity based on forgiveness and peace. In 2005 I was awed by the response of one Amish community after a gunman killed five of their children. A group of Amish elders visited the wife of the murderer to offer their forgiveness; the victims' families invited the widow to their own children's funeral; and the community requested that all relief money be shared with the widower and her three children. Finally, in a mesmerizing act of mercy, dozens of Amish families attended the murderer's funeral. The community's extraordinary demonstration of forgiveness was not an executive decision by a saintly individual, but a countercultural practice rooted in their understanding of Christian faith, a faith they saw as being directly at odds with the prevailing national culture of retributive justice.[7]

Around the same time, I stumbled upon Martin Luther King Jr.'s reflection on Gandhi, and I couldn't help noting how starkly his words contrasted those of my headmistress. "I believe that in some marvelous way, God worked through Gandhi, and the spirit of Jesus Christ saturated his life," wrote King in the *Christian Century*. "It is ironic, yet inescapably true, that the greatest Christian of the modern world was a man who never embraced Christianity."[8]

I began wondering why I had heard so little about these Christians who practiced and preached a radically different type of faith than the one espoused by condescending missionaries and the Religious Right. For years I had assumed that Christian political activism was limited to rallies against gay marriage and bombings of abortion clinics. Perhaps as an act of penance, I decided to write a book honoring the views of these Christians whose voices are so often muffled by the Religious Right and ignored by the secular left.

The Christian social justice activists profiled in this book believe in an interfaith global community based on ethics, a world with infinite potential for improvement, and an inclusive God of love. These activists may serve as our best hope in confronting the fearmongering and virulent intolerance of the neoconservative parties because they straddle the seemingly insurmountable divide between religious zealots striving for a Christian state and secular humanists prematurely bidding good riddance to God. Their middle way is a religiously pluralistic modern world in which people of faith play a unique role in protecting the weak, safeguarding the sacred, and promoting a just peace.

▬ ▪ ▬

In formulating this book, I decided to focus on Christians whose faith directly informs their progressive political views. Specifically, I wanted to find Christians who are actively challenging what so much of the Tea Party–inspired theology stands for in the United States. I was not interested in philanthropists who funnel their money to charitable causes but in radical activists who put their bodies on the front line of social justice struggles, struggles that are often mistakenly viewed as the domain of the secular left. I sought activists as famous as Daniel Berrigan—the Catholic priest who graced the cover of *Time* in January 1971—and as obscure as Joseph Land—a young Baptist who now leads a relatively anonymous life in suburban Michigan. Since most Christians involved in social justice struggles are driven by the politics of moral witness rather than the politics of pragmatism, I chose to profile not only activists who had achieved their vision (such as Jim Zwerg and SueZann Bosler), but also those who are tenaciously continuing their struggle despite bleak chances of success (such as John Dear and Charlotte Keys). I sought activists who have committed acts of civil disobedience and sacrificed their own welfare to live out their religious convictions but limited my examination to those who disavow violence—I do not wish to write a polemic on the merits and pitfalls of armed struggle.

I chose to concentrate on members of the Christian left but realized that, as with any division within the left and right wings of the political spectrum, such a label can only be an approximation since individuals often hold dissenting viewpoints. In general, though, the Christian left feels its religious obligations include the promotion of social justice and renunciation of power as well as the practice of humility, tolerance, and reconciliation. They note that the Bible contains accounts of Jesus repeatedly advocating for the poor, lost, and marginalized, not the powerful, wealthy, and pious. The Christian left largely opposes militarism, supports egalitarianism, and works to eliminate the conditions creating poverty in the first place. Aside from their views on abortion, most members of the Christian left are similar to the secular left in that they support universal health care, welfare provisions, subsidized education, no-strings-attached humanitarian aid, and affirmative action for the historically underprivileged. Perhaps Christian leftists do not seem nearly as organized as their right-wing counterparts, though this fact may have less to do with their numbers than with their unwillingness to voice political views in a confrontational and aggressive manner.

- ■ -

The Christian activists profiled in this book hope to serve as God's hands and feet rather than as his mouthpiece; they view faith as a personal commitment with public implications. For the most part, these politically progressive activists' worldviews are religiously informed but theologically discriminating and largely compatible with pluralism, science, and multiculturalism. They bear no resemblance to parochial, hierarchical, and exclusionary fundamentalists obsessed with determining who descends to hell. They seek to emulate the example of Jesus Christ, who they regard not only as the Son of God but also a Prince of Peace who committed nonviolent civil disobedience in the interest of the oppressed.

There have been a host of Christian martyrs throughout the past two centuries who have endured personal suffering in hopes of creating a path for social redemption. Early Christians disavowed all forms of violence and were routinely subjected to scorn and rejection, floggings and jail for preaching unpopular truths. Justin, martyred in AD 165, noted: "We have exchanged our swords for plowshares, our spears for farm tools . . . now we cultivate the fear of God, justice, kindness, faith and the expectation of the future given us through the crucified one . . . the more we are persecuted and martyred, the more do others in ever increasing numbers become believers." Maximilla proclaimed in a similar spirit, "Wish yourself a martyr's death. Blushing for shame you will be dragged before the public. That is good for you, for he who is not publicly exposed like this before people will be publicly exposed before God."

Millennia later, many Christians continue this self-sacrificial understanding of Christian testimony, this desire to make their stories reflect that of Jesus Christ. These activists often sacrifice not only their own safety, but also their religious organizations' approval: early Quakers excommunicated Benjamin Lay for staging a kidnapping to protest slavery; the Vatican excommunicated Father Roy Bourgeois for promoting female ordination; and Jesuits distanced themselves from Daniel

Berrigan when he burned draft cards during the Vietnam War. This book is not a defense of institutional religion but a defense of religion's ability to inspire heterodox individuals to follow their consciences.

-·-

The activists profiled in this book are part of an underreported American tradition that began with the nation's first Quakers who opposed the genocide of Native Americans at a time when so many self-avowed Christians justified pillaging foreign lands and massacring Native peoples by invoking God's name. Early Quakers—perhaps the forerunners of the Christian left—maintained a testimony against offensive violence, believing it was contrary to the spirit of Jesus' new covenant and his admonition to love one's enemies. While these Quakers were not immune to prejudice, many adopted fair land treaties with Native populations and readily aided them with advice, money, tools, and medicine.[9] In return, Native Americans shared their own expertise with Quakers and provided them sanctuary when they were persecuted by British authorities.[10]

Similarly, while many used the Bible to justify the exploitation of slaves, some of slavery's bravest opponents were empowered by their theology. In antebellum America, at a time when the law denied slaves any semblance of humanity and scientists espoused bogus theories of inherent racial inferiority, Christian abolitionists were among the first to confront these sentiments. Christian "fanatics" Nat Turner, Denmark Vesey, and Gabriel Prosser orchestrated three of this country's major slave insurrections, as well as John Brown's raid on Harpers Ferry. The scholar W. E. B. Du Bois notes that both Turner and Brown were messianic revolutionary leaders with "a steadfast almost superstitious faith in [their] divine mission."[11]

Even during the suffragist movement, women's rights activists evoked Christianity to support their cause in direct opposition to patriarchal pastors who claimed women should remain unseen and unheard. Sarah Grimké, one of the earliest suffragists and a devout Quaker, wrote in an openly published letter: "I ask no favors for my sex. . . . All I ask our brethren is that they will take their feet from off our necks and permit us to stand upright on that ground which God designed us to occupy."[12]

As remains true today, God is often co-opted for opposing political purposes. The Puritans appealed to the Bible, especially Romans 13:2, to justify the genocide of Natives.[13] A proponent of slavery, Reverend William Harrison, boasted in his pulpit that "Jesus Christ was a Southerner, born on Southern soil, and so were his apostles, except Judas, whom he denominated a Northern man."[14] Anti-suffragist Reverend John Cotton insisted, "God hath put another law upon women: wives, be subject to your husbands in all things."[15] In the final analysis, Christianity probably was less responsible for these instances of genocide, slavery, and patriarchal control than were simple human weaknesses for greed, selfishness, and power.

Religion is often a red herring for secular progressives who fail to realize that holy texts such as the Bible are flexible and resilient documents. As in the past, there remain stark differences today among those who call themselves Christians. The Christianity preached by Pat Robertson and the Christianity preached by Martin Luther King Jr. have little in common. The challenge is to understand what makes these two ways of practicing the same religion so different and to consider which one will lead us to a better future.

- ▪ -

Divine Rebels aims to show Christians' concern for *this* world, not just the next, and suggests that Christianity defies the contours of any specific political mold. While religious freedom must include the freedom to reject religion, perhaps a more challenging question for Americans is not if we will accept or reject God (most have already answered that question in the affirmative) but if we will revere a God who has infused every being with his sacred and loving essence or a God who establishes strict laws and religious supremacy.[16] Secular humanists who view religion as a thoroughly human invention have a point when they say people can be good without God. However, we all might benefit from recognizing the wisdom of Frederick Douglass, who simply but powerfully noted, "I would unite with anybody to do right and with nobody to do wrong."

At a time when Richard Dawkins's *The God Delusion*, Nicholas Everitt's *The Non-Existence of God*, and Christopher Hitchens's *God Is Not Great: How Religion Poisons Everything* are popular in literary circles, *Divine Rebels* reveals a religious tradition rooted in human empathy. The religious lacuna in current literature demonstrates the pervasive bias among social scientists to perceive religion as a conservative social force or archaic ideological manipulation. Although academics have grown increasingly cynical about religion, a global revival of faith is enrapturing the world.[17] Religion offers solace, community, and purpose. The union of religion and political power can often be corrosive; however, many religious adherents are far less concerned with gaining power than with checking its abuses.

Jean-Jacques Rousseau correctly noted that a person who separates politics from morals fails to understand both politics and morals. At a time of religious resurgence, morals are increasingly dictated by one's faith. As Roger Gottlieb, Shane Claiborne, and so many others have pointed out, even the staunchest atheist is faced with competing religious choices: If we choose not to embrace a God of love, we may inadvertently worship the civic God of militarism. If we choose not to regard the environment as holy, we may inadvertently be holding the corporate bottom line sacred. If we do not practice rituals of meditation, we may inadvertently embrace rituals such as shopping therapy. If we do not proactively choose to cultivate our religions, any number of self-appointed earthly deities will fill that void, from manipulative politicians to those who profit by luring us into their illusory TV heavens. The question is not if we are political or apolitical, religious or atheist, since we all undoubtedly embody some type of politics and religion. The question is what types of politics and religions do we embrace?

As political theorist Clive Hamilton mentions in *Growth Fetish*, the surge of self-help books in an era of frantic advertising and monomaniacal consumption may signal a search for meaning beyond the parameters of possession—an acknowledgment, if only subliminally, that the socially sanctioned recipe for happiness is a fraud.[18] The political propaganda machine and its vituperative pundits are only too happy to exploit the spiritual crises created by community deterioration and acute loneliness in contemporary America. *Divine Rebels* articulates a forward-thinking, faith-based alternative to both the conservative talking heads that warp religion as well as the political left's alienating cynicism. What distinguishes great spiritual leaders—from Gandhi and Martin Luther King Jr. to Aung San Suu Kyi and the Dalai Lama—is their courage to hitch themselves and their willpower to a higher cause and the compassionate pursuit of a more just world. As Thomas Merton said, "Without compassion, the protester tends to become more and more centered in anger and may easily become an obstacle to changing the attitudes of others."[19]

Secular and religious social justice activists must reconcile their differences to strengthen their common cause of making the world a better place. Secular progressives' best hope may lie in aligning themselves with religious progressives and working together to prevent political conservatives from cynically co-opting the language of religion as a convenient aegis for repugnant beliefs. In March 2010 conservative political pundit Glenn Beck suggested any church promoting "social justice" or "economic justice" was merely using code words for Nazism and communism.[20] Beck said "social justice" is a "perversion of the gospel" and told Christians to leave their churches if they heard that term used by their pastors or even found it on their churchs' websites. Reverend Jim Wallis—president of Sojourners (the largest network of progressive Christians in the United States)—denounced Beck's comments, noting that "Dr. King was a social justice Christian, the kind of Christian Mr. Beck constantly derides." Wallis also noted that ending the slave trade in Great Britain, ending legal racial segregation in America, and ending apartheid in South Africa took "vital movements of faith which understood the connection between personal compassion and social justice." Shortly after Wallis issued his response, Beck was flooded with more than fifty thousand messages from church leaders, members, and pastors proudly declaring that they are "social justice Christians."[21]

Indeed, there is a reason Beck shudders at the thought of religious organizations using the term "social justice." He knows the people who have rattled the cage, challenged the status quo, and revolutionized society—people like Dorothy Day, Abraham Joshua Heschel, and Dr. Martin Luther King Jr.—come out of this school of thought. A united front for moral renewal might be our best hope for a bold, strong, and defiant new social justice movement in America. Perhaps politically progressive Americans should do exactly what Beck fears most: encourage young visionaries to attend seminary, preach sermons of compassion, and raise hell from the pulpit to the streets until heaven is created here on earth.

1 JIM ZWERG

The Faith Driving the Freedom Riders

Any religion that professes to be concerned with the souls of men and is not concerned with the slums that damn, the economic conditions that strangle, and the social conditions that cripple them, is a dry-as-dust religion.

—Dr. Martin Luther King Jr.[1]

We're going to get left of Karl Marx and left of Lenin. We're going to get way out there, up on that cross with Jesus.

—James Bevel, *Southern Christian Leadership Conference*[2]

On May 4, 1961, one Greyhound bus and one Trailways bus left Washington, DC, for New Orleans, but neither bus ever reached its destination. Outside Anniston, Alabama, the Greyhound precariously tilted sideways, and the panicked driver realized his tires were slashed. As soon as the driver pulled off the highway, a mob of arsonists shattered the bus windows and lobbed a firebomb at the passengers, causing the fuel tank to explode. The mob proceeded to obstruct the bus's exits in hopes of cremating the passengers alive. Alabama state troopers belatedly dispersed the mob, allowing hysterical passengers choking on acrid smoke to narrowly escape death. Meanwhile, the Trailways pulled into the Birmingham, Alabama, station, where another mob greeted passengers with baseball bats, bicycle chains, and iron pipes.[3]

13

One survivor of the attack, James Peck, sustained head wounds requiring more than fifty stitches.

Both buses were part of the "Freedom Rides" in which blacks and whites traveled together through the South in hopes of breaking the segregation pattern in interstate travel.[4] A northern-based group dedicated to racial equality—Congress of Racial Equality (CORE)—organized the Freedom Rides as part of what Dr. Martin Luther King Jr. called "a full scale nonviolent assault on the system of segregation in Alabama." The civil rights leader Stokely Carmichael elaborated on the Freedom Riders' plan:

> In any sane, even half-civilized society [the plan] would have been completely innocuous, hardly worth a second thought or meriting any comment at all. CORE would be sending an integrated team—black and white together—from the nation's capital to New Orleans on public transportation. That's all. Except, of course, that they would sit randomly on the buses in integrated pairs and in the stations they would use waiting room facilities casually, ignoring the white/colored signs. What could be more harmless . . . in any even marginally healthy society?[5]

The Supreme Court had outlawed segregation in interstate bus travel back in June 1946 and then, in December 1960, had also outlawed segregation in waiting rooms and restaurants serving interstate bus and rail passengers. Nonetheless, Jim Crow travel laws remained throughout the South, since calculating Southern politicians rarely enforced these federal rulings lest they alienate Southern white leaders of the Democratic Party. Freedom Riders hoped to begin desegregation efforts themselves by blatantly violating Jim Crow laws and sparking a national debate on their legitimacy. "We were counting on the bigots in the South to do our work for us," explained one Freedom Rider, James Farmer. "We figured that the government would have to respond if we created a situation that was headline news all over the world and affected the nation's image abroad."[6]

As Farmer predicted, the mauled Freedom Riders did capture national attention and force Americans to question the morality of racial segregation. Supporters of the Freedom Riders saw them continuing a proud campaign of nonviolent civil disobedience that had begun with the Montgomery bus boycott and continued with student sit-ins at lunch counters.

These sympathizers commended the Riders' willingness to suffer for their moral convictions and hoped their sacrifices would awaken the country to the evils of racial segregation. However, the Freedom Rides coincided with the April 1961 Civil War Centennial celebration, and a resurgent siege mentality was in full force throughout the white South. Many Southerners regarded the Freedom Riders as needlessly antagonistic "professional agitators" from the North who were violating the "Southern way of life" and infringing on their state sovereignty. Memories of meddling abolitionists and invading armies were reawakened.[7]

After the burning in Anniston, Freedom Riders decided they could not allow their integrationist efforts to be derailed. Much to the surprise of the American public, the Student Non-Violent Coordinating Committee (SNCC) organized another Freedom Ride. Americans of every political persuasion wondered what drove these students to risk their lives attempting to integrate interstate travel. What gave them the courage to continue their campaign knowing full well that the previous Riders returned home bloodied and burnt? Why volunteer for what seemed like a suicide mission? Even those within the movement cautioned against continuing the Freedom Rides. When student leader Diane Nash called movement organizer Fred Shuttlesworth to inform him of the students' decision to commission a new ride, he responded sternly: "Young lady, do you know that the Freedom Riders were almost killed here?" Nash assured him that she did, adding: "That's exactly why the ride must not be stopped. If they stop us with violence, the movement is dead. We're coming."[8]

Whereas CORE had chartered their buses, members of SNCC decided they would obtain tickets and board a regular bus like any other travelers. They also then needed to choose the students who would be risking their lives to participate in the ride. A lanky twenty-one-year-old college student of German descent with verdigris eyes named Jim Zwerg was one of eighteen students who volunteered, and ultimately participated, in the potentially fatal mission.

In more ways than not, Zwerg was an unlikely candidate for the Freedom Rides. The short-tempered Wisconsin native had once scoffed at the idea of "nonviolent protest" as a way of transforming society. And, as a white man from a wealthy family, Zwerg had nothing tangible to gain from the movement's success. Zwerg, now a seventy-year-old former minister in the United Church of Christ, says that a remarkable two-year-long religious transformation led him to believe that protesting racial segregation was his higher calling and divine duty. Despite the tremendous risk involved, Zwerg insists he was deeply at peace with his decision to join the Freedom Rides. "My faith was never so strong as during that time," he reflected. "I knew I was doing what I should be doing."

— • —

Growing up in lily-white Appleton, Wisconsin, Zwerg led an all-American boyhood filled with hiking trips and Boy Scout excursions. He and his brother served as acolytes in the First Congregational Church of Appleton; they sang in the Sunday morning choir and participated in church summer camps. Taller and brawnier than other children his age, Zwerg preferred to settle his differences with his fists rather than words. Once in elementary school, he coldcocked a bully who cheated in kickball. A few years later, during a Boy Scout trip to a state fair in Milwaukee, Zwerg beat the hell out of a classmate who tormented his sick friend by jiggling the friend's cot to make him vomit. As a result, he lost his coveted spot on his school's honor committee, but even that did not cool his fiery temper.

Yet, Zwerg also had an introspective side that came out in his fondness for the outdoors. As an Eagle Scout, Zwerg spent countless hours tying complicated climbing knots, distinguishing poison ivy from innocuous weeds, and igniting bonfires with flint. Even after entering high school, Zwerg preferred exploring the wilderness to joining his friends at parties. Despite his propensity to wander away from crowds, Zwerg's natural charisma won him admirers, and, by his senior year, he was unanimously elected president of one of the largest church youth groups in Wisconsin. The gangly teenager with a blond crew cut had long considered himself a devout Christian. He dutifully attended church, read the Bible, and said grace before his meals, so when his church's senior minister abruptly relocated to Phoenix for a new job, Zwerg was happy to assist the church's associate minister by delivering that Sunday's sermon. He embraced his debut at the pulpit by preaching what he regarded as a "riveting message" on recharging one's spiritual batteries through regular church attendance.

— • —

In 1958 Zwerg began his freshman year at Beloit College, which was not too far from home. Without giving it much thought, Zwerg indicated on an incoming-student questionnaire that he felt comfortable rooming with someone of a different race. Four years earlier, the Supreme Court had struck down the "separate but equal" doctrine and mandated that segregated facilities be integrated with all deliberate speed. Zwerg ended up being paired with a short, stocky black roommate named Bob Carter. The two became fast friends. They played intramural college football and basketball together, crammed for exams over bottomless cups of coffee in the college's library, and spent many late nights attempting to decipher those enigmatic creatures called girls. [9]

Yet, it didn't take long for Zwerg, who was studying sociology, to notice that his and Carter's college experiences differed drastically. When Carter and Zwerg entered a cafeteria, people left the lunch counter. When Carter and Zwerg entered a barbershop, the barber refused to cut Carter's "nappy" hair. When Carter and Zwerg bought movie tickets, Zwerg enjoyed a front-row seat while Carter was segregated to the upstairs balcony. When Zwerg invited Carter to join his fraternity, Carter was informed that black students were prohibited from pledging; Zwerg eventually revoked his own membership. One September morning, Zwerg's parents visited Beloit and invited Carter to join the family for dinner at one of the fancier restaurants in town. The roommates welcomed the opportunity to escape the monotony of their college cafeteria's soggy hamburgers and overcooked vegetables and even dressed up for the occasion. At the restaurant, they regaled Zwerg's parents with stories about their professors, friends, and classes. After half an hour passed, Zwerg's father wondered out loud why their waiter had not yet taken their order. Finally, the maître d' appeared and crisply explained that the restaurant only served whites.

Zwerg was shocked by these racist double standards, but Carter and other blacks were accustomed to abuse in every facet of their lives. Nearly a century after the Emancipation Proclamation abolished slavery, racial segregation and Jim Crow laws still relegated African Americans to inferior and underfunded public schools and facilities. Disenfranchisement and voter harassment left many politically voiceless. Economic oppression, coupled with deep-seated prejudices, subjected blacks to impoverishment and exploitation at a level incomprehensible to whites. As novelist James Baldwin wrote to his nephew in an open letter in 1962:

"You were born into a society which spelled out with brutal clarity, and in as many ways as possible, that you were a worthless human being. You were not expected to aspire to excellence: you were expected to make peace with mediocrity."[10] But, by the early 1960s, black people across the country were beginning to more actively revolt against this unjust status quo. They sparked a movement rooted in the audacious belief that a subjugated minority could reclaim their humanity from an oppressive majority's iron grip on economic, political, and social structures. All over the nation, individual acts of resistance began snowballing into a collective movement for social change. Richard Wright spoke for many when he wrote in his classic *Black Boy*:

> The white South said that it knew "niggers," and I was what the white South called a "nigger." Well, the white South had never known me—never known what I thought, what I felt. The white South said that I had a "place" in life. Well, I had never felt my "place" to which the white South had assigned me. It had never occurred to me that I was in any way an inferior being. And no word that I had ever heard fall from the lips of Southern white men had ever made me really doubt the worth of my own humanity.

- ∎ -

At Beloit College, Zwerg was less interested in the national debate on civil rights than in his black roommate's college experience. One day during the second semester of his freshman year, Zwerg overheard a white student walk past Carter and say, "Do you smell a cigar? Nah, it's just a nigger." Passersby snickered loudly. Zwerg lunged for the white student's jugular, but Carter restrained him. Calling Carter a coward for refusing to defend himself, Zwerg snapped, "You take their abuse and you don't even smart-mouth them!" Carter walked away shaking his head and soon returned with a copy of Martin Luther King Jr.'s *Stride Toward Freedom: The Montgomery Story*. "Fighting doesn't prove anything," Carter said, handing his roommate the book. "But Dr. King did prove something."

Zwerg knew embarrassingly little about Dr. King or the Montgomery bus strike in Alabama. Who was this frail seamstress with wire-rimmed spectacles named Rosa Parks, and why did she refuse to relinquish her seat to a white man on a city bus in open disregard for city law? Zwerg read King's testimony and was struck by its pressing words: "Actually no one can understand the action of Mrs. Parks unless he realizes that eventually the cup of endurance runs over, and the human personality cries out, 'I can take it no longer.'" He was fascinated by the fact that King, at twenty-six, had been recruited to lead the Montgomery Improvement Association, the organization created to direct the nascent civil rights movement. Reading on, Zwerg was especially captivated by the young minister's emphasis on the Christian doctrine of love as an organizing principle. When Zwerg read "our action must be guided by the deepest principles of our Christian faith. Love must be our regulating idea. Once again we must hear the words of Jesus echoing across the centuries: 'Love your enemies, bless them that curse you, and pray for them that despitefully use you,'"[11] he put down the book and wondered if King were completely delusional. How could anyone tolerate, let alone love, people who forced them to attend inferior schools, drink from separate water fountains, and sit at the back of buses?

Zwerg had long considered himself a devout Christian who dutifully attended church and studied the Bible, yet he had never seriously entertained the idea that Jesus expected people to love their enemies. Now, a young preacher just a few years older than him was claiming "We must keep God in the forefront. Let us be Christian in our actions" as he rallied against the indignities that hundreds of blacks regularly suffered on Montgomery's buses. Dr. King also declared, "Love is one of the pinnacle parts of the Christian faith. There is another side called justice. And justice is really love in calculation."[12] The poetic quality of these orations impressed Zwerg, but he could not comprehend the depth of faith the Baptist minister must possess to actually pray for his enemies and love those who persecuted him. The sociology student was particularly amazed that King's singularity of conviction had not reduced him to a laughingstock—the minister's sermons had resonated with the dispossessed and inspired them to put the basic elements of Christian theology into action. He now understood why Carter had given him this gift, this message to transcend hatred rather than reciprocate in kind. But he still was not fully convinced of its validity.

Zwerg continued reading about how the black community in Montgomery organized carpools, preached messages of resistance from the pulpit, and persevered in their boycott even after the city retaliated by indicting one hundred boycott leaders. He sympathized with Reverend Fred Shuttlesworth's response to Police Commissioner Eugene "Bull" Connor's decree that no black minister should urge his people to stay off the buses: "Only God can tell me what to say in the pulpit. And I'm going to tell my people to stay off those buses if I have to go to Kilby prison."[13] Although Zwerg had never articulated this thought, he agreed Christians should pledge allegiance to God's divine law over unjust man-made ones.

Reading further, Zwerg was flummoxed to learn that Dr. King remained calm and composed even as segregationists harassed and heckled him. He wondered how the young minister managed to continue organizing the boycott after hearing an anonymous caller grunt, "Nigger, we are tired of you and your mess now. And if you aren't out of this town in three days, we're going to blow your brains out and blow up your house." Zwerg knew if someone were to threaten him with assassination, he would either react with rage or crumble with fear. The Baptist minister's steely resolve intrigued him, for it seemed simultaneously naive in its childlike simplicity and courageous in its ambitious vision. Zwerg wondered if King ever feared death or ever doubted that he was truly acting according to God's will.

Through King's writing, Zwerg soon discovered a mere mortal who experienced doubts and insecurities much like he did. But, Zwerg learned, King had overcome his paralyzing fear through a religious awakening:

> And I discovered that religion had to become real to me, and I had to know God for myself . . . I prayed a prayer out loud that night. I said, "Lord, I'm down here trying to do what's right. I think I'm right. I think the cause that we represent is right. But Lord, I must confess that I'm weak now. I'm faltering. I'm losing my courage." . . . And it seemed at that moment that I could hear an inner voice saying to me "Martin Luther, stand up for righteousness. Stand up for justice. Stand up for truth. And lo I will be with you, even until the end of the world." . . . I heard the voice of Jesus saying still to fight on. He promised never to leave me, never to leave me alone. No never alone. No never alone. He promised never to leave me, never to leave me alone. . . . Almost at once my fears began to go. My uncertainty disappeared. [14]

Zwerg wondered if God might actually be on the side of the weak and oppressed, might actually be a force more powerful than violence. After all, the Montgomery boycott had lasted over a year and led to a successful Supreme Court challenge to the Jim Crow law that relegated blacks to the rear of public buses.

Zwerg remembered the time he'd attended the state fair and beat up a classmate for bullying his friend. At the time, Zwerg had regarded this as a valiant act because, as the Bible says, an eye for an eye. Now Zwerg wondered if he had been mistaken in his approach and in his interpretation of Scripture. Even though he had protected his friend at the time, he wondered what had happened to the class bully. Had he simply grown into an abusive adult who continued tormenting others, or had he experienced a sense of remorse and turned his life around? Zwerg could not fully dismiss King's appraisal of the Montgomery protest as a testament to the power of Christian love and nonviolent resistance. He continued toying with the idea that nonviolence was more powerful than violence and wondered if early Christian martyrs were correct in believing pacifism was a mandate of their faith.

- ∎ -

Driven more by his interest in sociology than any sense of altruism, Zwerg increasingly wondered how he would react if whites—not blacks—were the oppressed minority. Much of Zwerg's college work examined patterns of association, exploring the interactions of people, communities, and organizations. Zwerg saw his vocation not as the study of people but as the study of the relationships among people and the products of human interaction such as culture, universities, and religion.

As little more than an academic experiment, Zwerg applied to and was accepted as an exchange student of Fiske University, a predominately black university in Nashville. When he arrived on campus in 1961, the disgruntled cabby stopped at the university gates, refused to assist him with his luggage, and muttered something about the "unfortunate mixing of the races." Before Zwerg could respond, the cabby sped off. Unfazed, he carried his own luggage to his new dormitory, unpacked, and headed to the campus rathskeller to make new friends.

While dancing the twist in the student union, Zwerg befriended a group of young activists involved with nonviolent demonstrations. The activists spoke of four students in Greensboro, North Carolina, who had sparked a national sit-in movement the previous year by refusing to leave a "whites only" Woolworth's lunch counter. The lunch counter closed for that day, but the students returned the next day with new recruits. By the third day, the number swelled to eighty-five.[15] Zwerg was amazed to hear that the protesters refused to retaliate when whites poured scalding coffee and ice-cold milkshakes on their heads. He wondered how he would have responded, as a black man, to racists. He decided he probably would have sucker punched each of the offenders yet suspected the police would simply arrest any black student who dared raise a finger against a white. Only later did Zwerg learn that the students were not simply reacting nonviolently for tactical purposes, but were also aiming to awaken a sense of moral shame in their opponents. They were emulating King's methods in hopes of winning their adversaries' hands in friendship and understanding.

Similar sit-ins had occurred in fifteen cities in five Southern states over the course of the next two weeks with King encouraging a rally of more than one thousand at White Rock Baptist Church in Durham, North Carolina, to support the student-led movement. Drawing on his own experience in Montgomery four years earlier, King told the students: "If there is one lesson experience has taught us . . . it is that when you have found by the help of God a correct course, a morally sound objective, you do not equivocate, you do not retreat—you struggle to win a victory."[16] King later added, "We have the power to change America and give a kind of new vitality to the religion of Jesus Christ. . . . He initiated the first sit-in movement."[17] By 1961 more than fifty thousand people—mostly black, some white—participated in similar demonstrations in a hundred cities. Over 3,600 people were jailed.[18] Ultimately, the desegregation of Nashville lunch counters came about due to cold economics rather than a reawakened sense of compassion. The activists' campaigns of nonviolent civil disobedience helped integrate Montgomery buses and desegregate Nashville lunch counters but did not catalyze a moral about-face in white society.

- ∎ -

At Fiske University, Zwerg's new friends had successfully integrated the nearby Wilson Quick drugstores by sending groups of students to "test the facilities" whenever someone reported having trouble accessing the lunch counters. The young activists told Zwerg their new focus was integrating local movie theaters. They introduced Zwerg to a professor who was beaten for nonviolently protesting segregation, and they invited him to join their next meeting at the professor's house. Zwerg paused. He had not come to Fiske to join a movement; he had come to dispassionately explore racial dynamics from a sociologist's perspective. The scholar in Zwerg wanted to passively observe the situation and take notes from the sidelines. Yet he remembered the frustration and sadness he felt when he invited one of his black friends to attend a movie only to have his friend smirk, "Well, you know we can't sit together, and they probably won't even let me in." Those words had pierced Zwerg, who, as a Christian, wanted to assure his friend that he disagreed with those arrangements and believed God had created everyone as equals. Now he had a choice between analyzing social relations from the safe distance of an academic or unequivocally condemning them and joining his brethren in changing those relations. As a Christian, Zwerg decided that reducing the suffering of others to a quaint academic exercise was insulting, especially since he, as a white man, was partly responsible for their suffering. After praying that evening, Zwerg decided he was a Christian first and a scholar second.

The next day, Zwerg joined his friends at their organizational meeting and learned more about their efforts to integrate movie theaters. A few weeks later, he took a bus downtown to witness firsthand the movie theater demonstrations and found that the students were far from the young revolutionaries he was expecting. The dozen well-dressed students idled in front of a movie theater as patrons strode past to buy their tickets. Nobody yelled and not a single scuffle broke out. Zwerg spent twenty minutes observing the modest, respectful wallflowers mill around and shuffle their feet. Exasperated, he confronted the group's spokesperson, John Lewis, and asked what in the world they were trying to accomplish. Lewis, a composed and resolute twenty-one-year-old, invited Zwerg to learn more about the group's efforts by attending the church meeting held after the demonstration.

Lewis and Zwerg were the same age, but Zwerg felt that Lewis's unflinching commitment to the movement and absolute certainty in its moral rightness made him seem far older and wiser than himself. Zwerg had never met anyone his age so focused and driven, and he longed to understand what gave Lewis the courage to pursue his unshakable vision of a radically different society. En route to the meeting, Zwerg learned that Lewis, a seminary student, shared King's faith in a benevolent God who sympathized with the oppressed.

The church meeting, unlike the movie theater protest, was full of verve. The animated group of students belted gospel songs, mulled over scriptural passages, and shared personal testimonies of their commitment to nonviolence. Everyone listened as soon as Lewis opened his mouth, and Zwerg wondered how he had cultivated such a strong faith and commanded such profound respect within the movement. After the meeting, the students passed an offering to defray the cost of sandwiches and newsletters. Buoyed by the enthusiasm of a collective spirit, Zwerg more and more frequently attended mass meetings at the church as well as other workshops designed to inform the community of the aims of the Student Nonviolent Coordinating Committee to desegregate society and spark a moral awakening.

— • —

The Student Nonviolent Coordinating Committee (SNCC) was more secular than Dr. King's umbrella organization, the Southern Christian Leadership Conference (SCLC), but Protestant theological terminology—exodus, redemption, salvation—was pervasive.[19] SNCC's founding statement was drafted largely by James Lawson, a Methodist minister and committed Gandhian. Since 1958, Lawson had trained Nashville students in techniques of nonviolent civil disobedience, explaining, "Under Christian non-violence . . . students reject the hardship of disobedient passivity and fear, but embrace the hardship (violence and jail) of obedience."[20] Lawson led many of the training sessions by delving into Gandhi's and King's philosophies of nonviolence, urging students to wrestle with their beliefs rather than accepting them blindly. Whenever the group heard of a situation where violence had erupted during a protest, they collectively brainstormed how to prevent it from happening again. All the while, Lawson and other leaders encouraged participants to examine their motivations and question their commitment to nonviolence constantly.

During the workshops, Zwerg and the other participants improvised situations they anticipated encountering during actual demonstrations. Selected students from the SNCC impersonated racists—punching, kicking, and threatening to extinguish cigarettes on demonstrators—while others monitored how the participants reacted. Whenever a participant emotionally cracked or physically retaliated, the role play stopped. A group leader would gently inform the participant that he or she was not ready to partake in an actual demonstration but could help distribute newsletters or transport volunteers. As one of only two white allies in the group, Zwerg was slandered as "white trash," "nigger lover," and "traitor to your race." The black students were similarly heckled: "You black son of a bitch, what are you doing here? Get the hell out of here! Hey boy, go on back where you belong!" A lewd suggestion about Zwerg and his black female friend almost caused the short-fused teenager to explode in rage. Each session, he feared he would be the next to go.

A brief religious service followed each workshop and a leader of the SNCC offered a sermon or testimonial to connect their struggle with those of Biblical heroes. Zwerg was especially captivated by movement leader Jim Bevel and his vivid allegories: *Here was Pharaoh with all his mighty chariots, horses, and armies . . . and here are all the racists with all their policemen, canines, and lynch mobs! All Moses has is a pathetic stick, but when Moses throws down the stick, it becomes a serpent with great power. And God says, "Grasp it!" And he does, and it changes back into the stick. We are similarly afraid of the stick—the stick of nonviolence—but, if we grasp it, we too will be free.* Listening to the story, Zwerg slowly decided that King was right; he could overcome fear without creating fear, overcome violence without becoming violent. Zwerg was struck by the idea that he already possessed the most powerful weapon in the world—God's love, as sappy as it sounded—and all he had to do was put this love into action via nonviolent civil disobedience. He came to regard nonviolent resistance as God's proverbial stick, which would provide strength and freedom against daunting odds. The more meetings he attended, the more the young activist genuinely believed that a person could fight a war with the deadliest machinery and most expensive weapons, but the power of love was the only force capable of intrinsically transforming people's hearts.

Zwerg drew strength from Biblical stories of captivity and slavery; the chosen people's wandering in the wilderness; the prophetic warnings of judgment and promises of justice; the Parable of the Good Samaritan; the many examples from Christ's ministry, including his final plea for unity; the Apostle Paul's seemingly endless quest to unite Jew and Gentile.[21] During subsequent role-playing workshops, the groups' synergism helped the once hotheaded young man overcome his desire to retaliate. The sociologist in him might have suggested that the movement's dynamics verged on groupthink, yet Zwerg, no longer a detached sociologist, saw the group strengthened by a benevolent spirit that defied measurement and quantification.

Although raised in the church, Zwerg says he first experienced a spiritual epiphany when asked to reread the Bible during workshops. Studying the Sermon on the Mount and seriously contending with the Biblical injunctions—love your enemies, pray for those who persecute you, live your life in service to others—led Zwerg to conclude that the Gospel's radical message was clearly that love, not violence, is how God binds people to him and to each other. Zwerg came to believe that a "good Christian" must not only nonviolently but also proactively change sinful social conditions. Convinced that Christian love could, nay, *must* be politically transformative, he began reading the Bible more carefully. For the young activist, the Scriptures felt alive and pulsating; they were no longer dry words written by deceased prophets. One day, in the middle of an especially vivacious meeting full of hand clapping and song singing, Zwerg realized the he did not have to love or forgive those who spat on him and called him names, but that he *did* love and he *did* forgive. He sang, "The Lord will see us through" with renewed gusto, and, for the first time, he genuinely believed in that divine promise. The once intemperate twenty-year-old swore to nonviolence not as a tactic but as a religious commitment.

— ∎ —

During Zwerg's sophomore year in college, after months of preparation, the SNCC determined their new recruit was ready to participate in an actual demonstration. Approaching the segregated neighborhood movie theater, Zwerg bought two tickets and gave one to his black friend Bill Harbor. As rehearsed in countless workshops, Zwerg nonchalantly asked Harbor, "Hey, do you want to see a movie?" The men proceeded to enter the theater but never made it past the carpeted hallways. An infuriated segregationist snuck up behind Zwerg and smashed a wrench against his skull. The blow immediately knocked Zwerg unconscious. His friends dragged him to the sidewalk and called an ambulance.

Discharged from the hospital days later with a bluish purple bruise protruding from his sandy blond hair like a nested ostrich egg, Zwerg continued his efforts. Repeatedly knocked down, beaten up, and spat upon, Zwerg recalled the abuses heaped on the Son of God and drew strength to resist lashing out in anger. Shortly afterward, the theater's management was sufficiently embarrassed by the negative attention and negotiated a settlement that included integrating its facilities. Recognized for his commitment, Zwerg was invited to join the steering committee of the SNCC in Nashville. With the same passion that Zwerg once used to analyze and dissect social relations, he now was in a position, with the aid of his religious convictions, to radically transform those relations.

- ! -

When Zwerg first found out about the Freedom Rides organized by CORE, he saw the participants as disciples of Jesus who adopted radically Christian methods to expedite social change that would ultimately reconcile victims and aggressors. When accepted and offered up in union with the suffering of Jesus, their own suffering would remit the just punishment of a society's sins and lead to a moral awakening. Most Americans regarded the Freedom Riders as either reckless Northern agitators or courageous national heroes, but Zwerg shared the Freedom Riders' steadfast belief in the promise of Psalm 27: *I am still confident of this: I will see the goodness of the Lord in the land of the living.*

Zwerg had once wondered how King survived a pummeling, blade attack, bomb explosion, and countless death threats without succumbing to crippling doubt. Now, Zwerg fully understood that the reason lay beyond the realm of the purely rational. Dr. King once explained in his writing, "I don't think anyone in a situation like this can go through it without confronting moments of real fear, but I have always had something that gave me an inner sense of assurance, and an inner sense of security. . . . I have always felt a sense of cosmic companionship."[22] The stronger Zwerg's own religious convictions grew, the more he too felt a sense of cosmic companionship that helped him overcome moments of fear.

When the SNCC decided to organize another Freedom Ride, from Nashville to Birmingham, student activist Ruby Doris Smith called the Department of Justice in Washington, DC, to ask for protection. She reported back, "The Justice Department said no, they couldn't protect anyone, but if something happened, they would investigate. You know how they do."[23] After witnessing the vicious reaction against the first group of Freedom Riders, SNCC organizers were well aware they were potentially chartering buses not for New Orleans but for the city morgue.

When Zwerg heard about the next ride, he immediately volunteered, seeing it as an opportunity to further live out his religious commitments. The SNCC, estimating it had sufficient funds to support ten Freedom Riders, had a lively debate into the twilight hours on how best to whittle down the list of eighteen volunteers. With only a few hours remaining before the Riders' departure, temporary chairman Jim Bevel announced his selection. The chosen included eight blacks and two whites, of which Zwerg was the only white man. Upon learning he had been chosen to participate in the potentially fatal mission, Zwerg reflected: "After we had talked it out and I was one of those chosen to go, I went back to my room and spent a lot of time reading the Bible and praying. Because of what had happened in Birmingham and in Anniston, because our phones were tapped . . . none of us honestly expected to live through this."[24]

■ · ■

After the steering committee adjourned around 10:00 PM, several of the newly elected Freedom Riders solemnly penned last-minute wills and letters to loved ones. The correspondence was marked "to be delivered if I'm killed." They also made emotional phone calls, communicating that these might be the last calls of their young lives.

Zwerg's mother was hysterical when she learned her son might die. She yelled into the phone, "You cannot do this to us, Jim. You cannot do this to us." When Zwerg replied he had never been more certain of anything in his life, his mother said he was foolhardy and selfish to participate in such a dangerous and provocative form of protest. She warned that Zwerg's decision could kill his father—who had a heart condition—and hung up. The heartbroken woman realized she did not want a saint but a son. She and her husband had raised their children to attend college, get married, and lead wholesome lives. Following Christian ethos, Zwerg's mother reasoned, required regular church participation and occasional donations to charities—it certainly did not require involvement in a radical fringe movement bent on breaking the law halfway across the country. Having seen the horrific images of the earlier Freedom Riders attacked by arsonists, Zwerg's mother wondered why her son thought this ride would be any different or make any bigger impact. She could not fathom what convinced her son to martyr himself for a cause that seemed so removed from his own life. Although she sympathized with her son's belief that God created all people as equals, she strongly believed that politics was best left to politicians rather than twenty-year-olds unversed in political nuances. She worried that her son was so radicalized that, even if he survived the Freedom Rides, he would continue sacrificing himself on subsequent rides like a lamb at the altar. And what next? Would her son's inflated confidence in nebulous principles lead him to partake in ever-riskier acts of protest in a country plagued by racial hatreds? Would an angry segregationist eventually kill her son and leave her a grieving mother?

Zwerg later reflected that his parents' disapproval "was very hard because these were the two people who taught me to love, and when I was trying to live love, they didn't understand." In the letter he wrote for them in the event of his death, Zwerg thanked his parents for providing the ethical foundation that led to his decision. That night he cried himself to sleep reading Psalm 27: *The Lord is my light and my salvation . . . though my father and mother forsake me, the Lord will receive me.* Unlike his parents, Zwerg saw his religious obligations as both personal and political.

- ■ -

Early on May 17, 1961, Zwerg and nine other groggy SNCC Freedom Riders rose from a fitful slumber, packed their bags, and boarded the 6:45 AM bus in Nashville. Nash, one of the student leaders, spoke in code to circumvent any eavesdroppers, informing Shuttlesworth that a shipment of ten chickens was scheduled to arrive in Birmingham by late morning. Nash also informed the Justice Department officials in Washington of the students' plans, remaining undeterred when they pleaded with her to cancel the ride.[25] "We signed our last wills and testaments last night," Nash calmly explained to John Seigenthaler, a Justice Department aide. "We cannot let violence overcome nonviolence."[26]

As the bus departed the terminal, a somewhat reckless Zwerg insisted on conspicuously sitting next to his black friend, Paul Brooks, near the front of the bus in violation of Alabama law.[27] When the racially mixed riders were stopped at the Birmingham, Alabama, city limits, the police started badgering Brooks and Zwerg. When Brooks was ordered to sit in the back of the bus, he politely explained that he was very comfortable where he was, thank you. The furious police instructed Zwerg to move so they could arrest Brooks, but Zwerg noted he was rather comfortable too, thank you. Both men were placed under arrest, removed from the bus, seated in a squad car, and hauled to the Birmingham jail.

Police officers proceeded to check the remaining passengers' tickets and became alarmed when they discovered that eight other passengers held identical tickets marked Nashville–Birmingham–Montgomery–Jackson–New Orleans. Convinced the group comprised outside agitators, the officers detained the remaining Freedom Riders and prevented them from leaving the bus. Maintaining the discipline learned in workshops, the Riders asked the officers whether they were World War II veterans and, if so, what had they fought for? They asked the officers if they were Christians and, if so, did they believe Christ had died for all people?[28] A crowd metastasized at the terminal as news spread of the Freedom Riders' presence in Birmingham. The Riders pleaded for over an hour with the police to respect their constitutional rights and let them disembark, but the police insisted on keeping the Riders in "protective custody" and forcibly obstructed the bus exit.

Zwerg, who wore an ill-fitting suit and held a pocket Bible, was thrown into a cell with twenty men in various states of inebriation. The police introduced Zwerg as a "nigger lover for the Freedom Riders." Frightened but forcing himself to remain calm, Zwerg spoke to his cell mates about the Freedom Rides and learned many of them were Catholics who themselves felt discriminated against in the predominately Baptist South. They did not agree with Zwerg's civil rights crusade but respected him enough to leave him unscathed, much to the policemen's chagrin.

The Riders, detained in separate facilities on the same jail block, communicated with each other through gospel songs. When Zwerg sang the lyrics "keep your eyes on the prize / hold on," ten of his cell mates joined in, their united voices wafting through the jail cell and communicating to Riders held in protective custody elsewhere that Zwerg was safe. Of all the sacred songs in the activists' repertoire, "We Shall Overcome" best captured the movement's religious, interracial, and nonviolent emphasis; Zwerg belted the verse, "God is on our side," throughout the night.

— ∎ —

When Zwerg was taken to court the next morning, a number of his cell mates confided, "Jim, we really don't agree with you, but we wish you all the best." Once released from jail, Zwerg reunited with the other Riders and agreed to continue the ride to Montgomery along with additional student volunteers from Nashville. Now nineteen students strong, the Riders returned to the Greyhound terminal. However, every bus driver adamantly refused to help. One driver explained, "I have only one life to give, and I'm not going to give it to NAACP or CORE." Without a bus to board, Zwerg and the other Riders spent the night at the Birmingham bus terminal as police reluctantly monitored a mob of three thousand disgruntled Southerners—led by Robert Shelton, Grand Dragon of the Alabama Ku Klux Klan—that lurked nearby. In *Parting the Waters*, Taylor Branch described the fear rippling through the air:

> At first, officers merely reprimanded stray whites who walked across the feet of the seated Freedom Riders or deliberately spilled drinks into their laps, but canine units eventually moved the whites back out of the terminal building. The Freedom Riders sang "We Shall Overcome." John Lewis and others began to preach in tandem. One of the more devout students could not help noting with satisfaction that fear seemed to deepen the reverence of a few skeptics who had been perfunctory about earlier religious devotionals. As night fell, bystanders tossed occasional rocks over the heads of policemen through the terminal windows.[29]

Despite the overall supine response of the Kennedy administration, Attorney General Robert F. Kennedy worried violence would erupt if the students remained in Birmingham and grew increasingly emotionally committed to their cause. Kennedy extracted a reluctant promise from Alabama governor John Patterson to protect the Freedom Riders and then called Greyhound's president to demand he procure a new driver.[30] When the ride resumed on the morning of May 20, the Freedom Riders were overwhelmed by the show of force—police cars with submachine guns attached to the backseats, planes whirring overhead—accompanying their bus. Fearful of a Klan ambush, the bus sped across the highway toward Montgomery.

When they arrived at the Montgomery Greyhound terminal, the squad car stationed there inexplicably took off. The lack of vehicular traffic in the vicinity left a pregnant stillness that made Zwerg uneasy.

At the terminal gates, reporters and cameramen eagerly awaited the group. Yet the terminal seemed too calm—eerily calm—and the Riders wondered if segregationists hadn't received news of their arrival. Zwerg disembarked first, looking for Reverend Ralph Abernathy or others from the organizing committee who were planning to chaperone the Riders to local homes and prepare them for the next leg of their journey. From the corner of his eye, Zwerg observed a burly man, lurking in the terminal's shadow, who approached the bus and made what looked like a signal. Within seconds, a terrifying whirlwind of livid segregationists raged through the streets and into the terminal. They surrounded Zwerg, calculating the best way to attack him for his audacity to "betray" his race. Zwerg felt his breath leave him, but he commanded his feet to remain planted firmly on the ground. He stuffed his clenched fists into his trouser pockets lest they act on their own accord and bowed his head in prayer: *God give me strength to remain nonviolent, please be with me, and forgive them for they do not know what they are doing.*

The mob descended with diabolical ferocity and screams of "filthy Communist, nigger lover, you're not going to integrate Montgomery!" One of the Klansmen pinned Zwerg's head between his knees, allowing others to use it as a punching bag. They methodically knocked out his teeth and stomped his face into the ground. White women clawed at his skin with their nails. Another Klansman stomped on Zwerg's back with his steel-tipped shoes to crack his spine, while yet another used Zwerg's own suitcase against him as a sledgehammer. Bleeding profusely and teetering on the edge of consciousness, Zwerg continued praying, but the words slurred together. The enraged mob broke three of his vertebrae, crushed his nose, shattered his teeth, dislocated his shoulder, and pummeled his right eye. Once Zwerg lost focus and his body went limp, his attackers tossed him over the railing of the bus-loading platform. He landed on the concrete ten feet below with a dull but chilling thud.[31]

Other Freedom Riders were summarily shoved over the terminal ramp wall and beaten unconscious by a mob wielding bats, pipes, and knives. A Klansman restrained one of Zwerg's friends, William Barbee, while another Klansman jammed a jagged piece of pipe in his ear, and a third cracked his skull with a baseball bat. The vigilante violence was directed not only at the Riders but also at journalists, photographers, black bystanders, and John Siegenthaler, aide to Attorney General Robert Kennedy, who had been dispatched to Montgomery to assist the travelers. For twenty excruciatingly long minutes, several hundred riot-ers were permitted free reign before police arrived to restore order.

Southern police demonstrated no urgency to help the mauled Riders. Zwerg was refused immediate medical attention on the pretext that no white ambulances were available for transport and no black ambulances were allowed to assist. Fearing their friend was on the brink of death, two Freedom Riders enlisted the help of a reporter and carried Zwerg to an empty taxi, but the white driver grabbed the keys from the igni-tion and disappeared. In the commotion, many of the Freedom Riders were separated. Zwerg faded in and out of consciousness. In a fleeting moment of lucidity, however, he realized he was in a moving vehicle and surrounded by deep Southern voices. *My God*, he thought, *I'm going to be lynched*. With that, he lost consciousness completely.

A full forty-eight hours later, Zwerg regained consciousness and real-ized, much to his surprise, that he was not hanging from a tree as he had expected. Instead, he lay incapacitated in a Montgomery hospital bed. The men who had transported him were law enforcement agents who had used the bus terminal's rear entrance to clandestinely load him in their car and shepherd him to the hospital. Shortly afterward, the attend-ing nurse learned a lynch mob was within half a block of the hospital and covertly administered Zwerg a sedative in hopes of preventing the trau-matized young man from regaining consciousness when they descended. However, at the last moment, the mob was prevented from entering the hospital. Zwerg remained hospitalized, in critical condition, for five days.

■ ∙ ■

Photos of Zwerg's bloody, mutilated face ran nationwide in *Time* and *Life* magazines and in Associated Press newspapers. In one iconic photo, Zwerg stands next to Freedom Rider John Lewis and holds a white hand-kerchief pocked with bloodstains as he uses his forefingers to fish several dislodged teeth from his mouth. In another, the lanky man with down-cast eyes and a blood-splattered suit slouches against a wall in a state of utter shock. When the images reached the public, police were asked why they waited twenty agonizing minutes before intervening. They responded that they knew nothing about the Freedom Rides. In truth, Birmingham's police commissioner, Eugene "Bull" Connor, was a mem-ber of the Ku Klux Klan himself.

In the white section of Saint Jude's Hospital, a physically battered but spiritually jubilant Zwerg told reporters essentially what they had heard from other Freedom Riders six days earlier. Wheezing for breath and straining each word, Zwerg confirmed the movement remained undeterred:

> Segregation must be stopped, it must be broken down. Those of us who are on the Freedom Ride will continue the Freedom Ride. I'm not sure that I'll be able to, but we're going on to New Orleans no matter what happens. We're dedicated to this. We will take hitting and we will take beatings. We're willing to accept death. But we're going to keep coming until we can ride from anywhere in the South to any place else in the South without anybody making any comments. Just as American citizens.[32]

Dr. King, who had followed the Freedom Rides closely, read a declaration at a press conference confirming the ride would persist through the heart of Mississippi, martial law or not, protection or not. The civil rights leader added, "We would not like to see anyone die. . . . We all love life, and there are no martyrs here—but we are well aware that we may have some casualties. . . . These students are willing to face death if necessary."[33]

Embarrassed by the national scandal, the Kennedy Administration called for a "cooling off period," a moratorium on the rides. Civil rights activists unequivocally rejected this call and redoubled their efforts. They organized a Freedom Riders Coordinating Committee to support interstate integration efforts through June, July, August, and September. Over sixty different Freedom Rides were held throughout the remainder of the year. Subsequent Freedom Rides included not only students but also two professors of religion from Wesleyan University and two clergymen from Yale.[34] Many participants in the movement were seminarians who shared Zwerg's faith in the redeeming love of Christ and the potency of nonviolent civil disobedience to overcome formidable obstacles.

Taking comfort in their belief in a higher arbiter of justice than Southern judges, the Riders shifted their strategy away from provoking segregationists and toward overwhelming county jails with their presence. They established a pattern where they were arrested and jailed while passing through Jackson, Mississippi, in an endeavor to supersaturate the Jackson and Hinds county jails. Later batches of Freedom Riders were transferred to the notorious Parchman Penitentiary and subjected to degrading treatment that included solitary confinement in the Maximum Security Unit (i.e., death row), issuance of only underwear, and no exercise. When Freedom Riders refused to stop singing freedom songs or comply with orders, prison guards routinely confiscated their mattresses, sheets, and toothbrushes. Wardens often removed the screens from the jail windows to invite mosquitoes to prey upon the Riders as they attempted to sleep in the excruciating summer heat. On more than one occasion, guards shocked Riders with electric cattle prods. An estimated 450 civil rights activists participated in one or more Freedom Rides, and the proportion of those jailed was roughly two-thirds college students, three-quarters male, and more than half black. Quakers and Jews (including several rabbis) were especially well represented among the whites.[35]

Behind the scenes, the Kennedy Administration brokered a deal with the governors of Alabama and Mississippi—the governors agreed to protect the Riders from mob violence, thereby ending negative media coverage, in exchange for the federal government agreeing not to intervene when police arrested the Freedom Riders for violating segregation ordinances at odds with federal laws. At a time when the Berlin Wall was going up and tensions with the Soviet Union flared, the Freedom Riders posed an unwanted distraction and major embarrassment for the White House by undermining the nation's image as the "land of the free."[36] The Kennedy Administration feared white vigilantes would carry out their threats of violence against prominent black churches, possibly sparking massive race riots. On May 29, 1961, Attorney General Kennedy pushed hard to secure a desegregation order from the Interstate Commerce Commission (ICC), personally requesting it to enforce the bus-desegregation ruling *Sarah Keys v. Carolina Coach Company*, which had been issued in November 1955 and explicitly rejected "separate but equal" in the realm of interstate bus travel. Kennedy also addressed US race relations in a broadcast beamed to over sixty countries via the Voice of America radio network. "[Mob violence] doesn't represent the vast majority of people in the South . . . and it certainly doesn't represent the feelings of the United States Government or the American people," he insisted. "There's no question that in the next thirty or forty years a Negro can also achieve the same position that my brother has as president of the United States."[37]

In September 1961 the ICC complied with Kennedy's request and established strict policies upholding the ruling against segregation—a full six years after it was first passed. By the end of the year, passengers of all skin colors sat wherever they wished on interstate vehicles for the first time in the nation's history. Within six months of the inaugural Freedom Ride, Zwerg and his friends rejoiced watching city officials remove "White" and "Colored" signs from bus terminals, drinking fountains, and waiting rooms.

— ∎ —

For a brief moment in time, Zwerg believes, he was blessed to see what "bearing the cross" might mean. "When I looked at Jesus of Nazareth, I saw someone living his faith, and during the Freedom Rides, I had a brief opportunity to dramatically live out my faith," he said. He later recalled that an incredible religious experience preceded his near-fatal beating:

> I knew that I was not alone so I was not scared. I felt God's presence on that bus platform. I felt that incredible bond of love, agape, that gives us worth and meaning. That love empowered all of us and made us so much more than what any of us were as individuals or even as a group. Love is the eternal motif of nonviolence, and it is how God binds us to each other and to Him.[38]

In 1961 King honored Zwerg with a Freedom Award from the Southern Christian Leadership Conference and also successfully encouraged him to enroll at Garrett Theological Seminary in Evanston, Illinois. Zwerg later went on to serve as a minister in the United Church of Christ.

For his part, Zwerg insists he's no hero. The Freedom Rides, he says, were full of extraordinary acts of courage on the part of countless ordinary people. He later learned that a black bystander, just off work, had stumbled into the mob violence. The elderly man diverted the mob's attention after they knocked Zwerg unconscious by insisting, "Stop beating that kid. If you want to beat someone, beat me."[39] And they did. The man was still comatose when Zwerg left the hospital. Zwerg credits this Good Samaritan for saving his life, saying, "I knew what I was getting into when I boarded that bus, but he sacrificed himself without a second thought." Zwerg believes the movement's ideals inspired complete strangers to exhibit unearthly courage on behalf of one another whether or not they called themselves Christians.

■ ● ■

The Freedom Riders achieved their goal of desegregating interstate travel but remained far from realizing their loftier ambition of catalyzing a moral reawakening throughout society. An undercurrent of violent racism continued to rear its ugly head in the following years, reminding Zwerg that the Beloved Community—King's vision of a completely integrated society, a community of love and justice wherein brotherhood characterized all social relations—was a far cry from contemporary America. On September 15, 1963, the Ku Klux Klan bombed the Sixteenth Street Baptist Church and killed four girls (ironically, during a Sunday-school class on "The Love That Forgives"). On November 22, 1963, King watched a breaking-news bulletin announcing John F. Kennedy's assassination and correctly predicted to his wife, "This is what is going to happen to me, this is such a sick society."[40] On June 21, 1964, James Chaney, a young black civil rights activist, and two white allies, Andrew Goodman and Michael Schwerner, were shot to death. Even after Jim Crow laws ended, blacks remained discriminated against in the housing and job markets, experiencing disproportionally higher rates of poverty and disenfranchisement than whites.[41]

Sociologists may see these shortcomings as the political limitations of a religious vision, but Zwerg agrees with Dr. King that the long arc of the moral universe slowly but surely bends toward justice. In 1986 Zwerg returned to Montgomery to join several former Riders in commemorating the twenty-fifth anniversary of the Freedom Rides. En route to the reunion, the civil rights activist sat next to a fifteen-year-old African American who had never heard of the Freedom Rides. "Here was a young man riding with me to Montgomery as if it were the most natural and uneventful thing in the world, which it thankfully was." Zwerg added, "So, yes, we truly accomplished something!"

2 DANIEL BERRIGAN

The Soul of the Vietnam Antiwar Movement

I had declared my conscientious objection. A veteran of D-Day and the Battle of the Bulge, my father said I was a chicken. I probably was. But I was also my father's son, and he had taught me to take religion seriously. I did. I took it both personally and politically, and that was the difference between us.

—JAMES FARRELL, *conscientious objector* [1]

I wake up in the morning each day, and don't know what to do.

I don't know what to do about what I see. Since I see, I can't rightly deny what I see. But what to do? I feel like a blind man ordered to paint a sunset or a quadriplegic in a marathon.

The best thing one can do in such a fix (the best I can do) is—not to do nothing.

—DANIEL BERRIGAN, *To Dwell in Peace*

On June 11, 1963, a Buddhist monk left Ouang Pagoda and drove to a busy traffic intersection in Saigon, Vietnam. The seventy-three-year-old man, Thich Quang Duc, descended from his rusted Austin sedan and quietly sat on the pavement in the classic Buddhist meditation pose, the lotus position. Nuns in gray headdresses and other monks in orange robes surrounded him and slowly began chanting a mournful sutra. One monk doused Duc with gasoline as if it were holy water. With his Buddhist prayer beads in his right hand, Duc calmly opened a box of matches and struck one. Fire instantly engulfed him. The chanting stopped. Fiercely bright flames leapt into the sky, leaving choking black smoke in their wake. From head to feet, Duc's body was subjected to inferno.

Duc's body was re-cremated during his funeral, but his heart miraculously remained intact and did not burn. Vietnamese Buddhists placed the organ in a glass chalice at Xa Loi Pagoda. Even today, his heart is regarded as a holy symbol of the compassion emanating from an enlightened soul.

— • —

Duc's self-immolation was his final act of protest against the puppet dictatorship of Ngo Dinh Diem, which the United States had sponsored in 1955 to prevent the unification of South and North Vietnam.[2] Although most Vietnamese were Buddhists, Diem was a Catholic and his regime denied religious freedom and violently quashed political dissent. A month earlier, when thousands of Buddhists had peacefully demonstrated against him, soldiers opened fire and trampled several monks to death.[3]

Photos of the monk ablaze spread across the wire services, appeared on the front pages of newspapers worldwide, and were seared into the public's collective conscience. Several monks followed Duc's example of self-immolation, and Diem's paramilitaries ransacked Buddhist temples, wounded thirty monks, arrested fourteen hundred people, and closed down the pagodas.[4] When demonstrations erupted across the city, police indiscriminately opened fire, this time killing nine people. When one protest drew ten thousand demonstrators, the United States secretly sent several thousand more troops to bolster Diem's limping regime. Diem's chief adviser, Ngo Dinh Nhu, announced she would "clap hands at seeing another monk barbecue show," which further turned local and world opinion against American support of the Diem regime in Saigon.[5]

— • —

Carlotta Ribar, Chris Kearns, and Tom Cornell were sitting in the New York City editorial office of *The Catholic Worker*—the progressive newspaper started by Dorothy Day in tandem with the Catholic Worker Movement to promote social and economic justice—when their colleague Bob

Steed stormed in, visibly agitated about the most recent string of self-immolations by Buddhist monks in South Vietnam.[6] The four decided they must react in accordance to their commitment to "the justice and charity of Jesus Christ." Cornell quickly drafted a memo to leaders of peace groups in New York City to discuss a joint protest against US policy in Vietnam.

With the monks' deaths fading from news headlines, Cornell and Kearns feared the weeks needed to coordinate a peace rally would make it less timely. So, they threw the memo into the wastebasket and decided to immediately choose a spot identified with South Vietnam to picket. But what spot? There was neither a Vietnam consulate in New York nor a state-sponsored airline, but the young Catholics located the apartment of Saigon's Permanent Observer to the United Nations. They spread the word that *The Catholic Worker* would be picketing him for two hours each afternoon for ten days and invited other peace groups to join on the final day. Over 250 antiwar activists answered Cornell and Kearns's call, arriving on the tenth day carrying signs outside the United Nations stating: "We demand an end to U.S. military support of Diem's regime."[7] They made national television coverage for staging the first Vietnam War protest.

Transcending religious loyalties but drawing on their Catholic faith for strength of conviction, Kearns and Cornell sparked what would become the largest antiwar movement in the nation's history. The August 23, 1965, issue of *Life* magazine featured a black-and-white photo of Kearns, an "all-American boy" with a crew cut and collared shirt, proudly holding a burning draft card. Eventually, the tradition of burning draft cards that was started by two young Catholic Workers would lead to 3,500 publicly destroyed draft cards despite Congress passing a law that made burning one a crime punishable by a $10,00 fine and five years in prison.[8]

Flag-waving counterdemonstrators frequently yelled, "Burn yourselves, not your draft cards." Much to their dismay, a handful of antiwar demonstrators began doing exactly that after President Johnson announced major troop increases and the bombing of North Vietnam.

- ∎ -

On March 16, 1965, an eighty-two-year-old survivor of Nazi terror, Alice Herz, set herself on fire in Detroit. Herz identified as a Quaker and was of Jewish and Christian background but explained in a letter to her daughter that her sympathies transcended religious affiliations: "I choose the illuminating death of a Buddhist to protest against a great country trying to wipe out a small country for no reason."[9]

In the late afternoon of November 2, 1965, the executive secretary of a Quaker community in Baltimore—thirty-two-year-old Norman Morrison—walked to the river entrance of the Pentagon and stood outside the office window of the secretary of defense, Robert McNamara. Emulating Herz, he doused himself with kerosene and set himself on fire. Morrison's widow later described him as a deeply religious man who was increasingly consumed by existential questions: "What can a man do with his life? How can he best show his beliefs? When must thoughts give way to deeds?"[10] According to his widow, Morrison decided to sacrifice his life after reading an article by a South Vietnamese priest about the bombing of a village there. Three decades later, McNamara confessed he was consumed with doubts about his recent remarks defending the war when he looked outside his window and witnessed Morrison burning alive. "I believed I understood and shared some of his thoughts." But instead of reversing course, McNamara said, "I bottle[d] up my emotions and avoided talking about them with anyone."[11]

On the chilly morning of November 9, 1965, a week after Morrison's death, Roger Allen LaPorte sat in front of the Dag Hammarskjöld Library at the United Nations in New York City with a canister of gasoline and a match. The twenty-two-year-old, six-foot-tall son of a lumberjack had enrolled at Columbia University after graduating from a Catholic high school but dropped out to join the Catholic Workers and serve soup to the Lower East Side's tenement dwellers. LaPorte chose the tranquil winter hour of 5:00 AM to assume the lotus position of a Buddhist monk in front of a granite wall chiseled with a quote from the Book of Isaiah: *They shall beat their swords into plowshares, and their spears into pruning hooks; nation shall not lift up sword against nation, neither shall they learn war anymore.* Twenty minutes later, LaPorte doused himself with gasoline and lit himself on fire cap-a-pie. He died the next day at Bellevue Hospital with second- and third-degree burns covering 95 percent of his body. When asked why he had set himself aflame, a grotesquely disfigured LaPorte calmly and lucidly replied, "I'm a Catholic Worker. I'm against this war, all wars. I did this as a religious act."[12]

Fewer than a dozen Americans cremated themselves alive in opposition to the Vietnam War, but those who did captured the urgency and intensity of sentiments that the antiwar, religiously inspired Left would continue expressing throughout the Vietnam War. Although Herz, Morrison, and LaPorte did not share the Buddhist monks' religion, they viewed the US involvement in Vietnam as an affront against God. Many Vietnamese regarded Herz, Morrison, and LaPorte as heroes; the government of North Vietnam even issued a stamp in Morrison's honor and named a street after him in Hanoi.[13] Reactions in the United States, however, were far more mixed and created schisms that would only widen in the coming decade, especially within the Catholic community—a community long accused in American history of not being sufficiently pro-American and patriotic. Cardinal Francis Spellman of New York immediately labeled LaPorte's self-immolation as sinful, sanctified the involvement of the United States in Vietnam as morally justified, and concluded that LaPorte had disregarded the law of Christ's compassion by leaving behind a grieving family. The left-leaning *Catholic Worker* issued a statement in diametric opposition to Spellman's:

> [LaPorte] was trying to say to the American people that we must turn away from violence in Vietnam, and he was trying to say something about the violence that is eroding our own society here in the United States and our city of New York. And so he made this sacrifice, attempting to absorb this violence and hatred personally, deflecting it from others by taking it voluntarily to himself.[14]

Mainstream Catholics who regarded suicide as the worst possible moral transgression—a cardinal sin implying despair and a loss of faith in God—recoiled at the *Catholic Worker*'s defense of LaPorte and redoubled their support for the constituted authority of both church and state.

However, one renegade Jesuit priest with sunken eyes, chiseled features, and an elfin stature, Daniel Berrigan, refused to refer to LaPorte's death as a suicide. His close friend, the Vietnamese Buddhist monk Thich Nhat Hanh, had explained to him that immolation was sometimes an offering to humanity through "the willingness to take suffering on yourself to make yourself suffer for the sake of purification, for the sake of communication."[15] Berrigan's superiors forbade him to make public statements about the death, but he delivered the homily at LaPorte's funeral anyway. At the mass, Berrigan asked, "What if the death reflected not despair, but a self-offering attuned to the sacrifice of

Christ? Would not such a presumption show mercy toward the dead, as well as honoring the living?"[16]

The questions Berrigan dared raise—and all their implications about the meaning of Christianity in times of war—infuriated Cardinal Spellman, who had long resented Berrigan's prominent role as an organizer of Clergy and Laity Concerned About Vietnam (CALCAV), a committee of some forty antiwar clergy including Abraham Joshua Heschel, Richard John Neuhaus, Harvey Cox, and William Sloane Coffin.

Spellman had no sympathy for antiwar radicals such as Berrigan; Spellman had supported Ngo Dinh Diem for the presidency of Vietnam as far back as the early 1950s when the Catholic Diem was attending a New Jersey seminary during his two-year exile. After Diem took power in 1954 and was threatened by Ho Chi Minh forces, Spellman had ratcheted up his support for an American intervention to stabilize Diem's regime. The cardinal was increasingly alarmed at the sight of Catholic refugees fleeing the communist North, and he regarded the war effort as the best way to keep Catholic-friendly Saigon safe from falling to Godless communists.

Spellman, who was a key financial donor to the New York Jesuits, ordered Berrigan immediately expelled from New York City, and, within two weeks of delivering the homily, the disobedient priest was banished to Latin America, where his Jesuit superiors assigned him to the editorial board of a missionary magazine. Berrigan was shocked and hurt by the Church's harsh retaliation against anyone refusing to toe the official line. In a letter to his close friend and confidant Thomas Merton, the Trappist poet-monk and forerunner in the Catholic pacifist tradition, Berrigan questioned his allegiance to the Jesuit order and spoke of looming depression. Merton himself had previously considered abandoning the Trappists but now wrote to Berrigan, "We must stay where we are. We must stay with our community, even though it's absurd, makes no sense, and causes great suffering."[17] The suggestion of suffering for the sake of an unwelcoming community would anger or confuse most people, but Merton's words comforted the pariah priest. Over the years, Berrigan had come to believe his religious commitments required perpetual acts of sacrifice—perhaps, one day, sacrifices as extreme as the one LaPorte had made in setting himself on fire. Berrigan saw himself waging an epic battle on behalf of the mild, meek, and nonviolent Jesus, whose image the Church hierarchy wished to warp into an armed mercenary. He took comfort in the prophets of Israel in the days of Elijah who spoke of a remnant of true believers who would remain faithful to their God, never bending their knees to Baal.

= ∎ =

Although Cardinal Spellman temporarily succeeded in banishing Berrigan, he ultimately failed to extinguish the polemical questions that the subversive priest incited though his homily, questions that he would continue inciting throughout the protracted Vietnam War. During the 1960s and early '70s, Berrigan organized the radical core of the Vietnam peace movement and emerged as the nation's most controversial and heterodox Catholic priest. The father of the Catholic "Ultra-Resistance"—a group of antiwar activists determined to end the Vietnam War using any means short of violence—Berrigan led his supporters in everything from burning their own draft cards to theatrically raiding draft boards and burning the draft cards of others.

On May 17, 1968, in a media spectacle infused with religious symbolism that ultimately ended in a cinematic FBI chase, Berrigan and eight other pacifists invaded the Selective Service System office in suburban Baltimore, doused draft cards with homemade napalm, and recited the Lord's Prayer in full view of the public. The draft board raiders, who came to be known as the "Catonsville Nine," reinvigorated the antiwar movement by inspiring over one hundred similar acts of protest, shook the foundation of the tradition-bound Catholic Church, and enraged patriotic Americans who saw Berrigan and his younger brother, Philip, as communist apologists, treasonous criminals, or, at best, unwitting puppets of the Vietcong. Many Catholic Americans were particularly distressed by what they regarded as the Berrigans' hooligan tactics, and they insisted that a priest's job was to hold mass and celebrate the Eucharist, not appear on the nightly news in prison shackles, ranting against their wartime president. Even within the antiwar movement, stalwarts grumbled about a cult of personality around the Berrigans and a perceived dismissive attitude toward anyone unwilling to aspire to a similar level of martyrdom. Yet the Berrigans' staunchest supporters insisted they were modern-day prophets whose civil disobedience harkened back to Thoreau's protest of slavery, Gandhi's protest of British colonialism, and Dr. King's protest of segregation.

- ∎ -

Daniel Berrigan was born May 9, 1921, in the snowcapped Mesabi Iron Range of Minnesota and, with his six Irish-Catholic brothers, shared a bleak, drifting existence similar to that of *The Grapes of Wrath*'s Okies. His socialist-leaning father—a subscriber to the *Catholic Worker*—led them all on a four-mile trek to church each Sunday regardless of blizzards or thunderstorms, and he routinely subjected his peripatetic family to his mercurial moods, impossible-to-fulfill demands, and bouts of violent rage.

A sensitive child who expressed himself through images rather than words, Berrigan regarded his father as a capricious tyrant who manipulated virtuous sentiments to justify his "extraordinary conglomerate of passion and illusion," as he later wrote in his autobiography, *To Dwell in Peace*. Berrigan described his "Dado" as a railroad union-organizer whose egalitarian principles stopped short of his own family; he notes that "we grew inured, as the price of survival, to violence as a norm of existence" since "power, rightly, sanely used—this was an enigma to my father."[18] A failed poet whose work was rejected even by parochial Catholic magazines starved for material, Dado may have "lost in the world, [but] he won with us," writes Berrigan. "We, not his peers, were the pawns in his game of power and dominion . . . the shame of it all mounted in his guts like a lake of bile. It overflowed on us."

Young Berrigan seemed to find in his mother the opposite of everything he despised in his father. His German immigrant mother, a brunette milliner named Freda, waged her own private war against her husband using the traditional "weapons of the weak": nonviolent resistance, patient endurance, and indirect confrontation. Berrigan writes, "It was a slave rebellion. She created, within the strait limits set by husband and church a kind of slave culture; within it she breathed free." Noting Catholicism's condemnation of divorce, Berrigan never seriously questioned why his silently suffering mother—a pious Catholic depicted as a paragon of womanly selflessness—did not leave her husband rather than mold her entire life around his tyranny, eventually thriving off her need to resist his overexertion of authority.

When Berrigan was about five years old, his father was fired for attempting to unionize railroad workers, and the family was forced to relocate to Syracuse, New York, where they eked out a living on a ten-acre farm. Dado eventually founded the Electrical Workers Union, the first of its kind in Syracuse, as well as a Catholic interracial council. Spindly and afflicted with weak ankles, Berrigan took refuge in books while his father instructed his more brawny brothers in carpentry, raising crops, and animal husbandry. While not protecting her sons from their father's wrath, Freda cooked so many free meals for hobos during the Great Depression that one marked their barn with a special sign indicating to friends that a warm meal and night's shelter were available there. Berrigan and his brothers meanwhile completed their studies under the tutelage of stentorian Catholic nuns who, he says, thrived on tormenting their young charges by pulling out their hair and pounding their heads against blackboards.

Berrigan later reflected that his parents shared a profound commitment to social justice—"They had an acute sense of the underdog"—but only one of them lived out her ideals in each and every quotidian act. Freda never changed her husband, but she outlived him, even though he died at the age of ninety.

— ∎ —

Berrigan announced before he was old enough to grow facial stubble that he felt called to enter the priesthood. Enamored with the poetry of the Psalms and encouraged by his rosary-reciting mother who had uncles in the Church, Berrigan joined the Society of Jesus at the age of nineteen and underwent rigorous training as war erupted across Europe. Years later, Berrigan explained in an interview with the *Boston Globe* why he decided to join the Society of Jesus despite never having met a Jesuit in his life: "I chose the Jesuits because they offered the longest, the most difficult study."[19] With a tinge of pride, Berrigan said he embraced the Jesuits precisely because of the hardship and toil they promised in their brochures—promises that differed markedly from the plum offers of other orders who showcased communal swimming pools and recreational areas in the glossy pamphlets they circulated to potential recruits.[20] Berrigan, a young ascetic, appreciated that the Jesuits' booklets had all the glitz and glamour of an Amtrak train schedule. The arduous, demanding, and, at times, self-abnegating discipleship of the Jesuits was in keeping with the austerity that Berrigan would choose to live out for the remainder of his long life.

After his ordination in 1952, Berrigan spent the next two years living with a Jesuit community in Lyon, France. In the bucolic French countryside, Berrigan learned about the Jesuits of the so-called worker-priest movement who lived in voluntary poverty. These politically militant worker-priests had strong ties to the country's labor movement and told a young, eager-to-please Berrigan that struggling for social change was a mandate of his Jesuit vows. Several priests regaled Berrigan with stories of leading the French Resistance during World War II, and a few even told him that they once traveled to Germany to clandestinely shepherd persecuted minorities out of the country.

The thirty-three-year-old Berrigan was intensely fascinated by the extreme suffering endured by these macerated Good Samaritans, many of whom had survived the torturous conditions of slave labor camps. At times, Berrigan seemed less concerned with what the priests had achieved than with what they had sacrificed. In his mind, their stories took on Biblical proportions and their righteous suffering seemed to echo that of the Son of God, who so loved the world that he faced societal scorn and sacrificed his own life so others might live forever. The more time Berrigan spent with the French Catholic avant-garde, the more he wondered if, as a sworn disciple of Christ with a vocation as a social redeemer, ostracism and martyrdom lay in his future.

■ ● ■

Berrigan returned from France and started teaching at LeMoyne College in Syracuse, during which time he befriended Catholic Worker Movement founder Dorothy Day. He often took his students on field trips "to get to know certain aspects of the city that they wouldn't be meeting in their own backyard," among them the Catholic Worker houses. In the same way that Berrigan found inspiration in his mother's charity toward hoboes during the Great Depression, he now felt inspired by Day's passion for social causes. He later credited Day—a former journalist who'd traded her Greenwich Village bohemian lifestyle for a nun's vows—for helping him draw his own connections between the poverty and misery of the world and his government's foreign policy. He recollected, "Down at the Bowery, Dorothy used to tell me, 'God has created enough for everyone, but there's not enough for human needs and perpetual warfare. We've got to stay with those at the bottom and those who oppose war.'"[21]

Around that time, Berrigan struck up a mail correspondence with Thomas Merton after reading an article the Trappist monk wrote in the *Catholic Worker* newspaper about possibilities of nuclear war. Merton, along with Day, was one of the most prominent pacifist voices in the country and had a profound influence on Berrigan. "Violence today," Merton wrote, "is white collar violence, the systematically organized bureaucratic and technological destruction of man. . . . Modern technological murder is not directly visible, like individual murder. It is abstract, corporate, businesslike, cool, free of guilt-like feelings and therefore a thousand times more deadly than the eruption of violence out of individual hate."[22]

Seeking deeper guidance and a fatherly mentor, Berrigan frequently visited Merton at Gethsemane Abbey near Louisville, Kentucky. In March 1965 he attended a three-day retreat there, titled "The Roots of Protest," and met renowned antiwar advocates including Gordon Zahn, Tom Cornell, A. J. Muste, Jim Forest, and Howard Zehr. At the retreat, Merton spoke animatedly about Franz Jägerstätter, a Catholic conscientious objector who refused to serve in the army of the Third Reich and was later beheaded for his defiance. Berrigan found himself emphatically nodding when Merton asked, "Was Jägerstätter the only one to uphold the Gospels' dictum of nonviolence? Why should others like him ever again have to stand alone?"[23]

Back at LeMoyne College, Berrigan emerged as a firebrand preacher of Gospel poverty, prodding his students to "get poor," nudging friends to liquidate their assets and relocate to the ghetto, sending students to the Deep South where his younger brother, Philip, was organizing CORE and teaching at an all-black New Orleans high school.[24] In *No Bars to Manhood*, Berrigan explained his early opposition the Vietnam War by saying, "It seemed to me spiritually absurd and suicidal to be pretending to help the poor at home while we bombed the poor abroad."[25]

By early 1965, Berrigan joined Dr. King and other prominent religious leaders—such as Yale's Reverend William Sloane Coffin and the Jewish Theological Seminary's Rabbi Abraham Joshua Heschel—in publicly condemning the war for squandering resources needed to fight poverty, requiring African Americans to bear an unfair share of the risks, mocking the principles of nonviolence, and killing innocent Vietnamese. Berrigan deeply admired King and agreed with the young Baptist minister's prediction: "If America's soul becomes totally poisoned, part of the autopsy must read Vietnam."[26]

That same year, Berrigan cofounded Clergy and Laity Concerned About Vietnam (CALCAV) and spoke publicly about his calling to follow Christ in discipleship committed to justice, solidarity with the poor and oppressed, and prophetic resistance to all warmongering. Berrigan had few supporters at the top of the Catholic hierarchy since the Church overwhelmingly supported the doctrine of "just war" and warned that evil would triumph "in the absence of good men defending liberty." The paradox of the Vietnam War was a familiar one: the people who supported escalating violence and the people who advocated a cease-fire often drew on the same Judeo-Christian God. In Catholic circles, the pro-war impulse was augmented by fears that communists in North Vietnam were persecuting Catholics and pushing them into refugee camps in the South. Cardinal Spellman visited Vietnam and proclaimed the conflict a "war for civilization" and its combatants "soldiers of Christ."[27] For Spellman, the Vietnam conflict was similar to the Spanish Civil War and required Catholics to defend their faith by defeating the "Godless" North Vietnamese government.[28]

- ■ -

After Spellman banished Berrigan to Latin America for his comments on LaPorte's self-immolation, antiwar clergy quickly organized the "Committee for Daniel Berrigan" and mobilized a campaign in his defense. Students at Notre Dame University launched a hunger strike upon learning of Berrigan's expulsion. By Christmas 1965, a full-page ad had appeared in the *New York Times* lambasting Cardinal Spellman for censoring Berrigan and more than fifty supporters had demonstrated outside Spellman's Madison Avenue office holding signs saying, "Merry Christmas, Dan, wherever you are." A rallying point for the emerging Catholic Left, Berrigan's exile generated enough attention to embarrass the Jesuit order, and by March 1966, he finally received a telegram recalling him to New York. Immediately upon returning to his Manhattan apartment, Berrigan snipped a newspaper photo of Cardinal Spellman in full military regalia and plastered it on the inside lid of his toilet along with the beatitude "Blessed are the Peacemakers."[29]

A wounded Berrigan resumed assailing the church for its silence on the Vietnam War, busied himself with organizing the increasingly radicalized Catholic Left, and reoccupied his cochairmanship of CALCAV.

Three weeks after returning, he led a peace march of interfaith clergy through Manhattan, stopping to pray on Fifth Avenue under Saint Patrick's Cathedral, where Cardinal Spellman presided. Berrigan also worked with the Catholic Peace Fellowship to launch a campaign forbidding Catholic priests from acting as military chaplains. Through his writing and speaking engagements, Berrigan called for a more prophetic church that would confront pressing social issues. He traveled with International Pax Christi, a Catholic peace and activist group, to Italy, where he lambasted his country's involvement in Vietnam. As part of CALCAV, Berrigan joined Reverend William Sloane Coffin Jr. in urging nonviolent resistance and affirming the right to selective conscientious objection.

Antiwar clergy increasingly recognized they were in a unique position to win over influential parts of the American middle class—church- and synagogue-goers who would never have responded to the call of the radical Left but who did take notice when their spiritual leaders denounced the war.[30] With this knowledge in mind, Berrigan arrived on Cornell's campus in August 1967, a time when the United States had more than half a million troops in Vietnam and showed no signs of withdrawing. As an assistant director of Cornell United Religious Work, Berrigan counseled students against enlisting in the war and helped run a veritable Underground Railroad to Canada. He attended and led teach-ins against the war at local coffee shops and also busied himself protesting a military research facility on Cornell's campus—a facility that he later referred to as "poison in the Ivy."

Berrigan thrived most when opposing injustices, perceived or real, and soon emerged as a personal nightmare for Cornell's president, James A. Perkins. The outspoken priest used his classes to vivisect the operating procedures of his employer: How did the agricultural school treat the seasonal migrant laborers hired during the apple harvest? What about Cornell's investments in apartheid South Africa? What were the moral consequences of the university's receiving military research grants while bombs rained down on Vietnamese citizens?[31] Many members of the Cornell faculty resented Berrigan's pontificating and accused him of undermining their scientific research as well as heightening campus tensions by lending moral support to draft dodgers. On the other hand, the resolutely secular members of Students for a Democratic Society (SDS) canonized Berrigan as their personal messiah, saw themselves as his disciples, and followed him to activist Mecca: antiwar demonstrations on the Pentagon lawn.

- · -

Despite his frequent arrests at national antiwar protests he had helped organize, Berrigan grew both frustrated by the ongoing bombing campaign and consumed with guilt that he was not doing enough to end the war. In January 30, 1968, Berrigan traveled to Vietnam with Howard Zinn, the World War II air force bombardier and progressive American historian renowned for his prolific scholarship. Flying over the demilitarized zone between North and South Vietnam, Berrigan and Zinn landed in Hanoi shortly after the Tet uprising started in the South. A survey of the damage done by American bombing raids led Berrigan to record his disgust in *Night Flight to Hanoi*: "I felt like a Nazi watching films of Dachau."[32] He went on to elaborate in *The Dark Night of Resistance*, "In our ears was the blaze of air-raid sirens, in our being the shame of the war. We had had certain lessons during that week; crouching in air-raid shelters, hearing the drone of lethal motors and the obscene thud of bucket upon bucket of wrath dropped by those pirate birds."[33] After spending days touring the city and countryside, Berrigan returned home angrier than ever at his country and even less forgiving of himself.

Berrigan increasingly felt with a somewhat alarming certainty: the war was wrong, resistance was right, and pacifism was the only salvation. He once told a lawyer friend with a tinge of cruelty, "If the government were coming for your TVs and cars, then you'd be upset. But, as it is, they're only coming for your sons."[34] Consumed with his antiwar activism, Berrigan sometimes overlooked the complexities of the million and a half "boat people" drowned in the sea by the government of Hanoi, the increasingly violent tactics employed by the left-wing radicalism he once supported at home, and the Molotov cocktail a militant later lobbed at the Cornell chapel.

- · -

Berrigan was no longer content with polite prayer vigils and marches on Capitol Hill. He no longer believed it was enough to distribute leaflets, march, chant, or write checks for charities. He now dismissed the tepid response of CALCAV, whose protests felt safe and even fashionable. So, he began brainstorming more dramatic, expiatory means of protesting the ongoing carnage in Vietnam. What was needed, he decided, was a far larger and bolder sacrifice that would atone for his country's collective sins and testify to his personal willingness to endure handcuffs and prison cells. Although he rejected the "romantic revolutionary" sentiments of violence and maintained that the "means determine the ends," he felt increasingly frustrated that the ends remained the same: the war continued unabated. Somehow, nothing he did seemed to make any difference, and he took that as his personal failure. Berrigan was thoroughly convinced that an extreme, powerful act of self-abnegation on the behalf of greater humanity would catalyze a moral reawakening throughout American society.

Shortly after he returned from Vietnam, Berrigan was sitting at his office desk overlooking the Ithaca gorges when he received a phone call from his brother Philip, who was awaiting sentencing for raiding a Baltimore Customs House and dousing 1-A draft files with blood. Philip explained that the "Baltimore Four," as the media called them, had decided the act of pouring blood in a draft office was a prophetic stroke worthy of Amos and Hosea; the blood could be seen as a surrogate for the blood of Christ and destroying draft files would stall a part of the Pentagon's induction machinery.[35]

Philip, a former second lieutenant who was so disgusted by warfare that he followed his older brother into the priesthood and similarly committed himself to pacifism, proposed that they partake in an upcoming massive, nonviolent break-in at the Catonsville Selective Service Center. Initially, Berrigan balked at the idea of entering a government building and destroying draft cards since he feared it might lead to real violence. However, Philip explained to him that burning draft cards was no more violent than when Moses burned the wayward Israelites' pagan golden calf and Martin Luther incinerated the papal bull of excommunication and the canon law.

The idea of directly engaging the government's war-making structure by raiding Catonsville deeply appealed to Berrigan. But he knew from his experience defending LaPorte that participating in such a radical form of protest would evoke the extreme ire of his superiors, who might very likely banish him forever from the Society of Jesus. If excommunicated, Berrigan would be stripped of the title of priest and ostracized from his community permanently. Meditating for twenty-four hours, Berrigan weighed his next move and, as he later put it, sweated out his options.

Berrigan was uncertain if Catonsville would have any impact on ending the Vietnam War, but he did know his participation might mean the ultimate sacrifice of his lifetime. His whole life would irreversibly change if he waltzed into a government facility, pulled out draft cards, and set them aflame. He would have to say goodbye to his career, his friends, and his stable future. Berrigan decided that God was testing him as He had so often tested prophets in Biblical times who were called to shepherd humankind from the chasm of despair toward the mountaintop of peace. Appealing to God for guidance, Berrigan wondered if he truly possessed the vision and mettle of Biblical prophets such as Isaiah, Jeremiah, and Ezekiel. He came to see the invitation to participate in raiding the draft board as the ultimate test of his Christian faith. Anne Klejment, who has written extensively about the Berrigan brothers, convincingly suggests that Berrigan ultimately decided to participate because Catonsville represented an unprecedented level of sacrifice: "He could not claim religious leadership among students unless he began to take some actions against the war that entailed risks to himself."[36] He picked up the phone in his office and dialed Philip's number. "You know, I'm in," he announced resolutely.

- ◼ ∎ ◼ -

Preparations for Catonsville were minimal since Philip faced sentencing for the previous Customs House raid. To make sure everyone was equally implicated, the nine antiwar activists collectively concocted homemade napalm by following a recipe in the Green Berets' handbook: two parts gasoline, which provided the flames, and one part Ivory Flakes, which provided the gelatinous adhesive. As their location, they chose the working-class town of Catonsville, where, as Berrigan later recollected, "the draft board was a tawdry little shack of a place and fairly accessible."[37] The draft files were public records available upon request, so the group did not anticipate any trouble locating and compiling the papers before destroying them. They enlisted the support of a lawyer, Philip Hirschkop, who was the principal attorney for the peace movement in Washington, DC, and who shared their steadfast commitment to nonviolence. The protest's goals were to stunt the Pentagon's induction machinery and save as many young men as possible from the draft, force the nation to openly debate the morality of the Vietnam War, and use the courtroom as a public forum to denounce the war and the injustice of conscription.[38]

On May 17, 1968, shortly after lunchtime, the Berrigan brothers, along with seven others, walked into the draft board office in Catonsville,

Maryland, where three secretaries sat at their desks typing and arranging papers. One of the peace activists, Tom Lewis, announced the pending raid, yet the secretaries seemed unperturbed until the other raiders glided into the room with two wire incinerator baskets under their arms. The activists then grabbed the 1-A records that signaled the most likely to be drafted, and a clerk started screaming. Philip tried to explain that no one would get hurt, and when she kept screaming, one of the activists tried drowning her out by loudly explaining his opposition to the war. Their purpose, they said, was to halt the influx of soldiers to Vietnam: "We do this because everything else has failed."

The nine activists confiscated over 378 files and then proceeded to the facility's parking lot, where they doused the files with napalm. Since the media had been alerted beforehand, a small group of reporters and photographers and a TV crew were on hand to witness the priests strike a match and send the government documents flaking up to the heavens. For ten minutes, the dumbfound crowd watched the flammable jelly used by the American military to incinerate the jungles of Southeast Asia work its magic equally well on draft cards. The group, known as the Catonsville Nine, released a press statement:

> This sacrificial and constructive act is meant to protest the pitiful waste of American and Vietnamese blood in Indochina.[39] . . . We charge that America would rather protect its empire of overseas profits than welcome its black people, rebuild its slums and cleanse its air and water. . . . We destroy these draft records not only because they exploit our young men but also because they represent misplaced power concentrated in the ruling class of America. [40]

When the police arrived, the trespassers had solemnly clasped hands and were reciting the Lord's Prayer in the parking lot while encircling the incinerated draft cards. The definitive photograph of the event shows the Berrigan brothers in clerical dress—Philip big and bearish, Daniel waifish and puckish—serenely awaiting their imminent incarceration. Several FBI agents appeared moments later. One yelped when he saw Philip Berrigan, whom he remembered from the Baltimore Customs House raid seven months earlier. The agent scowled, "Good God, I'm changing my religion."[41]

Philip responded to Catholicism's higher echelons:

One asked his soul, in near despair with such a church: What of the children of Vietnam, what of the victims of the merciless air raids, what of the Buddhist monks driven to self-immolation, what of the destruction of peasants and land and streams? And equally to the point, what was one to make of a church that could live, in a kind of spurious peace, with such crimes? Did we deserve the name Christian?[42]

Thomas Merton, however, voiced caution and said the act "bordered on violence." For the first time, Berrigan felt disappointed and questioned his involvement in the raid, but he decided that he did not regret his actions. The Catonsville Nine responded to Merton and other skeptics by saying their action was life-affirming and noted that violence against material objects is justifiable when protecting human lives: "Some property has no right to exist. Hitler's gas ovens, Stalin's concentration camps, atomic-biological-chemical weaponry, files of conscription and slum properties are examples."[43]

Many secular antiwar activists were similarly shocked by the Berrigans and called them "elitist," "Irish mafia," "arrivistes," and worse.[44] Philip Berrigan responded with righteous indignation, claiming, "I will refuse to indict anyone's conscience, but I don't have to cheer their work, which seems to me safe, unimaginative, staffish, and devoid of risk or suffering. . . . To stop this war, I would give my life tomorrow, and I can't be blamed if I have little time for those who want to run ads in the *New York Times*."[45] Ultimately, the Berrigans may have played as little a role in ending the Vietnam War as did the armchair activists they disdained, but the raid did turn the brothers into poster priests of the Vietnam antiwar movement.

The trial of the Catonsville Nine generated a sympathetic crowd of over two thousand people and featured luminaries such as Noam Chomsky, I. F. Stone, Abraham Joshua Heschel, Harvey Cox, and Dorothy Day. Among the draft raiders' supporters was Howard Zinn, who wrote in defense of his Vietnam travel companion: "Dan Berrigan is facing prison because he decided to protest the mass murder of the Vietnam War by destroying draft card files in Baltimore. Of course he violated the law. But he was right. And it is the mark of enlightened citizens in a democracy that they know the difference between law and justice, between what is legal and what is right."[46] As if the Vietnam War itself were on trial, the police barricades outside the courthouse separated peaceniks holding signs saying "Free the 9" and "End the War" from a handful of counterdemonstrators carrying their own signs: "Peace Creeps Go Home" and "We Want Dead Reds." Capturing the divided response of the American public in general and Catholics in particular, one of the Berrigans' longtime supporters—actor Martin Sheen—later quipped, in direct contrast to the FBI agent, "Mother Teresa drove me back to Catholicism, but Daniel Berrigan keeps me there!"

-・-

On October 7, 1968, the decorated war veteran and much-admired jurist Judge Roszel Thomsen presided over the Catonsville trial in US District Court. In 1952, two years before the Supreme Court struck down the "separate but equal" ruling in *Brown v. Board of Education*, Thomsen had helped end school segregation locally as a Baltimore school board member. In the Catonsville case, Thomsen rejected the "justification" defense—which allowed defendants to speak to the court and jury about their motives—but was fascinated enough by the antiwar activists to allow them to speak about their lives and rationales in their closing remarks.[47]

When Daniel Berrigan took the stand dressed in his black suit and white collar, he succinctly explained to the jury in a voice that poorly hid his fury, "I burned some paper because I was trying to say that the burning of children was inhuman and unbearable." After offering their testimony, Berrigan led the court in the Lord's Prayer—a move that mesmerized even their defense attorney, William Kunstler—and later summarized the group's sentiments in a poem that read in part:

> Our apologies good friends
> For . . . the fracture of good order
> the burning of paper instead of children[48]

The prosecution responded, "If these people were entitled to be acquitted by virtue of their sincerity and religion and conviction, then according to the same logic, should not the man who commits any other crime be also entitled to acquittal?"[49] After three hours of deliberation, the jury returned a verdict of guilty on three charges—interference with the Selective Service Act of 1967, destruction of Selective Service records, and destruction of US government property. After the verdict was read and all nine were sentenced to three years in prison, a man in the courthouse yelled out, "Members of the jury, you have just found Jesus Christ guilty!"[50]

- • -

When Christ was found guilty, he was sent to the cross to the die; when Berrigan was found guilty, he went underground to hide. After fruitlessly appealing his conviction, Berrigan decided he could no longer submit to the authority of the American courts, especially after Nixon extended the war to Cambodia and Laos. Berrigan wrote at the time that the courts "had become more and more the instruments of the war-makers."[51] Over the span of four months, the impish priest eluded a flabbergasted and increasingly irate FBI Director J. Edgar Hoover while taking shelter with thirty-seven families in twelve cities. While on the lam, the "outlaw priest" surfaced occasionally on television newscasts and in church pulpits to blast the war. The antiwar movement followed the cat-and-mouse chase with zeal, cheering for their underdog and rejoicing each time he further embarrassed FBI officials. At one point, Berrigan appeared at Cornell's Barton Hall incognito—in a motorcycle helmet and goggles—for an antiwar rally. Despite undercover FBI agents peppering the audience disguised as hippies (perfectly costumed except for their dangling earpieces), sympathetic students successfully smuggled Berrigan out inside a giant papier-mâché puppet head created by the Bread and Puppet Theater. When a reporter asked Berrigan how he managed to foil the FBI agents' mission on several occasions, he replied, "You could say that my survival is a triumph of the love and the humanity of the people who shelter me over the FBI."[52]

Finally, on August 11, 1970, agents with binoculars posing as bird watchers captured Berrigan on Block Island off the Rhode Island coast in a refurbished former horse stable. Far from contritely surrendering, Berrigan seemed to get the last laugh even in defeat: the iconic photo that ran in newspapers and magazines across the world shows a jubilant priest being carted off by two disgruntled federal agents. Berrigan subsequently served eighteen months of a three-year sentence in Danbury Federal Correctional Institution in Connecticut before he was paroled.

The *New York Times* estimated that the Catonsville Nine's actions inspired over one hundred similar acts. In 1968 the Boston Two and the Milwaukee Fourteen destroyed over ten thousand draft files combined. The DC Nine burned files of the napalm-producing Dow Chemical Company in March 1969. The Pasadena Three, the Silver Springs Three, and the Chicago Fifteen destroyed over forty thousand draft records combined in May 1969; the East Coast Conspiracy to Save Lives was responsible for the destruction of thousands of draft files in Philadelphia.[53] The most prolific draft record destroyers were the Boston Eight, who struck four draft boards and destroyed over one hundred thousand files. However, in the early morning hours of Sunday, August 22, 1971, Hoover and Attorney General John Mitchell announced that FBI agents had arrested twenty-eight antiwar activists, four of whom were priests, in and near a draft board office in Camden, New Jersey. The raid resulted in another high-profile trial that was seen by many as a referendum on the Vietnam War and led to yet another series of copycat raids.[54]

■ • ■

In January 1971 the cover of *Time* magazine featured a sepia-toned courtroom sketch of Daniel and Philip Berrigan with the title "Rebel Priests: The Curious Case of the Berrigans." As the article notes, "To those who read the Berrigans' writing and ponder the Berrigans' lives, the greatest fascination lies not with the collision between conscience and state, but rather that between the Berrigans' conscience and their own."[55]

The Vietnam War officially ended in April 1975, but the Berrigans continued full throttle in protesting what they considered bellicose US foreign policy. Although their theatrical protests never again generated as much media attention as Catonsville had, the Berrigans publicly opposed aid to alleged anti-Communist forces in Southeast Asia, the use of American forces in Grenada, the installation of Pershing missiles in West Germany, aid to the Contras in Nicaragua, intervention in Afghanistan during the Soviet invasion, the Cold War, and the Gulf War.[56] Berrigan also opposed the US wars in Afghanistan and Iraq. On April 2002, less than a year after the World Trade Center attacks in New York City, he delivered a speech titled "Lamentations and Losses: From New York to Kabul" to students at the College of the Holy Cross. In his speech, Berrigan referred to the World Trade Center and the Pentagon as symbols of idolatry signifying both monetary and military world domination: "The ruin we have wantonly sown abroad has turned about and struck home. . . . Thus: sin, our sin, has shaken the pillars of empire. What has befallen, we have brought upon ourselves. The moral universe stands vindicated."[57] Though it only further demonized him in the eyes of the US right wing, Berrigan's declaration that Babylon reaped the terror it sowed echoed the analysis of the attacks that antiwar scholars such as Noam Chomsky and Howard Zinn would later provide in resolutely secular language.

Arrested more times than he can count—but "fewer than I should have been," he says—Berrigan has spent over half a century digging mock graves on the Pentagon's front lawn, pouring vials of his own blood on Capitol Hill, vandalizing army airplanes, hammering on nuclear nosecones, turning his back on judges during his sentencing hearings, staging hunger strikes in prisons, undergoing strip searches for educating his fellow inmates, and standing in court on charges ranging from criminal mischief to destruction of government property to, most egregiously, failure to quit.[58] He's also emerged as something of a cultural icon: he's appeared in the film *The Mission* with Jeremy Irons and Robert De Niro, hawked the "mocha fudge" flavor of Ben & Jerry's ice cream, and written thirty-odd books, including the play *The Trial of the Catonsville Nine*, which won an Obie Award. Berrigan has been nominated for the Nobel Peace Prize twice.

In 1996, nearly fifty years after Catonsville, the Jesuit order publicly honored Berrigan's lifelong commitment to peacemaking. In a tribute to him on his seventy-fifth birthday, Peter-Hans Kolvenbach, S.J., the superior general of the Society of Jesus, wrote, "Christian conviction demands that we be people of peace, people who insist that a world without war is possible. And so, it is right that we celebrate Father Daniel Berrigan, because peace took root in his heart."[59] On Berrigan's eightieth birthday, over eight hundred friends and allies gathered with him at Saint Paul the Apostle Church. Folk singer Dar Williams crooned the song "I Had No Right," which she wrote in honor of the Catonsville Nine. When an acquaintance asked the gracefully aging Berrigan how he was doing, he responded with a hint of melancholy, "Well, things are a little weird; I haven't been in jail for a while."[60]

— ∎ —

In the summer of 2010, after badgering members of the Catholic Worker community across the country, I finally tracked down the lefter-than-Left priest, who now keeps a relatively low profile when not attending antiwar rallies. When I arrived at Berrigan's Lower West Side friary on Thompson Street in Manhattan, I half expected to find a Bible-toting warrior, but on that warm June morning, I walk into the friary's cozy hallway to find a slightly hunched, elderly man with a meek smile and skin crinkled like aluminum foil. Greeting me with the softest, gentlest "hello" that I've heard since my first day at Montessori school, Father Daniel Berrigan clasps my hand in his own. The man in front of me in a breezy flannel shirt, khaki pants, and navy blue bedroom slippers certainly does not look like an outlaw whose mug shot once appeared on the FBI's Ten Most Wanted Fugitives list. Berrigan's thick, still-black eyebrows contrast with the thin layer of white hair that coats his balding head like peach fuzz. His tastefully decorated office showcases posters of freedom fighters such as Mahatma Gandhi, a child's drawing of a circus clown, and framed quilts of butterflies. Among his impressive collection of books are volumes by his longtime heroes: Dorothy Day, Martin Luther King Jr., and Thomas Merton. Just shy of his ninetieth birthday, Berrigan speaks with me for an hour and a half, patiently answering my questions and stopping only twice or so to cough.

The secretary who manned the draft boards at Catonsville later testified in court that she felt terrified when the draft raiders started snatching up 1-A files, so I ask Berrigan if, in retrospect, he regrets upsetting her. Berrigan smiles and explains with a dash of old-world chivalry, "Well, we made sure to send her flowers from Danbury jail—her name was Ms. Murphy, I believe. We were very careful that nobody got hurt during the raid, especially the women."

"Why did you decide to participate in Catonsville?" I ask.

"I took this as a summons . . . " he says before trailing off. "Also, I loved my brother very deeply and I wanted to be faithful to him."

His words remind me of Proverbs 17:17, *A friend loveth at all time, and a brother is born for adversity.* Philip died of cancer in 2002, at the age of seventy-nine, at a commune for pacifists he founded in Baltimore.

"Why aren't there more acts of resistance against the Iraq War?" I ask.

"There's resistance all the time today, but there's no media. The media is a total sellout. You're not going to know the earth is shaking if nobody reports it, but there are still plenty of people who are trying to read the

Gospel and act as if were true." He points to his niece, Frida Berrigan, as an example.

In 1969 Philip had secretly married a nun named Elizabeth McAllister—the public acknowledgment of his marriage, in 1973, led to his excommunication and removal from the priesthood. Defrocked but undeterred, Philip and Liz decided to continue their social justice activism. Back in the 1970s, they agreed they could not have children because their activism did not permit them the energy or time; however, their misplaced faith in the rhythm method soon led to the birth of Frida.

— ∎ —

Frida Berrigan grew up in a resistance community started by her parents, and her parents' idealistic notions largely dictated her extremely unconventional childhood.[61] Frida learned to accept her father's absence on Christmas morning—and the absence of his legendary peanut-and-raisin pancakes—for the notion that a father who truly loves his child will tirelessly protest nuclear weapons to make sure she doesn't wake up suffocating in radioactive dust. Frida grew up in crime-ridden inner-city Baltimore for the notion that a child sheltered in suburbia will never understand the oppression faced by the majority of the world's people. Both her mother and father intermittently spent years locked in jail for the notion that a weapon that can murder hundreds of thousands of people should not exist.

Protest and resistance were such a part of Frida's upbringing that she remembers watching her little sister (Kate was "accident" number three) sprinkle sugar on homemade cookies while singing out, "Sprinkle it on like ashes on the White House, like blood on the Pentagon!"[62] As her father lay dying of cancer in 2002, Frida and her sister-in-law used scraps of his clothes to sew a banner to hang over his coffin: *They will hammer their swords into plowshares and their spears into pruning hooks. Nation will not lift up sword against nation, and never again will they learn war.*

Some children might have rebelled by joining warmongering neoconservatives or simply lapsing into political apathy, but Frida, as an adult, largely shares her parents' sentiments. Shortly after the War on Terror began, she carried on her father and uncle's legacy of the Catholic Ultra-Resistance by spearheading the grassroots organization Witness Against Torture (WAT). In a phone conversation, Frida explained:

It began with a question: how could we act in such a way that resisted the War on Terror? We weren't thinking about consequences or what would happen to us. We decided that Jesus's questions were simple: Did you visit me when I was in prison? Did you feed me when I was hungry? Did you clothe me when I was naked? . . . We came out of the Catholic Worker experience of doing the draft board raids and creative actions in the 1960s. It happens that, at this moment, the issue is torture.

In the winter of 2005, Frida and twenty-four American members of WAT—mostly Catholic Workers—flaunted the travel ban against Cuba and voyaged to the US Naval Base at Guantánamo Bay. Camped outside the detention facility, the peace activists fasted every Friday in solidarity with the hunger strikers and explained to the media, "The definition of what it means to be Catholic is acts of mercy." The activists were unsuccessful in entering, let alone closing down, the prison at Guantánamo Bay. However, one of the prisoners' lawyers later confirmed the detainees knew about the antitorture vigil and, for the first time since their arrests, were hopeful that regular American citizens cared about their nation's purported ideals such as the right to a fair trial and the right not to be subjected to cruel punishment. Out of the twenty-five activists, ten received notices from the Office of Foreign Assets Control with an "invitation to self-incriminate" for the amount of money they spent in Cuba, but the office took no further action against them. After the activists returned to the United States, they continued organizing more broadly to shut down Guantánamo by working with interfaith human rights activists.

On May 29, 2008, Frida Berrigan and thirty-three other anti-torture activists knelt and prayed on the Supreme Court's steps while wearing orange jumpsuits and black hoods similar to the ones worn by Guantánamo detainees. Once inside, they attempted to unfurl a four-by-thirty-foot banner reading "Close Guantánamo." They were promptly arrested and handed a maximum of 120 days in jail. Tim Nolan, one of the arrested activists, reflected: "Guantánamo is so striking in its immorality and lack of justice. . . . If humans were created in God's image, torture is clearly a defilement of that."[63] Charges against the activists were later dropped and they resumed their work.

— • —

Daniel Berrigan tells me he's extremely proud of his niece and the new generation of Catholic Workers who are carrying on the tradition of agitating for peace, loving their enemy, and beating swords into plowshares.

As my interview with Berrigan wraps up, I ask him if he continues to get arrested.

"Oh yes, just the other week." He adds with a laugh, "But prison is a younger man's job."

I ask him about the subtler differences between religious and secular humanists. Berrgian notes there's a common quest to live in a supportive community and find something worth living for, such as peace or justice—or, for religious people, *someone* worth living for who embodies peace and justice. "The more I read about Howard Zinn, the more I find myself drawn to him, although he was secular," says Berrigan. "He knew how to widen the circle."

I ask my last question with trepidation, "Are you afraid of death?"

"No; not yet, at least," he says. "I already know what I want written on the tomb."

"Really?" I ask.

"Oh, yes. I want it to say, 'It was never dull, hallelujah!'"

Listening to Berrigan, I realize for the first time that warriors and peacemakers are not opposites, but two sides of the same coin. The opposite of a warrior or a peacemaker, I realize, is an apathetic person who somnambulates down life's middle road. Warriors count their battle wounds, and peacemakers count their years in prison. Warriors take their orders from generals, and peacemakers take their orders from their conscience or their God. Warriors are memorialized in statues, and peacemakers are memorialized in folk songs. Both see themselves fighting absolute good over absolute evil, and both insist their sacrifices promote the common good. But there is one critical difference between warriors and peacemakers: a warrior will sacrifice his own life and the lives of others, but a peacemaker will sacrifice only his life and never the lives of others. As a pacifist, Berrigan survived a Depression-era boyhood, an abusive father, and countless wars to emerge with a startlingly simple message: sacrifice ends where the suffering of others begins.

If Berrigan had lived during slavery, he would have fought with the abolitionists, but he would not have joined John Brown in leading violent slave insurrections. Today, he participates in candlelight vigils outside abortion clinics but refuses to tolerate violence against abortion providers. Even at the height of his Vietnam antiwar activism—or, as his detractors would say, the height of his arrogance—Berrigan never condoned violence. A tape-recorded message to the Weatherman Underground, attributed to Berrigan in 1971, pleads with the militant group to return to nonviolence, warning that "no principle is worth the sacrifice of a single human being." It is a stunning statement coming from a man who has molded his entire life around principles of sacrifice, a man who many accuse of having emblazoned a Superman *S* on his own chest, a man who seems to understand the world in jarring absolutes. There is something exceedingly humble about acknowledging that one's own subjective worldview is never compelling enough to rob another human being of his or her well-being.

— • —

Leaving the friary, I step into the stiflingly hot New York summer afternoon, where women in stilettos are sipping mocha lattes in vegan-friendly cafes and shirtless men listen to music emanating from their iPods while jogging alongside their panting canines. Before reaching the uptown subway station, I realize that I forgot my audio recorder's case in the friary. Returning to Thomspon Street, I knock on the friary's door, but there is no response. Peering through the tinted window, I expect to see Berrigan in the background, perhaps reading a play by T. S. Eliot or a book on the psychology of Nazi doctors. Instead, my own face stares back, and I realize the window is not a window but actually a mirror. The mirror captures the world whirring behind me—a world largely unaware that this week marks the war in Afghanistan as the longest war in US history; a world largely apathetic to the fact that over a million civilians have died in Iraq; and a world largely oblivious that a man named Daniel Berrigan once existed, and continues to exist. Inside, somewhere, Berrigan must be looking back at the world—a world for which he has sacrificed so much, a world that will never fully understand him, and a world that he still does not understand.

3 ROY BOURGEOIS

The Crusade to Close the School of the Americas

I hope you come to find that which gives life a deep meaning for you. Something worth living for—maybe even worth dying for—something that energizes you, enthuses, you, enables you to keep moving ahead.
            —ITA FORD, *one of four churchwomen raped and murdered in El Salvador by SOA-trained government troops* [1]

[School of the Americas] provides professional education and training for civilian, military and law enforcement students from nations throughout the Western Hemisphere. . . . Our motto is "Libertad, Paz y Fraternidad," which means Freedom, Peace, and Brotherhood.
—COLONEL GLENN R. HUBER JR., *Commandant of SOA/WHINSEC* [2]

On March 24, 1980, Archbishop Oscar Romero celebrated Mass at a small chapel run by the Carmelite sisters in San Salvador that is nestled in an oncology hospital, La Divina Providencia. The elderly bishop with a large forehead, bushy eyebrows, and aviator glasses preached a prophetic gospel denouncing the cancer of militarism in his country. The landholding oligarchy comprised 2 percent of the population but owned 60 percent of the land. These elites operated notorious "death squads" that tortured, raped, murdered, and disappeared trade unionists, landless peasants, community organizers, student activists, and others daring to oppose the oligarchy's centuries-old hold on power.[3] During the two decades of civil war, over seventy thousand people were killed.

Making appearances in the slums and countryside, Romero emerged as the lone public defender of Salvadoran peasants and urged them to create self-reliance groups in opposition to the military junta.[4] His message was simple yet potent: the spirit of God ennobles and ultimately guarantees the victory of the downtrodden. The archbishop was aware of the lethal danger he faced for refusing to bow to authority. By 1980, death squads were murdering more than three thousand people each month, strewing corpses across San Salvador's streets as a warning to potential dissidents. Romero remained undeterred and used his weekly radio sermons to command the oligarchy to halt the killings. Distancing himself from both Marxism and capitalism, the archbishop associated himself with liberation theology by viewing the teachings of Jesus Christ in terms of liberating marginalized members of society from unjust political, economic, and social conditions. Romero further alarmed the ruling powers by urging peasants to struggle for their own liberation rather than rely on handouts from the church or the government.

In February 1980, shortly after the National Guard and National Police opened fire on a crowd of protesters in front of the Metropolitan Cathedral and killed twenty-four civilians, Romero sent a personal letter to President Jimmy Carter asking him to suspend military aid to El Salvador.[5] The Carter administration ignored the request, regarding El Salvador's leftist opposition, FMLN (Farabundo Marti National Liberation), as a communist-led insurrection. The United States continued channeling millions of dollars in military aid to the country.

When a parishioner asked Romero if he feared assassination, the archbishop declared: "I do not believe in death without resurrection. If they kill me I will rise again in the people of El Salvador . . . if God accepts the sacrifice of my life, then may my blood be the seed of liberty and a sign that hope will soon become a reality."[6]

On March 24, 1980, in the modest chapel of La Divina Providencia oncology hospital, Romero elevated the chalice at the end of the Eucharistic rite. Then a gunshot shattered the silence. A sniper had crept into the chapel and shot Romero in the heart, making him the first bishop in eight centuries to be killed at the altar. Of the estimated 150,000 people who dared to attend his funeral, dozens were gunned down by the military.[7]

Human rights organizations speculated that Roberto D'Aubuisson, a leader of the right-wing ARENA party and a US favorite, was responsible for Romero's assassination. However, D'Aubuisson had the protection of Nicolas Carranza, vice-minister of defense, who at the time received $90,000 a year from the CIA.[8] Elliot Abrams, Assistant Secretary of State for Human Rights, insisted that D'Aubuisson "was not involved in murder."[9] When Ronald Reagan took office in 1981, US military aid to El Salvador rose steeply despite its government's worsening human rights record.[10] In 1993 a United Nations commission revealed that D'Aubuisson, indeed, "gave the order to assassinate the Archbishop and gave precise instructions to members of his security service, acting as a death squad, to organize and supervise the assassination." Most disturbingly, El Salvador's notorious army officer had graduated from the School of the Americas (SOA)—a combat training school in Fort Benning, Georgia—eight years before orchestrating Romero's assassination.

It would take another renegade priest, Father Roy Bourgeois, to expose the sordid secret of the School of the Americas and its trail of death. Through a campaign spanning two decades, Bourgeois revealed that D'Aubuisson was just one of over sixty thousand Latin American soldiers trained by the US military at US taxpayer expense on US soil at the School of the Americas. The forty-five-year-old priest with a cherubic face and bright, twinkly eyes as blue as lapis lazuli dedicated his life to fulfilling Romero's hope that his murder would serve as "the seed of liberty." Three years after a bullet punctured the archbishop's heart and desecrated the church's altar, Bourgeois made sure that El Salvadoran paramilitaries heard Romero's resurrected voice boom through their barracks.

■ ● ■

Bourgeois grew up in the swampy sawmill town of Lutcher, which is nestled between the Cajun capitals of New Orleans and Baton Rouge on the East Bank of the Mississippi River.[11] Lutcher was a close-knit town of under four thousand residents—a town where elderly churchwomen whiled away the long summer days on their porch rocking chairs sipping ice-cold lemonades and gossiping about neighbors. Bourgeois's father worked for Louisiana Power & Light Company and, after finishing his day's work of reading electric meters, would fry up fresh bass while Bourgeois's mother prepared a wicked shrimp gumbo. As adventurous as Huckleberry Finn, Bourgeois spent his childhood fishing in ponds along the levee, checking the pits of neighborhood trappers for alligators, and borrowing horses from friends' stables for joyrides. In high school, Bourgeois played football for the Lutcher Bulldogs and respected Coach Buckner, who, like most people in the town, considered God, football, and the US military as a holy trinity. Before every game, Buckner led his players in prayer to request that God obliterate the competition.

Bourgeois and his childhood sweetheart—Gerry Landry, the head cheerleader at their high school—attended senior prom; soon afterward, overbearing but well-intentioned neighbors prodded the couple to get married, settle down, and raise children. Engaged to Landry, Bourgeois enrolled at the University of Southwestern Louisiana, in Lafayette, home of the Ragin' Cajuns. He paid his way through school working as a roughneck on oil rigs in the Gulf of Mexico and hoped his degree in geology would help him strike it rich working for a multinational oil company in South America. Bourgeois spent countless hours daydreaming about the world beyond the Mississippi River, and he imagined traveling to the exotic places that he heard about from other roughnecks. At his college's student center, Bourgeois met navy recruiters who promised him a ticket out of rural Louisiana, a ticket to an adventurous life abroad complete with a steady salary, plenty of booze, and endless parties. Bourgeois loved his fiancée, but also wanted to travel the world—he wanted to run his hands across the Great Wall of China, ride in a rickshaw in India, and fall asleep in the shade of a palm tree in Costa Rica. Most of all, Bourgeois wanted to wake up unencumbered by responsibilities, free to explore each new day. He reconsidered making such an early commitment to marriage and unceremoniously broke off his engagement in his third year of college. Although his parents were disappointed about his plans to delay marriage, they were patriotic Catholics who were proud of their son for deciding to serve his country.

In 1962 Bourgeois graduated from Officer Candidate School in Newport, Rhode Island, and joined the navy. Shortly after the Cuban Missile Crisis he was assigned to a research ship heading for the Caribbean. In Trinidad and Jamaica, Bourgeois witnessed acute poverty for the first time. Although he joined friends for rowdy nights on the town, he was perturbed by the sight of malnourished street children with stomach muscles too weak to hold in their guts. He couldn't help thinking, "Thank God that I wasn't born in this hellhole." Bourgeois applied for a transfer at the Pentagon assignment desk and requested a "sophisticated" European city such as Paris, Rome, or London. He was relocated to a NATO base outside of Athens, Greece. Yet, even when sharing beers with friends on the base or snapping photos of the Acropolis on his days off, the memory of scrawny-armed children with protruding collarbones and glassy eyes haunted Bourgeois.

Shortly after the Johnson administration claimed the North Vietnamese had attacked a US destroyer in the Gulf of Tonkin, Bourgeois volunteered to swap his rollicking life on US bases in Europe for active duty in the miasmal jungles of Vietnam. His parents tried to dissuade their son from putting himself in such danger, but Bourgeois insisted that the cause was noble and the military needed experienced officers. He was hungry for a taste of active combat and also attracted by the promise of a week of R&R in a tropical paradise such as Thailand. That summer, the antiwar movement organized in opposition to the administration's announced plans to double the monthly draft quota and increase troop deployment to Vietnam from 75,000 to 125,0000. Dismissive of peaceniks, Bourgeois parroted the official line: "If we don't fight the Commies in Vietnam, then we'll have to fight them in California next!" He was disgusted by the protestors and often smirked, "What the hell do those cowards know?" In the spring of 1965, Bourgeois left for Vietnam with the verve of Saul setting off for Damascus.

■ ● ■

During a grueling weeklong POW survival training in Hawaii, Bourgeois learned how to resist proffering information in the most torturous of circumstances. The navy hired Filipinos to dress as Vietnamese and capture, humiliate, and break down new recruits during mock interrogations. By frantically reciting "Our Fathers" in his head, Bourgeois endured sleep deprivation, physical violence, and water boarding without cracking. During an intense three-day survival test, he befriended a former schoolteacher from New Jersey, Ray Ellis, who shared his patriotic spirit. Ellis was classically handsome with the six-foot-two physique of a competitive swimmer, wavy blondish-brown hair, and dimples.

Upon arriving in Vietnam, General Westmoreland greeted Bourgeois and the new recruits in the aircraft hangar, saying, "Boys, give it everything you've got! We're going to have you boys out of here in a year." Bourgeois and Ellis were initially stationed at navy bases in Nha Trang and Qui Nhon in the coastal lowlands, but later relocated to Saigon in

September 1965, where they were attached to the US Military Assistance Command Headquarters.

That autumn, Bourgeois and his fellow navy lieutenant Ellis were assigned to river patrol in the Mekong Delta. The open stretches of the fetid swamps reminded Bourgeois of the Louisiana bayou. He whispered to Ellis, "This does not look good; we're going to get our asses shot. You can't see the enemy around the river bend, and they've set up explosives everywhere." Bourgeois refused to participate in what he considered a suicide mission, but Ellis brushed off such concerns. A few weeks later, Ellis's River Assault Group boat was ambushed with mortars and machine gunfire. The young schoolteacher and his Vietnamese crew were killed. Years later, Bourgeois would find Ellis's name on the Vietnam War Memorial's wall and trace each granite letter.

In the wake of Ellis's death, Bourgeois's sense of immortality was profoundly shaken. Grasping for a way to explain his friend's death, Bourgeois sought out Catholic churches in Vietnam. In the village of Binh Loi, a few miles outside Saigon, Bourgeois met Father Lucien Olivier. The French Canadian missionary ran the Thanh Mau Orphanage and an adjacent refugee camp. Olivier spent each day caring for 150 orphans and 350 war refugees, including many suffering from amputated limbs, chronic malnutrition, and infected sores. They all lived in thatch-roofed huts and slept on the rocky ground. The Catholic priests back home pontificated in a condescending manner that made Bourgeois acutely uncomfortable, but Olivier seemed different. The Redemptorist priest with a wispy beard and dark cassock donned a conical sedge hat similar to the ones traditionally worn by the Vietnamese working in the rice paddies. In the wake of his friend's death, Bourgeois spent more time with Olivier, observing him tend to the myriad needs of the orphans and refugees. Olivier told Bourgeois he'd arrived in Vietnam seven years before the US invasion and enlisted the help of local nurses and teachers. Although deeply critical of the war, Olivier welcomed Bourgeois's efforts to recruit GIs as volunteers at the camp. Still mourning Ellis's death, Bourgeois came to regard Olivier as a pillar of peace in a world full of madness. He and other GIs organized outings to the local zoo for the orphans and pitched in money for their school supplies.

Bourgeois visited the children more frequently and learned about their personal tragedies. Some were pocked like pincushions from shrapnel; others were severely burned by the napalm and Agent Orange made by

Dow Chemical. Vietnamese nurses told Bourgeois they believed napalm firebombs and Agent Orange defoliants contributed to miscarriages and deformities because an alarming number of babies were now born with twisted arms, mangled legs, and missing eyes. One day an orphan with a chemically burnt face tugged at Bourgeois's military fatigues and asked, without a hint of malice, "Why is the United States doing all this?" While Bourgeois still trumpeted the war effort, he no longer had a satisfactory answer.

Bourgeois wrote letters back home to raise money for the orphans. His local church in Lutcher came together as a community and sent multiple five-pound care packages full of clothes, toys, and medicine for the orphans, which cost two dollars to send to servicemen abroad and usually took ten days to arrive. Several department stores, including Neiman Marcus in Texas, heeded Bourgeois's appeals by sending crates of clothes and toys.

In March Bourgeois acquired enough seniority to relocate from the bottom floor to the fourth floor of the ten-story Victoria Hotel in Saigon, where he and two hundred other officers were quartered. On April 1, in the eerily quiet hours of early morning, Vietcong gunmen opened fire on the MPs guarding the hotel entrance. Within minutes, a truckload of explosives reduced the bottom three floors of the hotel to rubble, killing several people, including the officer who was assigned Bourgeois's old room. Rumors of Bourgeois's death spread throughout his hometown when, in fact, he sustained moderate wounds in his neck and legs from ricocheting metal and glass shards.[12] The near-death experience triggered a period of intense introspection for the young officer. Reiterating the orphan's question, Bourgeois asked himself why he was in Vietnam in the first place.

The enviable salary, bachelor lifestyle, inebriated parties, and officer clubs no longer held much allure for Bourgeois, who increasingly felt empty and lonely. He questioned his once steadfast commitment to a military career. After observing Olivier's unshakable equanimity, Bourgeois no longer considered the life of a warrior a noble calling and began entertaining ideas of becoming a missionary. He admitted to an army chaplain that he was not at peace with his life. "I'm Catholic and my faith is more important to me now than ever before," confided Bourgeois. "I think God is calling me, but I can't be a priest because I'm not holy enough. I was thinking, maybe, I could become a brother?" The chaplain laughed, "Don't think you're unworthy; none of us are truly holy or deserving of the honor of priesthood." He recommended that Bourgeois investigate Maryknoll, a missionary order that served in Africa, Asia, and Latin America. "They work with the poorest of the poor and go where other missionaries don't want to go," said the chaplain.

During his week of R&R, Bourgeois visited the Maryknoll order in Hong Kong and felt at peace for the first time since leaving the bayous of Louisiana. The community leader took Bourgeois on a tour of the clinics and schools they had built for refugees, but he omitted showcasing their place of worship. Bourgeois was impressed by the Maryknollers, who bore no resemblance to the "holy rollies" whom he had feared encountering. Instead of pontificating, these people seemed more like social workers concerned with building schools and hospitals. Watching the Maryknoll community at work lifted Bourgeois's spirits after the despair of combat and gave him a glimpse of what he regarded as his own pathway to redemption. Within a few days of living with the Maryknollers, Bourgeois knew he wanted to spend the rest of his life among these missionaries who reminded him of Father Olivier back in Vietnam. On the flight back to Saigon, an elated Bourgeois experienced a sense of purpose again after his long spell of depression. He listlessly finished his tour of duty and, with great sadness, bid farewell to the orphans, promising to return soon.

— ∎ —

Bourgeois, a Purple Heart recipient, returned to Cajun country in June and received a war hero's welcome home. Joyful to reunite with his family, Bourgeois's anguish and loneliness gradually dissipated. Still, his commitment to join the Maryknoll seminary did not waver. Bourgeois's friends and family were flabbergasted by his desire to trade his military fatigues for a clerical collar. His high school buddies dismissed his aspiration as the aftershock of combat and even placed bets on how many days would pass before Bourgeois came to his senses. After all, the 1960s' sexual revolution was building momentum, priests were leaving their orders en masse, and the civil rights movement was riveting major cities across the country. Seminary life seemed as antiquated as crew cuts and poodle skirts. Bourgeois's brother exclaimed, "There's more chance of my becoming president of the United States than Roy becoming a priest!"

In the autumn of 1966, Bourgeois settled into Maryknoll College in Glen Ellyn, Illinois, where he befriended Monsignor John Egan, who had marched in Selma and walked in union picket lines. Among Egan's friends was legendary community organizer Saul Alinsky, who visited Maryknoll College one weekend to conduct a workshop for the seminarians. Alinsky turned Bourgeois's idea of the Bible upside down by celebrating the community organizing skills of Paul and Moses and referring to the Gospels as a blueprint for curbing the abuses of power. Upset that garbage was overflowing on the curbsides of poor neighborhoods, Alinsky suggested the seminarians get organized, hire a pickup truck, and load it with the neighborhood's banana peels, babies' diapers, and fetid meat. Then, Alinsky nonchalantly continued, "go dump all the garbage on the steps of city hall." Bourgeois was shocked and humored by the gutsy rabble-rouser who had no qualms about urging otherwise respectable seminarians to engage in civil disobedience.

After a year in Glen Ellyn studying philosophy and working with community organizers, Bourgeois attended the Maryknoll seminary in Hingham, Massachusetts, for a year of spiritual formation that included working alongside inner-city Boston's poorest residents. During this time of reflection, Bourgeois made a trip to Walden Pond and read Henry David Thoreau. He was attracted to the transcendentalist's idea of simple living and decided life was too ephemeral to waste on chasing riches on South American oil rigs. For Bourgeois, Thoreau's idea of living modestly was a message that resonated throughout the Bible. He thought he finally understood what Jesus meant when he told a rich man: "If you want to be perfect, go, sell your possessions and give to the poor."[13]

As Bourgeois began his metamorphosis, the Church in the late 1960s was undergoing a parallel transformation under the Second Vatican Council. After centuries of alignment with those in power, the church asserted that working for justice was commanded in the Gospel.[14] The council's document, *Gaudium et Spes*, urged wealthy individuals and nations to aid the millions tormented by hunger and poverty. As is customary with Catholic documents, the title comes from the first sentence and means "Joy and Hope" in Latin.[15] In no uncertain terms, the document declared: "If one is in extreme necessity, he has the right to procure for himself what he needs out of the riches of others. . . . The greater part of the world is still suffering from so much poverty that it is as if Christ Himself were crying out in these poor."[16]

In January the Tet offensive and images of the US embassy under fire consumed American television screens, shattering any remaining illusions that the war was winding down. The massacre of civilians during the destruction of Ben Tre, a city of three thousand people, further angered a war-weary United States, as did a military official's doublespeak, "It became necessary to destroy the town in order to save it." The escalating cost of the war continued draining money from Johnson's antipoverty programs.

The twin polemics of war and poverty increasingly consumed Bourgeois's thoughts. He felt assaulted by the Scriptures, which seemed to refute everything that he had learned in boot camp and on the gridiron.[17]

— ∎ —

Bourgeois traveled to local high schools to share stories of the orphans he met, show slides of Vietnam, and raise money for Father Olivier's mission. He remained in close contact with the elderly priest and brainstormed ways to return to Saigon. Although most seminarians fulfilled the "apostle work" component of their curriculum by mowing the seminary's lawns or working at a nursing home, the rector granted Bourgeois permission to complete this component in Vietnam. To raise funds for the trip, Bourgeois wrote to dozens of newspapers, offering his services as a freelance photojournalist. The *Burlington Press* in Vermont agreed to finance Bourgeois's trip in exchange for his photo essays.

Bourgeois arranged to spend three months working at a Vietnamese orphanage and refugee camp. When Bourgeois returned to Saigon in the summer of 1968, the third battle for the decimated capital had just ended, and General Creighton Abrams was succeeding Westmoreland as the badly battered marines retreated from Khe Sanh.

Walking down the barely recognizable streets of war-torn Saigon, Bourgeois surveyed the massive craters from mortar attacks and found the destruction far exceeded even the most horrific depictions on network news. Dozens of orphanages and refugee camps had cropped up on the banks of the Saigon River. Homeless children slept in the gutters and paced through alleys, rummaging for scraps of food like feral animals. During the war, about half of Vietnam's forest cover was obliterated and a fifth of its agricultural land was destroyed. Bombs left 25 million craters in their wake, and US troops drained Tram Chim, which oxidized the iron sulfides in the soil into acid; the water became so toxic that even the mosquitoes died out. The few remaining Maryknoll missionaries in

Saigon told Bourgeois the river cranes—symbols of hope in Vietnamese culture—had disappeared from the delta and were feared to be extinct in Southeast Asia.[18]

While delivering supplies with the Catholic Relief Services to refugee camps in collaboration with Maryknoll nurses, Bourgeois eventually located his old friend, Olivier. The exhausted missionary told him the Thanh Mau Orphanage had been evacuated after his Vietnamese assistant was killed and several children were injured. Olivier took Bourgeois to the new orphanage he had built in a house in Saigon. Although Bourgeois worried the children might not remember him, they ran into his outstretched arms and thanked him for returning.

Bourgeois spent most of his mornings at Go Vap orphanage, the largest in the city, and his afternoons with Olivier's orphans. The malnourished children at Go Vap suffered from dry, scaly skin and bleeding gums. Each day, they ate only two bowls of rice with powdered milk. Polio crippled almost three dozen children, but the most heart-wrenching case that Bourgeois says he encountered was a four-year-old girl named Phuong. Blinded in one eye by a piece of shrapnel and badly disfigured on the left side of her face, Phuong was still in shock when she first met the former military officer. For two hours, she sat motionless in the seminarian's lap. Then, suddenly, Phuong grabbed his arms and refused to budge. Bourgeois continued visiting the traumatized girl and wrote to his hometown newspaper to raise money on her behalf, since Phuong was in jeopardy of losing her good eye if her blind one wasn't surgically removed. Bourgeois took the child to see a US Army ophthalmologist, but the doctor refused to treat Phuong because she was a Vietnamese child, not a US soldier. Bourgeois insisted that the United States had a responsibility to help because its bombs had scarred Phuong's face. The doctor curtly dismissed the indignant seminarian: "We don't make the rules." For the first time in his life, Bourgeois was viscerally angry at the US military. Bourgeois realized he and the surgeon were speaking entirely different languages—he spoke of "moral obligations" while the surgeon spoke of "military protocol"—and Bourgeois suspected this difference in vocabulary reflected a much larger, irreconcilable schism. He left the hospital sickened that his country considered the child in his arms as "collateral damage" rather than a human being.

The little girl who eventually lost her eyesight showed Bourgeois a part of the war he was previously blind to. The once gung-ho military

officer had scorned Daniel Berrigan, the Catholic antiwar activist convicted in 1968 of burning Selective Service files with homemade napalm,
but now Bourgeois regarded Berrigan as the true patriot: he was guilty
of burning draft files, not children.

As Bourgeois was leaving Southeast Asia in the middle of August 1968,
he read newspapers voraciously to better understand the true cost of the
Vietnam War. He learned that under Robert McNamara the Pentagon's
budget increased to $74.9 billion in fiscal year 1968, from $48.4 billion in
1962, and had bankrupted domestic social uplift programs for the inner-
city poor. Worse, tens of thousands of American combat troops had
arrived in Vietnam and American warplanes were pounding the enemy
in a bombing campaign code-named Rolling Thunder, which had sent
148,000 flights with 128,000 tons of bombs over North Vietnam, without
stymieing the flow of enemy arms and soldiers into South Vietnam.[19]
Bourgeois prayed fervently for courage to take up the mission of a healer
and atone for his sins, sins that increasingly left him feeling ashamed
and self-loathing. He now understood why early Christians refused to
serve in any army and followed literally the Biblical commandment to
lay down the sword.

— ∎ —

Back in the United States, Bourgeois began four years of study at Maryknoll's major seminary in Ossining, New York. He lectured at high
schools and colleges across Westchester County about the war's effect on
uninvolved civilians. He spoke of Olivier, his missionary friend, who had
shown him a meaningful way to spend one's life by making the world
safe for the most vulnerable. In 1969 Bourgeois timidly attended his first
peace demonstration in an effort to more authentically embrace what he
saw as his new vocation, that of a peacemaker.

After Nixon ordered the invasion of Cambodia and Ohio National
Guardsmen shot thirteen students protesting at Kent State University,
Bourgeois ratcheted up his antiwar activism. The tone of his speeches
intensified as he encouraged students to join the antiwar movement and
lobby members of Congress.

On June 13 the *New York Times* began publishing *The Pentagon Papers*,
a clandestine government history of the Vietnam War. When Bourgeois
learned of the deceit surrounding the Gulf of Tonkin incident—the

pretext used to elicit congressional authority to launch an undeclared war—he realized that he had gambled his life for a glaring lie. That realization not only enraged him, but also led him to deeply resent the military apparatus. In the fall, Bourgeois read Saul Alinsky's book, *Rules for Radicals*, which delineated the difference between realistic radicals and rhetorical ones.[20] He came to agree with Alinsky, the father of modern community organizing, that political engagement is the key to maintaining America's democratic tradition.

On November 11, Bourgeois was arrested for the first time when he joined the "daily death toll" demonstrations in Washington, DC, protesting the more than three hundred civilian casualties that occurred daily in Southeast Asia. Police arrested the demonstrators as they alternated obstructing the sidewalk in front of the White House. In April 1972 US B-52s started bombing Hanoi. Bourgeois grew increasingly disgusted by what he regarded as Nixon's unjustifiable, inhuman, and immoral assault on North Vietnam. Over beers at a local pub, the seminarian and a close friend from Vietnam who now worked as a social worker decided to launch the Westchester, New York, chapter of Vietnam Veterans Against the War. Bourgeois also circulated a petition against the bombing that he published in New York's *Citizen Register*; he secured 90 percent of his fellow seminarians' signatures, including that of Father Miguel D'Escoto, Maryknoll's communications director who would years later become president of the United Nations. Through his friendship with D'Escoto, Bourgeois learned to appreciate the difference between Western notions of charity and third-world theologians' quest for justice.

— ∎ —

On May 27, 1972, Bourgeois and his classmates were formally ordained. In August, during the reign of General Hugo Banzer, Bourgeois was assigned to serve at a mission in La Paz, Bolivia. During his five years in South America's poorest nation, Bourgeois learned the average Bolivian earned a paltry $300 per year and lived in constant fear of torture, rape, and disappearances—clandestine kidnappings and hidden murders—at the hands of Banzer's paramilitaries. Among Bourgeois's friends was Ita Ford, a nun from New York who patiently tutored him in Spanish. Barely more than five feet tall, Ford was once nicknamed "Pixie" by her high school friends at the Catholic-run Visitation Academy in Brooklyn, New

York. Now, Ford helped her exceptionally slow new pupil conjugate his verbs and roll his Rs during hour-long classes. She shared with Bourgeois her efforts to organize local communities to oppose the social structures that condemned them to lifelong poverty, such as failing schools and subpar hospitals. Years later, members of El Salvador's military death squad would torture, rape, and murder the demure schoolteacher who blinked often and was easily startled by loud noises.

In 1972 Banzer imposed a nationwide state of siege after factory workers, tin miners, and union leaders protested his austerity programs and demanded wage increases to offset soaring prices caused by devaluation of the peso by 39.4 percent in October.[21] When peasants blockaded roads leading to Cochabamba to protest the doubling of food prices, security forces imposed curfews, arrested workers, and raided the homes of suspected dissenters. Bourgeois published a letter in the *New York Times* on February 18, 1973, saying the lack of electricity, potable water, and medical equipment at the Cochabamba orphanage and city hospital caused gratuitous deaths. He concluded on a sarcastic note: "Cochabamba received as a gift from the United States three helicopters, the combat type used in Vietnam. . . . I would like to say to my country, thank you very much for your gift because this is just what we need."[22]

Even after contracting typhoid, Bourgeois decided to forego the relative comfort of the Maryknoll mission house, opting instead for Villa El Carmen, a barrio home for the poorest. He rented a mud brick house with dirt floors for ten dollars a month and lived without running water or reliable electricity as if punishing himself for his prior involvement in the US military. There were nights the transplanted Creole wept and wondered if there was a God.

Bourgeois had arrived in Bolivia planning to teach but was relieved to learn that nobody expected him to have all the answers. The peasants embraced the priest as their own—their "Padre del Pueblo"—and taught him the virtue of generosity, offering him their last freeze-dried potatoes. He held Mass in an open field. When members of the community approached him offering to erect a church, he shook his head. "You, the people, are the church," he replied. Bourgeois figured Christ was content with a squalid manger, the humble life of an itinerant preacher, a loaned tomb. He knew his community would benefit more from schools and clinics, not fancy churches with gilded pulpits. Bourgeois explained to the poor that the elite built regal cathedrals because they wanted to adorn Christ rather than emulate his example.

Around this time, liberation theology sprouted all over Latin America with a new Biblical perspective emphasizing social justice. The new theology maintained that God fervently wanted the poor to have their basic needs met, but the societal sins of political and economic exploitation forced them to live in dehumanizing conditions. It was a radical departure from the belief that the poor should silently accept the status quo and then reap the reward for their righteous suffering in the afterlife. Liberation theologians found resources and space to organize within religious organizations, benefiting from the popular legitimacy and political protection the Latin American Church enjoyed.[23]

Aside from offering spiritual guidance, Bourgeois also ran community meetings to discuss the specific needs in the barrio. He collaborated with Jorge Rosso, a community leader with a comically expansive mustache and deep belly laugh, who helped him secure education and health care for the poor. Together, they empowered indigenous Aymara women to start a fair-trade weaving cooperative.

Meanwhile, Banzer usurped more and more power. Opposition newspapers and radio stations were forcibly silenced, and sixty-eight journalists fled into exile along with leftist politicians and trade unionists.[24] On December 30, 1973, the *New York Times* reported that Banzer's regime not only held people without trial, but also violated "all the fundamental laws protecting human rights" and that torture was "commonly used on prisoners during interrogation . . . beaten, raped and forced to undergo simulated executions . . . hung for hours with their hands tied behind their backs."[25] Security forces harassed and disappeared tin miners—most of whom suffered from silicosis, a chronic pulmonary disease—and students seeking better wages, better working conditions, and political freedom.

Bourgeois encouraged the formation of Christian "base communities," small groups who would gather to read the Bible and reflect on their lives vis-à-vis the Scriptures. These communities came to discover a loving God, a creator who did not will their suffering. Many of the women told Bourgeois they closely identified with Mary, a mother who saw her son accused of sedition, tortured, and executed. With the vast majority of the Bolivian population living in dire poverty, many parents were forced to instruct their children to chew on coca leaves to curb their chronic hunger. In winter months, parents gave their children "chicha," a potent corn liquor, to stay warm. Many of these parents watched their infants waste away before their first birthday.

Working with Jesuit Father Luis Espinal, Bourgeois's appreciation for liberation theology deepened as he drew connections among what he saw as the institutional violence of Banzer's regime, the sinfulness of unjust social structures, and the economic crucifixion of the poor.[26] Bourgeois regarded liberation theology as a new model for the church, a chance to escape the patriarchal, hierarchal model in favor of a circular model that encompassed base communities and empowered the dispossessed to speak for themselves without intermediaries. Bourgeois explained to his community that priests did not have a monopoly on the word of God and often asked, "If our theology is not liberating, *para que sirve?*" What good is a theology that does not liberate?

The most subversive book in Latin America, Bourgeois decided, was not written by Karl Marx, but by the four gospel writers who called out for justice. Apparently, the Carter and Reagan administrations agreed. The Sante Fe Report in 1980 warned against liberation theology: "Marxist-Leninist forces have utilized the church as a political weapon."[27] Bourgeois would later say the Reagan administration disdained liberation theologians since they "applied the Ten Commandments not just to individuals, but to institutions, corporations, and countries."

In October 1975 a US missionary, Father Raymon Herman, was found strangled and shot twice in the head near Cochabamba, where he had just finished transforming an abandoned building into a hospital for the destitute. Bourgeois and other priests learned of a secret government operation to discredit, arrest, expel, and execute progressive clergy considered hostile to the regime. The scheme, known as the "Banzer Plan," was developed in early 1975 after church officials began denouncing violence by the military. The CIA aided the Interior Ministry by compiling detailed dossiers on priests, fully knowing the plan called for "dirty tricks" to be used against undesirable clergy, including the planting of subversive documents on church premises.[28]

Bourgeois suspected he knew exactly why progressive clergy threatened the military status quo: a priest living among dispossessed, marginalized, and subjugated peasants would inevitably come to sympathize with their plight and use his pulpit to boost their morale and fortify their spiritual stamina in the arduous struggle for their God-given right to political freedom and economic security.

During his ongoing spiritual formation, Bourgeois had come to agree with Paulo Freire's explanation of "solidarity" in *Pedagogy of the Oppressed*:

> The oppressor is solidary with the oppressed only when he stops regarding the oppressed as an abstract category and sees them as persons who have been unjustly dealt with, deprived of their voice, cheated in the sale of their labor—when he stops making pious, sentimental, and individualistic gestures and risks an act of love. True solidarity is found only in the plenitude of this act of love, in its existentiality, in its praxis. To affirm that men and women are persons and as persons should be free, and yet to do nothing tangible to make this affirmation a reality, is a farce.[29]

Bourgeois accepted that by living with the poor in true solidarity, as an ally in their struggle for justice and liberation, he too risked suffering their fate.

On November 21, 1976, Bourgeois met with university activists and barrio leaders to compile names of political dissenters who had mysteriously disappeared. After the meeting, Bourgeois was accosted by two plainclothes agents from the Ministry of the Interior, who pushed him inside the back of a Volkswagen Bug with tinted windows. When he inquired why he was detained, Bourgeois received a blow to his stomach with the blunt end of a rifle. He prayed for strength to protect his friends' identities and responded to the agents' questions by feigning language difficulties and repeatedly saying, *"No comprendo."* Bourgeois was blindfolded, interrogated, beaten, and dumped outside a cemetery as a warning to other priests and agitators. According to the regime, he was guilty of organizing and educating peasants as well as denouncing the military. Not wanting to endanger his friends, Bourgeois decided to leave Bolivia. Upon exiting the country, his passport was stamped in red: *Prohibido Entrar.*

- ∎ -

In the spring of 1977, Bourgeois's family and friends did not recognize the radical young man who returned home full of anger and resentment toward his own government. What was all this talk about economic exploitation, US-sponsored terrorism, greedy multinational corporations, and imperialistic foreign policies? Why couldn't Bourgeois talk about fishing, hunting, and football over a bowl of crawfish gumbo? During a discussion with members of a conservative prayer group, Bourgeois chastised them for living in a suburban bubble. "The greatest problem in our country is our ignorance of the effects of American foreign policy on those on the receiving end," hissed Bourgeois. "You can say the rosary all you want, but it won't change anything!" Antagonized by the confrontational young man, the demure church ladies shook their heads in disapproval and kept saying, "Who are you? Why are you so angry? We don't know you anymore."

Banned from Bolivia and a social pariah in his own hometown, Bourgeois felt acutely lonely and frustrated. Over the next two years, he slowly began connecting with antiwar communities across the nation. On February 18, 1979, he went to Washington, DC, and led a protest against the arms trade, evoking Psalm 33: *Rulers are not saved by their armies, nor can they find hope in their weapons. Despite their power, they cannot bring peace.* Crossing the barricade, Bourgeois was dragged away by police while holding a "Bread Not Arms" sign. Over the next year, Bourgeois went to a new parish each week with the same message: weapons expenditures are not only a theft from the poor, but they also make their oppression possible; poverty and exploitation, not communism, are the cause of instability in Latin America. Attracted by Dorothy Day's Catholic Worker movement and its commitment to the poor, Bourgeois hoped to serve those whom society had abandoned while seeking to change the system that had forsaken them.

— • —

On March 22, 1980, Jesuit Father Luis Espinal, who had educated Bourgeois in liberation theology while working on the human rights commission in La Paz, was tortured to death by paramilitary forces connected to the Bolivian army. Two days after Espinal's murder, Archbishop Oscar Romero was assassinated while offering Mass. Demoralized and enraged, Bourgeois mourned their murders and renewed his commitment to social justice; he was determined to continue Romero's legacy.

— • —

On May 25, 1980, Pentecost Sunday, Bourgeois and a group of supporters recited Mass on the lawn of the Pentagon with a prayer that the country would "beat its swords into plowshares" as prophesied in Isaiah. On Monday, Bourgeois entered the navy office in the Pentagon and returned his Purple Heart to "let go of the past and to purify the heart." Bourgeois explained, "Isaiah, the prophet of the Hebrew Scriptures, said it so well: 'They will take evil and they will call it good. They will take the lie and give it to you as truth.' This is what our leaders did about Vietnam."

Bourgeois left the medal with a letter of explanation, in which he denounced US militarism and policies that "exploit and oppress our sisters and brothers in developing countries and here at home." In an act of civil disobedience, seven antiwar activists planted wheat on the Pentagon lawn while Bourgeois and two others each splattered a pint of their own blood on the pillars at the building's main doorway. It was, Bourgeois said, symbolic of the blood wantonly spilt by US-backed militaries, especially the blood of Romero and Espinal.[30] From that day onward, Bourgeois started each morning praying for forgiveness for his complicity in the eight years of US warfare that deposited an estimated 2.5 million tons of bombs on North Vietnam.[31]

Bourgeois wrote home to his family, who increasingly feared for his sanity:

> I do not answer to President Carter or the generals. I answer to God for all that I do or don't do. One of the greatest wrongs that we as Christians can be accused of is our silence and indifference to other people's suffering. I've come to the conclusion that we are not made for war . . . our God, a loving God, a creator who has given us a life that is sacred and precious did not make us for war. And I as many have come to the conclusion in our journey of faith: God does not bless war. God does not bless killing. God does not bless discrimination in its many forms.

When Bourgeois's family visited him in jail, his mother confessed, "We love you, but we don't understand you." One of his sisters cried, "You're gonna break Daddy's heart, he's so proud of you for bravely fighting in 'Nam." Another said softly, "God brought you back safely from the war, and God will see you through this, too." On subsequent prison visits, Bourgeois's family slowly learned why he insisted on protesting war and, far more slowly, reluctantly came to support his activism.

On December 4, four US churchwomen—including Bourgeois's friend, Ita Ford—were found dead in a makeshift grave about thirty miles from San Salvador. On Good Friday, Bourgeois flew to El Salvador to witness the brutality firsthand. After a harrowing trip, the Maryknoll priest returned to testify:

> I must say that I've never seen anything like El Salvador. I was more frightened there than I was in Vietnam or Bolivia. It was the slaughter of the innocent. So many disappeared. A knock would come in the night; there's a list. It was campesinos, labor leaders . . . those who threatened that system of power and wealth. The army was brutal and our country knew exactly what was going on there.[32]

Bourgeois reprimanded the Reagan administration for backing what he called "the homicidal regime in El Salvador" and issuing a white paper falsely claiming that the Soviet Union was arming the rebels.[33] Thousands of declassified State Department, Defense Department, and CIA documents later confirmed that the Reagan White House was fully aware of who ran, funded, and protected the El Salvadoran death squads in the 1980s and planned the assassination of Romero.[34]

In late May, Bourgeois was shocked to read in the *New York Times* that 525 soldiers from El Salvador were being flown to Fort Benning, Georgia, to commence their training on US soil. He wondered, what right had they to come to the United States? What would they learn while at Fort Benning? Who would suffer at their hands when they returned home? Bourgeois remembered the words of slain Archbishop Romero: "If I don't speak for the victims, who will?" Bourgeois and two other activists decided that El Salvadoran soldiers must hear Romero's immortal message again: *Thou Shalt Not Kill.*

- ■ -

On August 9, 1983, Bourgeois and two of his close friends purchased jungle fatigues with insignias of high-ranking officers from Ranger Joe's Army surplus store outside of Fort Benning, Georgia. Bourgeois, Larry Rosebaugh, and Linda Ventimiglia had spent weeks scaling pine trees and perfecting military decorum. Rosebaugh, who resembled gentle Saint Francis despite donning pseudo-military regalia, had spent his formative years ministering to the homeless of Rio de Janeiro. Ventimiglia, a future nurse, had worked at a Catholic Worker house in Texas and wanted to "become an instrument of peace." Now, they loaded their Land Rover with pepper, a rope ladder, tree climbers, and a high-powered Sony cassette player with four speakers. Most important, they carried a tape recording of Romero's last sermon, delivered on March 23, 1980, in the San Salvador cathedral just moments before he was assassinated.[35]

Plastered with Fort Benning stickers, their Land Rover rolled toward the army checkpoint and the three antiwar activists offered shaky salutes to the military personnel on duty. He hesitated, then ushered them forward with one brisk hand motion. The three friends exhaled in unison. They had penetrated the high-security, restricted area where the US military was training a brutal El Salvadoran rapid deployment force. Bourgeois was certain that this army, instructed in the art of warfare on US soil, would return to its homeland and use every weapon in its arsenal to bolster a Salvadoran elite minority at the expense of an impoverished majority. He was aware that the mastermind of the El Mozote massacre, Major Jesús Natividad Cáceres Cabrera, had attended classes on the base eight years earlier, putting his education into action by throwing a baby into the air and impaling her on his bayonet to encourage his soldiers to kill even children.[36]

The three antiwar activists chose a towering hundred-foot pine outside the barracks where the Salvadoran soldiers slept. Rosebaugh sprinkled the base of the tree with pepper to avert guard dogs from tracking their scent. Bourgeois strapped tree climbers to his boots and slowly scaled the pine tree. A branch cracked. Soldiers ran outdoors and illuminated the trees with floodlights. The activists murmured frantic prayers over the sounds of their violently thumping hearts. Silence resumed.

Bourgeois threw the rope ladder to Ventimiglia and Rosebaugh. They aimed their tape player at the barracks and waited for nightfall to shroud them in darkness. When the last lights on the base dimmed, the moment they had long awaited finally arrived. Bourgeois whispered in his mellifluous Cajun drawl, "Oscar Romero, my brother, this is for you." He pressed the play button on the tape recorder. Suddenly, the slain Salvadoran archbishop's voice bellowed from the treetops in Spanish:

I would like to make a special appeal to the members of the army and specifically to the ranks of the National Guard, the police and the military. Brother, each one of you is one of us. We are the same people. The peasants you kill are your own brothers and sisters. When you hear the voice of a man commanding you to kill, remember instead the voice of God: *Thou Shall Not Kill.*

The archbishop's last Sunday homily, once again, implored the Salvadoran military to lay down their weapons:

No soldier is obliged to obey an order contrary to the law of God. There is still time for you to obey your own conscience, even in the face of a sinful command to kill. The church, defender of the rights of God, of the law of God, and of the dignity of each human being, cannot remain silent in the presence of such abominations.

Romero's resurrected voice boomed through Fort Benning, causing discombobulated soldiers to race outside, some livid and others terrified. All recognized the archbishop's distinct baritone voice, but did not know where to point their weapons. "It was a sacred moment," Bourgeois later recalled. "Those soldier, coming out the barracks, looking in the sky, not being able to see us, hearing the words of this prophet." Suddenly, flood lights beamed. Sirens hissed. Military police with M-16s swarmed around the grounds and released snarling police dogs.

Through the commotion, Romero's voice continued piercing the darkness, "In the name of God, in the name of our tormented people whose cries rise up to heaven. I beseech you, I beg you, I command you, stop the repression!"

The cursing MPs finally located and cocked their rifles at the antiwar activists camouflaged in the majestic pine. Bourgeois stalled for time, saying they no longer had the rope ladder. When the elated priest finally began a leisurely descent, he left the cassette running. One MP climbed nearly sixty feet up the tree to yank Bourgeois down to earth and silence Romero's voice, at which point Bourgeois started shouting the bishop's words in Spanish. The priest was bludgeoned from behind, thrown against the tree, and promptly strip-searched.

-¡-

The frustrated guards found no drivers licenses, passports, or other identification cards on the three activists. When interrogated at the provost marshal's office, Bourgeois insisted on calling himself Oscar Romero. Rosebaugh went by the name Rutilio Grande, a Jesuit priest slain by the Salvadoran military. Ventimiglia assumed the identity of Jean Donovan, one of the four US churchwomen tortured to death by Salvadoran security forces. Police brusquely escorted the three activists to the Muscogee County jail, eventually charging them with criminal trespassing and impersonating officers.

The case of *United States of America v. Linda Ventimiglia, Roy Bourgeois, and Larry Rosebaugh* was assigned to the octogenarian US District Court Judge J. Robert Elliott. The July/August 1983 issue of *American Lawyer* magazine declared Elliott was the worst judge on the federal bench and called him "an old-line segregationist who flaunts his deep-rooted prejudices against blacks, unions, and criminal defendants." Elliott once used an injunction to halt Dr. King from marching in Albany, Georgia, on the grounds that the demonstration violated the rights of local whites opposed to integration.[37] In 1974 Elliott had reversed the court-martial conviction of Lieutenant William Calley, who had been jailed for his role in the My Lai massacre.

Bourgeois said in his opening statement, "I stand before this court as a priest of the Maryknoll Order trying to take my faith seriously." He continued, "At Fort Benning, Salvadoran soldiers are being trained by my country to kill innocent men, women, and children who are struggling for justice. When a law of my country contradicts the law of God, then I have no choice but to disobey the law of my country. Some call it civil disobedience; I call it divine obedience."

The federal prosecutor—assistant US attorney Sam Wilson—dismissed Bourgeois's argument, saying it was equivalent to "the devil made me do it," only in reverse. Bourgeois couldn't help thinking the US attorney failed to appreciate the significant differences between the devil and God. At the end of the trial, Judge Elliott—who had freed the army officer found guilty of ordering the 1968 My Lai Massacre in which up to 504 unarmed civilians were murdered—sentenced the peace activists to the maximum prison terms of fifteen to eighteen months.

Bourgeois was sent to a federal work camp in Terre Haute, Indiana. He soon landed in solitary confinement for requesting to teach English and GED prep to Hispanic inmates and, when denied, refusing to perform menial labor. The forty-five-year-old priest with dove-gray eyes was an unusual candidate for a treatment normally reserved for hardened criminals. The soul-destroying loneliness of living in a windowless five-by-nine-foot prison cell gnawed at Bourgeois, first nibbling away his memory, then attacking his muscles, and eventually shaking his once steadfast faith. "Was I a fool for Christ, or just a fool?" he wondered. The priest's thoughts soon slurred together like static-laden transmission warbling from a rusty radio.

On the brink of despair, Bourgeois wondered if his sacrifices had made any difference. Perhaps he should have gotten married, settled down, and found a well-paying job. Then the priest began rereading psalms and Saint Paul's epistles from prison. The Scriptures resonated more profoundly than they ever had in the seminary. Bourgeois later recollected, "Through divine grace, I could feel His presence, understand His mercy, receive His love. It was as if He said, 'I will not desert you.' I felt this deep inner peace, this sense of freedom."[38]

Bourgeois regarded his first two weeks of solitary as a proverbial desert experience, a period of desolation and despair similar to the one described by Saint John of the Cross in his epic poem *Dark Night of the Soul*. In his prison journal, Bourgeois noted the words of Saint Thérèse of Lisieux: "suffering gladly borne for others converts more people than sermons." Bourgeois prayed to God to purify his heart, fortify his faith, and solidify his commitment to continuing Romero's legacy. After fully embracing his solitude and emerging with his faith intact, Bourgeois confided to the warden, "You know, I'm a priest and this is the best retreat I've ever been on!" Shortly before his release on September 21, Bourgeois gave thanks for the "gift of prison," a sacred time when he'd whetted his faith and sensed a divine presence. Bourgeois later reflected that he could not have dealt with the high cost of peacemaking—the loss of friends, the loneliness of prison, the pain it caused family members—without reaffirming his faith.

When Bourgeois was imprisoned again for partaking in subsequent protests, he insisted that "it's a privilege to speak for the poor and the martyrs of El Salvador . . . I don't fear prison—I fear apathy and indifference." Bourgeois wrote hundreds of letters, gave several interviews to the media, and educated sympathizers from his prison cell. Whenever he worried if his work mattered, he took solace in the words of Oscar Romero:

We accomplish in our lifetime only a tiny fraction of the magnificent enterprise that is God's work. Nothing we do is complete, which is another way of saying that the Kingdom always lies beyond us . . . We cannot do everything, and there is a sense of liberation in realizing that. This enables us to do something, and to do it very well. It may be incomplete, but it is a beginning, a step along the way, an opportunity for God's grace to enter and do the rest. We may never see the end results, but that is the difference between the master builder and the worker. We are the workers . . . prophets of a future not our own.[39]

Bourgeois noticed that Romero's words were echoed in the writings of Dorothy Day and Thomas Merton; both Catholics focused on spiritual integrity, humility, and patience over short-term results in their lifelong struggles for social justice. Bourgeois stopped fretting about the efficacy of his actions; however, he was elated when he later learned that at least one El Salvadoran paramilitary defected after hearing Romero's speech posthumously broadcasted across Fort Benning.

■ ● ■

Meanwhile, Jesuits in El Salvador cautioned people about the sin they called "idolatry," the worship of the false Gods of wealth and power. As Eduardo Galeano noted in his banned book, *Open Veins of Latin America*: "Our defeat was always implicit in the victory of others; our wealth has always generated our poverty by nourishing the prosperity of others."[40] The Jesuits evoked Leviticus: God says to Moses, "Do not abandon me and worship idols. Do not make gods of metal and worship them." The Jesuits dared to name those institutes and individuals that were worshipping wealth. In the middle of the night on November 16, 1989, an elite unit of the Salvadoran army retaliated by dragging six Jesuit priests from their beds, ordering them to lie face down in the ground, and blowing out their brains with high-powered assault rifles.

Bourgeois was horrified to learn that those responsible for the murders were trained by the US Army at Fort Benning, at a place called the School of the Americas (SOA). When Bourgeois left prison, he continued his effort to, as he said, "unite the will of the spirit to the work of the flesh." The more Bourgeois learned about SOA, the more determined he became to shut it down. Through restless days and sleepless nights, Bourgeois uncovered that the school graduates between six hundred and eight hundred police and military officers annually, and it trains several hundred more via mobile training teams dispatched to Latin America. Initially established in Panama in 1946, the school was expelled from the country in 1984 under the Panama Canal Treaty. Former Panamanian president Jorge Illueca stated that the School of the Americas was the "biggest base for destabilization in Latin America." After studying reams of declassified information and perusing countless witness testimonies, Bourgeois concluded that SOA was manufacturing Latin American despots favorable to US economic interests in the region. But who in their right mind would believe a raving priest who probably suffered from post-traumatic stress disorder?

Renting a modest apartment near the school, Bourgeois launched SOA Watch in 1990, an independent grassroots organization that aimed to close SOA through vigils, fasts, demonstrations, and nonviolent direct action.

In November of that year, Bourgeois and three activists gathered outside Fort Benning to remember the six Jesuits killed on November 16, 1989. They vowed to return every year until the school closed. Each year, more peace activists and human rights organizations joined the annual protest. In 1993 the Leadership Conference of Religious Women passed the first resolution calling for the closing of SOA. Shortly afterward, the Presbyterian Church passed a similar resolution. The Lutherans, Methodists, United Auto Workers, NAACP, Vietnam Veterans Against the War, Unitarian Universalists, United Church of Christ, Amnesty International, all peace churches, and over half of the country's Catholic bishops signed similar resolutions calling for the school's closure.

— ∎ —

In the summer of 1993, a lone reporter named Doug Waller finally heeded Bourgeois's countless pleas to further investigate the School of the Americas. With Bourgeois's assistance, Waller wrote a groundbreaking article for *Newsweek* magazine titled, "Running a 'School for Dictators.'" The exposé detailed how SOA indoctrinated Latin American soldiers in counterinsurgency techniques, sniper training, commando and psychological warfare, and military intelligence and interrogation tactics. Waller wrote that these graduates consistently used their skills to wage war against their own people, especially educators, union organizers, religious workers, student leaders, and others working for the rights of the poor. The article noted that hundreds of thousands of Latin Americans had been tortured, raped, assassinated, disappeared, massacred, and forced into exile by those trained at the school. Waller stated that nineteen of the twenty-seven Salvadoran officers implicated in a U.N. Truth Commission report for the Jesuit murders were graduates of the school.[41]

Once *Newsweek* shattered the silence, even Capitol Hill took note of the issue. Massachusetts congressman Marty Meehan was among the first to express outrage: "If the School of the Americas held an alumni association meeting, it would bring together some of the most unsavory thugs in the Western Hemisphere."[42] Larry King, CBS, CNN, and NBC covered the story and interviewed Bourgeois, who continued uncovering manuals of the school that advocated "any means necessary" to achieve US military or political goals. Bourgeois disclosed to an aghast public that a fruit picker named Daniel Arcila traveled to Colombia's capital, Bogota, to inform officials that their paramilitary allies—allies who attended the School of the Americas—were terrorizing peasants by prying off fingernails with pocket knives, using blowtorches to burn bodies, and dismembering penises with chainsaws.[43]

In 1994 Susan Sarandon narrated a short documentary, *School of Assassins*, which was later nominated for an Academy Award. In 1996 the Pentagon was forced to release training manuals used at the School of the Americas, which detailed torture, extortion, and execution tactics. The *New York Times* reported, "America can now read for themselves some of the noxious lessons the United States Army taught thousands of Latin Americans." Newspapers across the country ran editorials demanding the school's closure.

Massachusetts congressman Joseph Kennedy took a special interest in closing down SOA and told Bourgeois his staff had discovered additional passages in the manuals that he said came right out of SS manuals. In July 1999 the House of Representatives voted to cut approximately $2 million from the SOA budget, an act that would have effectively abolished the school had it been upheld by the Senate.[44]

The negative publicity forced the school to dismantle its Hall of Fame, which included photos of notorious dictators such as Bolivia's Banzer—the dictator who had orchestrated the disappearance, torture, and murder of Bourgeois's friends. In an attempt to sanitize its image, the school also removed an ornate sword bequeathed by the Chilean dictator Augusto Pinochet that had once been proudly displayed at the school's entrance. In January 2001 the Pentagon attempted to disassociate the school with its horrific past by renaming SOA the Western Hemisphere Institute for Security Cooperation (WHISC). Bourgeois agreed with Representative Joe Moakley—who had spearheaded the congressional investigation into the Jesuit massacre—that the school was "pouring perfume on a toxic dump." Protesters gathered with signs warning, "You Can't WHISC Away the Past." Confirming activists' fears that the school's mandate had not changed, Salvadoran Colonel Francisco del Cid Diaz graduated from WHISC-SOA in 2003 despite being cited by the 1993 U.N. Truth Commission for commanding a unit responsible for shooting civilians at point-blank range.

Today, defenders of the school claim it doesn't teach abuse and that the new curriculum now includes human rights as a component of every class. They also argue that no school should be held accountable for the actions of a "few bad apples."

In 2008 over twenty thousand people descended on Fort Benning to demand the school's closure. Recent protests have included a rainbow coalition of antiwar activists, Buddhist monks, Grandmothers for Peace, Latin American solidarity groups, union workers, NAACP members, and college students.

Vietnam veterans like Charles Liteky, who was awarded the Medal of Honor and became the only recipient to renounce the prestigious recognition on antiwar grounds, also participate in demonstrations. Singer Pete Seeger and actor Martin Sheen have lent their stardom to illuminate the cause. On the TV show *The West Wing*, Sheen's character used his presidential power to accomplish on network television what the movement has yet to accomplish in real life: closing the School of the Americas.

-■-

Since 1990, over 275 protesters have been arrested for nonviolently taking their message to the headquarters, which requires trespassing over barbed wire fences. Bourgeois calls them "prisoners of conscience" who have energized the movement.[45] According to Bourgeois, nuns comprise the largest contingent of such prisoners. He notes, "Many Catholics who have integrated social justice into their life understand this issue, and they understand why not speaking is irresponsible." One prisoner of conscience, sixty-eight-year-old Franciscan sister Gwen Hennessey, elaborated on her reasons for joining the movement:

> We are here on earth to build the Reign of God—to live out our humanity, to share the God-giftedness within, in solidarity with all of our brothers and sisters and all of creation. We are here to live out our humanity in love, compassion. . . . Today we cry out for those who are not afforded their dignity. Today we cry out for the voiceless. Today we cry out against unjust structures that teach oppression, rape, and murder, those structures held up by U.S. tax fund, our corporate sin! In the name of God we must shut down the SOA and all that it stands for.[46]

Although the bourgeoning movement is the result of one man's deep faith, Bourgeois downplays his own significance. "If anything happened to me," he said, "it wouldn't really matter because the movement would live on."

Bourgeois spent the next decade working with peace and justice ministries across the nation instead of officiating at any single church. "Whenever I'm invited to say a mass, I spend a few minutes talking about Oscar Romero," explains Bourgeois. "Then I invite the audience to partake in a meeting on closing down the School of the Americas." In more recent years, Bourgeois has traveled across South America to meet with labor unions, university students, indigenous leaders, church groups, and government officials to muster support to withdraw their troops from SOA. "Our movement is connected to the victims in Latin America," says Bourgeois. "We want to have one foot in Latin America and one foot here." In March 2006 Bourgeois led a delegation of citizen diplomats—including Salvadoran torture survivor Carlos Mauricio—to Bolivia, the country that once blacklisted Bourgeois for organizing peasants. President Evo Morales warmly received the delegation and agreed to gradually withdraw the Bolivian military from training programs at Fort Benning, making Bolivia the fourth country, after Argentina, Uruguay, and Venezuela, to announce its withdrawal from the SOA.

Upon returning to the United States, Bourgeois continued visiting universities, churches, and other groups around the country to speak out against bellicose US foreign policy. For the last three years, Bourgeois has also spoken out against what he regards as a serious injustice much closer to his home and church: the exclusion of women from the priesthood. "As a Catholic priest for thirty-six years, in conscience, I cannot remain silent about injustice in my Church," says Bourgeois. "I have come to the conclusion that the exclusion of women in the Catholic Church is a grave injustice." In August 2008 Bourgeois took part in a ceremony to ordain a member of the group called Roman Catholic Womenpriests. With unusual swiftness and severity, the Vatican informed Bourgeois that he would face the harshest form of ecclesiastical punishment—excommunication—unless he recanted within thirty days. Bourgeois insisted that having an all-male clergy implies that men are worthy to be Catholic priests but women are not. "After much prayer, reflection and discernment, it is my conscience that compels me to do the right thing," wrote the renegade priest to the Vatican. "I cannot recant my belief and public statements that support the ordination of women in our Church."[47] Bourgeois went on to note that ordaining women would help fill the current deficit of priests in Catholic communities. More controversially, he suggested that the presence of women in the Catholic Church—an institution he's previously called an "All Boys Club"—might have prevented predatory priests from preying on children. "We need women priests in our Church for it to be healthy and complete," wrote Bourgeois.

On November 24, 2008, the Vatican excommunicated Bourgeois *latae sententiae*—automatically—for not recanting his public statements supporting the ordination of women. Shortly after his excommunication, Bourgeois told the *Catholic Review*, "It's a silencing; it's trying to get rid of you . . . in Bolivia [as a missionary] they kicked me out of the country. Now they're kicking me out of the church."[48]

Bourgeois still considers himself a priest in good standing with God and he continues to celebrate Mass privately in his apartment in Columbus, Georgia, where he carries on his twenty-year-long campaign against SOA. These days Bourgeois spends most of his energy advocating in favor of women's ordination, but he was recently reminded of the urgency of closing down the School of the Americas. On June 28, 2009, General Romeo Vásquez Velásquez, a graduate of SOA, led a military coup in Honduras against President Manuel Zelaya. Bourgeois quickly flew to Tegucigalpa to join protesters outside the US embassy in demanding that the United States stop training Honduran soldiers, withdraw its ambassador from the country, and pull out American troops on nearby bases. Meanwhile, SOA Watch coordinated a "Global Day of Action for Honduras" in major cities across the United States to pressure the State Department to legally define the de facto regime in Honduras as a military coup and cut off all aid to the country until President Zelaya was unconditionally reinstated.

A new Honduran president, Porfirio Lobo Sosa, took office on January 27, 2010, forcing Zelaya into exile. For Bourgeois, the political coup echoed the dirty wars of the 1980s and confirmed the necessity of closing down SOA once and for all.

— • —

In November 2009 Bourgeois and SOA Watch were nominated for the Nobel Peace Prize for their sustained, faithful, nonviolent witness against the disappearances, torture, and murder of hundreds of thousands of civilians by foreign military personnel trained by the US military at US taxpayers' expense. Bourgeois says he will continue speaking out against what he calls US imperialism even if SOA closes because, he says, SOA is symptomatic of US political and economic hegemony in Latin America and the post–cold war world. "The school is not an aberration of US foreign policy, but a clear illustration of it," explains the priest.

Shortly before the Iraq War, Bourgeois spoke at a church in Ridgewood, New Jersey, and warned about the perils of military interventions. An angry audience member hollered, "How dare you! This is an antiwar talk!" Bourgeois replied, "Yes sir, this is an antiwar talk because we are in church to worship a God of love and peace."

4 JIM CORBETT

Convictions of the Hearth in the Sanctuary Movement

I always believed that America opened its arms to the persecuted, but I'm afraid to walk the streets here.
> —CLEMENCIO GONZALES, *who left El Salvador after his friends were found decapitated in the fields outside his village; he was denied political asylum in the United States*[1]

We are writing to inform you the Southside United Presbyterian Church will publicly violate the Immigration and Nationality Act, Section 274(A). . . . We take this action because we believe the current policy and practice of the United States Government with regard to Central American refugees is illegal and immoral.
> —REVEREND JOHN FIFE, *in an open letter to US Attorney General William French Smith*[2]

Jim Corbett, a philosopher-turned-rancher, led a quiet life in a dusty corner of Tucson, Arizona. The soft-spoken, painfully shy Wyoming native with a long face, droopy eyes, and scraggly goatee had attended Harvard on a scholarship to study philosophy. He had hoped to become a professor but later joked, "The main thing I learned from studying philosophy was that I knew nothing to teach." Embracing rural life, Corbett studied the husbandry of goats and bees, wrote a paper on "the goat cheese economy," and considered moving to an impoverished

96

country to share his expertise.³ Even after crippling arthritis splayed his toes sideways out of his sand-dusted huaraches, he continued chasing cows across the pasture of his ranch along the San Pedro River, where he lived with wife, Patricia. The proud descendent of a Blackfoot Indian and Ozark Mountain mule trader, Corbett embraced the Quaker faith in the early 1960s and attempted to live a simple, humble life.⁴

On May 4, 1981, a series of events forever changed that life, turning the anonymous rancher into a legendary outlaw. That morning, Corbett learned that his friend and fellow Quaker, Jim Dudley, had given a ride to a Salvadoran hitchhiker when Border Patrol agents stopped his car at the Peck Canyon roadblock and promptly arrested the young Salvadoran for Entry Without Inspection (EWI). Dudley informed Corbett that the agents planned to deport the petrified Salvadoran back to his war-torn homeland and had practically arrested him, too, for assisting the undocumented immigrant. Corbett had given little thought to the border fence to the south of his ranch, but he was aware of the violence engulfing Central America and wondered if the Salvadoran refugee faced life-threatening dangers back home.

Hoping to better understand the confusing news coming out of Central America, Corbett decided to locate the detained El Salvadoran for, if nothing else, an animated political discussion. Coincidentally, Corbett shared his name with the previous mayor of Tucson, so Border Patrol mistook his identity and proffered information about the detainee's whereabouts. Corbett discovered that the Salvadoran, "Nelson," was being held in the Santa Cruz jail on the edge of Nogales, Arizona, a border town that spreads over the international fence separating Mexico and the United States.⁵ When Corbett arrived at the jail, he discovered twenty-by-twenty-foot cells, each crammed with over thirty men nearly suffocating in the desert heat. The Quaker could not locate Nelson but spoke at length with two other exhausted, dehydrated detainees who begged him to notify their families that they were being deported. Although Corbett was fluent in Spanish, he struggled to understand the torrent of words pouring from the delirious men who recounted gruesome details of paramilitary death squads terrorizing their homelands. What was all this talk about thugs with machetes and nighttime disappearances at gunpoint? Spooked by the intensity of the detainees' pleas for help, Corbett decided to present G-28 forms on their behalf, which would legally guarantee them a hearing before an immigration judge. Upon filling out the forms, Corbett returned to the jail only to learn that Border Patrol had removed both Salvadorans.[6] However, instead of leaving, Corbett began gently prodding other detainees about their pasts. Some had been tortured in unimaginably barbaric ways—electrical shocks, fingernail extractions, gang rape, eyeball removal, torch burns, and submersion in rat-infested pits.[7] The rancher was so disturbed by their accounts that he impulsively obtained a $4,500 lien on one of his trailers and bonded out four Salvadoran women and one baby. Acting as an intermediary, Corbett mailed letters to the refugees' relatives and strategized with them about legal routes that might allow them to stay in the country.

The more time Corbett spent listening to refugees' stories, the more their stories raised philosophical and theological questions on the moral obligation of bystanders confronted with the suffering of others. What responsibilities do individuals bear in alleviating the suffering of strangers? What responsibilities do they have to hold accountable those who have created the conditions for this suffering? And how is an individual complicit in the continuance of violence—how does a person contribute to and benefit from the status quo? As someone now privy to the refugees' debilitating fear, Corbett grew increasingly concerned about his own responsibility as a Quaker—a Christian pacifist—living in a country that denied these refugees asylum.

Corbett spent much of his life studying moral philosophy as an academic pursuit and was acutely aware of the "bystander effect," the social psychological phenomenon where individuals fail to offer assistance in an emergency situation when others are present because they assume someone else will intervene. He knew that extremely few people had dared to protest antebellum slavery, as had the Quaker Benjamin Lundy, or the Nazi Holocaust, as had the Franciscan friar Maximilian Kolbe. Corbett believed that these few dissenters had drawn on their deep spiritual beliefs to resist falling prey to the bystander effect. Praying and meditating, the contemplative goat herder slowly came to see the Central American refugee crisis as his own moment of truth. Directly confronted by the refugees' immediate trauma, Corbett questioned whether assisting a few survivors financially was really enough, or if he should dedicate himself fully and unequivocally to protesting the political warfare decimating Central America as well as the squalid conditions he had witnessed in INS detention camps. He remembered the profound sadness he felt upon learning that a *coyote* (a professional smuggler) had abandoned twenty-six Salvadorans in the scorching Arizona desert a year earlier. Half of them died from heat stroke or severe dehydration, and the other half barely survived by drinking their own urine.[8] Although church members in the area assisted the survivors by raising money to pay for their bonds and legal representation, the Salvadorans were deported. Back home, they faced an uncertain fate: for some, a mercifully quick bullet in the brain; for others, mutilation, rape, and the drawn-out agony of torture.[9]

For Corbett, his chance encounter with fleeing refugees posed the moral conundrum of his lifetime. Ultimately, he decided that he could not live with himself if he cowered, so he vowed to his God to fully dedicate himself to the cause of the refugees.

— ∎ —

Seeking to qualm the refugees' fears of outsiders, Corbett donned a priest's cassock and began calling himself Padre Jaime, assuring jittery detainees that he shared the sentiments of their native clergy, including Archbishop Oscar Romero, who showed mercy to peasants. By appealing to local churches for funds and liquidating his own assets, Corbett bonded out a dozen refugees and helped them file claims for political asylum. However, he soon learned, much to his anger, that the refugees bonded out were denied work permits and forced to join the underground economy of sweatshops and restaurant kitchens in order to survive. These jobs did not lead to the American Dream, but dead-ended in nonnegotiable hours, emotional humiliation, and physical danger. The refugees' status as "illegals" also meant employers could deny them health insurance, public assistance, and hospitalization. Still, the refugees confided to Corbett that they preferred a slow death in exile to returning home and facing a gruesome death at the hands of roving paramilitaries who sought out those who had dared to flee.

Corbett began single-handedly sheltering over twenty refugees in his two-room converted garage, only to realize his home and finances could not accommodate the flood of Central Americans. The overwhelmed rancher began envisioning a loose network of support and assistance for undocumented Central Americans—an informal network of secret routes and safe houses reminiscent of the Underground Railroad that helped slaves escape to free states in antebellum America.[10] He believed one of the biggest problems for Central Americans fleeing violence was that the Mexican informal, church-based system of protection and transportation buckled at the US border. To compensate for this void, Corbett decided to form a "border ministry" that would safely guide Central Americans into the United States where they could contact lawyers and apply for asylum.[11]

Still, Corbett lay awake consumed with the fear the he was not doing enough for his brothers and sisters south of the border. Haunted by the refugees' stories of sadistic armies who yanked out fingernails with iron pliers, he grew increasingly convinced that he must do more. But what else could he do besides organize, pray, fund-raise, and provide legal council on behalf of the refugees? Then one day, in the women's section of the prison, Corbett observed mothers surrounded by their children as they covered a nightstand with a white cloth to create a makeshift altar. To the Quaker's surprise, the prison priest did more than pray before they were loaded into trucks and sent off—he suggested an alternative route past the Mexican checkpoint near Hermosillo if the women attempted to escape en route. After listening to the subversive priest, Corbett decided to use his intimate familiarity with the daunting desert terrain to advise refugees on how to evade Border Patrol agents while trespassing over the US border.

Donning his wide-brimmed cowboy hat, the long-faced shepherd drove his jeep to the US-Mexico border where refugees faced impending separation from their families, humiliation, imprisonment, coercion, deportation, and death. Heeding the soft whisper of what he believed was the Holy Spirit, the rancher sent word to Catholic churches sheltering refugees in Mexico that he would work as a *coyote* free of charge. Exceedingly knowledgeable on the desert's nuanced dips and labyrinthine turns, Corbett drove through strawberry hedgehog cacti and golden cane cholla to shepherd Central Americans across the border through holes in the fence. In a Quaker pamphlet, he shared with his brethren the plight of refugees he encountered on the border:

> I [looked] for a doctor to remove a bullet from a woman without reporting it. She had been running and hiding for weeks after being shot in the groin by a Salvadoran soldier. On the border, I once tried to comfort a

woman who had been raped and then sold to be used as a prostitute. . . .
A few blocks from my home in Tucson, I once spent the small hours of
the night searching for accident victims who were hiding from ambulance attendants and police. When I found them, I then had to locate doctors who would set their broken bones without informing the police. On
another occasion, I watched helplessly as a woman hit by a car was turned
over to a policeman and held for the Border Patrol within minutes of her
arrival at a hospital emergency room. She became hysterical. . . . These
people preferred rape and untreated injury to dealings with local police
and emergency services because they were refugees who had fled some
of the most atrocious tortures that military regimes have ever devised for
suppressing social unrest.[12]

The more time Corbett spent studying topographical maps pointing
out riverbeds and crossing points, the more obsessed he became with
outfoxing Border Patrol. Although an introvert by nature, Corbett's
self-assurance grew exponentially, and he began relishing the experience of outmaneuvering local officials. The self-fashioned *coyote* spent
three years transporting an estimated seven hundred refugees across the
border to safety.[13] From Chiapas to Hermosillo to Monterey to Tucson,
the humanitarian smuggler penned letters to friends, refugees support
groups, church leaders, and Quaker councils along the Rio Grande. By
1983 INS officials had plastered Corbett's mug shot on "Most Wanted"
posters across their office walls. Convinced of his divine mission, Corbett
later noted, "Just as refugees are outlawed, hunted down, and imprisoned,
if we choose to serve them in Spirit and Truth, we also will be outlawed."

- ■ -

Between 1980 and 1991, nearly one million Central Americans illegally entered the United States seeking asylum from the political violence erupting across Guatemala, El Salvador, and Nicaragua. In Guatemala, government-backed mercenaries killed fifty thousand, abducted
one hundred thousand, and raided 626 villages.[14] In El Salvador, Oscar
Romero was only one of the dozens of clergy members assassinated
by roving paramilitaries.[15] One exiled missionary described the death
squads' vicious campaign targeting civilians:

People are not just killed by death squads . . . they are decapitated and their heads are placed on pikes and used to dot the landscape. Men are not just disemboweled by the Salvadoran Treasury Police; their severed genitalia are stuffed into their mouths. Salvadoran women are not just raped by the National Guard; their wombs are cut from their bodies and used to cover their faces. It is not enough to kill children; they are dragged over barbed wire until the flesh falls from their bones while parents are forced to watch.[16]

Human rights groups estimated that political violence killed eighty to one hundred thousand Salvadorans, and even more were uprooted.[17] The war in El Salvador created more than one million refugees. Fugitives forcibly repatriated potentially faced rape, imprisonment, torture, and death upon returning.[18] Political violence also left as many as fifty thousand Nicaraguans dead.

In the 1980s the United States heavily influenced the political landscape of Central America in what President Ronald Reagan described as an effort to curb Soviet influence in the hemisphere. Fearing the Soviet hammer and sickle lurking behind every popular uprising across Central America, the United States spent more than $4 billion on economic and military aid during El Salvador's civil war and provided funds, training, and arms to the Salvadoran and Guatemalan governments throughout the 1970s and 1980s.[19] The president explained his foreign policy to CBS News's Walter Cronkite, "What we're doing is . . . trying to halt the infiltration into the Americas by terrorists, by outside interference, and those who aren't just aiming at El Salvador but I think are aiming at the whole of Central America and possibly later South America—and I'm sure eventually North America."[20]

The Reagan administration also lent covert and overt support to Nicaragua's contra guerrillas against the country's revolutionary Sandinista National Liberation Front. Referring to contras as "the moral equivalent of the Founding Fathers," Regan funneled $1 billion to the guerrillas despite human rights organizations such as Americas Watch frequently accusing the contras of killing civilians.[21]

The Reagan administration was aware of the abysmal human rights records of its puppet dictators in Central America but insisted its policies were securing a brighter future for the region. Assistant Secretary of State for Human Rights and Humanitarian Affairs Elliot Abrams delivered a speech in Miami in 1982 articulating the administration's long-term policy. "We want to be very sure that in a situation such as that in El Salvador, we do not trade the serious but solvable rights problems of today for a permanent Communist dictatorship," he said. "Resisting the expansion of communism is a key human rights goal." He added, "I am always amazed when people come to me to voice their concern about refugees from El Salvador, yet who oppose the Administration's effort to avoid enlargement of that refugee problem by giving the aid it needs to defeat Communist-led guerillas."[22]

Reagan's admirers credited him for stamping out communist sentiments and nurturing free-market systems across the region. They saw his administration as responsible for opening Central American markets to what they regarded as favorable neoliberal economic policies that led to El Salvador's adoption of the US dollar as its official currency. Applauding Reagan's determination to leave no trace of communist sympathizers close to US borders, these admirers opposed amnesty for refugees, saying they were economic immigrants who depressed wages for domestic workers, leeched off social services, and contributed to urban crime. By 1980, the Census Bureau and INS speculated that an estimated six million illegal aliens lived in the United States. "Not only do they suffer, but so too does U.S. society," the US Select Commission on Immigration and Refugee Policy conjectured in 1981. "The presence of a substantial number of undocumented/illegal aliens in the United States has resulted not only in a disregard for immigration law but in the breaking of minimum wage and occupational safety laws, and statutes against smuggling as well. As long as undocumented migration flouts US immigration, its most devastating impact may be the disregard it breeds for other U.S. laws."[23]

Reagan proposed a plan to heavily fine employers who hired illegal aliens, and requested Congress to appropriate $40 million to construct additional detention facilities and hire Border Patrol agents. By 1983, Salvadorans were being deported at the rate of about one thousand per month. Still, Border Patrol officials estimated that for every illegal alien they caught, between two and five got past them undetected.[24]

Reagan's opponents, including Corbett, regarded the president as a cold-hearted, anti-communist zealot who perpetrated crimes against humanity with US taxpayers' dollars. They contended that US arms and military interventions inflamed and prolonged Central America's civil wars, arguing that the real issue was not communism versus freedom, but human rights in economic and political terms. These opponents insisted that the widening economic disparities between ruling oligarchies and disenfranchised peasants, not godless communism, precipitated the guerilla revolutions that the Reagan administration sought to quash at any cost. Rejecting what they believed was Reagan's paranoid view of global reality as divided between Kingdoms of Light and Darkness, opponents sought asylum for refugees in the short run and a more humane US foreign policy toward Central America in the long run. Reverend William Sloane Coffin later quipped, "I think the most powerful ideology in this world in terms of unexamined slogans and premises is not communism but anti-communism."[25]

— ▪ —

In an open letter published in late 1981, Corbett began documenting the treatment of Central Americans by the INS—the inhumanely cramped cells, brutality of Border Patrol agents, and atmosphere of crippling fear—and formulated a theology of an underground railroad that incorporated elements of Latin American liberation theology. The erudite rancher's letter also introduced the religious concept of "sanctuary" as a focal point for the movement and sought support from a wide coalition of interfaith organizations. Corbett believed in a single church united in human compassion—whether run by a priest or a rabbi or imam—and he mailed five hundred letters to religious groups throughout the United States asking for their support in starting a widespread sanctuary movement.[26]

As a Quaker, Corbett regarded sanctuary as a religious activity of community solidarity with the dispossessed and forgotten. He called his approach "civil initiative" and defined it as the "community practice of acting together on recognized and ratified human rights." In one of his letters he wrote: "I can see that if Central American refugees' rights to political asylum are decisively rejected by the U.S. government or if the U.S. legal system insists on ransom that exceeds our ability to pay, active resistance will be the only alternative to abandoning the refugees to their fate."[27] Reflecting on his own religion's relationship to social justice movements, Corbett noted, "Unlike peace churches that withdraw from a war-making society in order to establish islands of nonviolence, the Quaker meeting usually aspires to be fully engaged while remaining radically unassimilated. . . . . As a faith practice, sanctuary brings back into focus our community's covenant to serve the Peaceable Kingdom."[28]

One of the first people Corbett enlisted to help him illegally harbor refugees was Jim Fife, pastor of the adobe-style Southside Presbyterian Church and a member of the steering committee of the Tucson Ecumenical Council. In addition to the church, Fife had access to a few dilapidated buildings that Corbett envisioned renovating for the purpose of sheltering refugees. Fife sympathized with the plight of asylum seekers but was constrained by his commitments to his congregants and required to bring any decisions before his Session to decide. In October 1981 Fife presided over a church meeting on the topic of sanctuary and read a statement by Corbett:

> For those of us who would be faithful in our allegiance to the Kingdom, there is also no way to avoid recognizing that in this case collaboration with the government is a betrayal of our faith, even if it is a passive or even loudly protesting collaboration that merely shuts out the undocumented refugee who is at our door. We can take our stand with the oppressed, or we can take our stand with organized oppression. We can serve the Kingdom, or we can serve the kingdoms of this world—but we cannot do both. . . . When the government itself sponsors the crucifixion of entire people and then makes it a felony to shelter those seeking refuge, law-abiding protest merely trains us to live with atrocity.[29]

After four hours of prayerful reflection, the Session voted (with two abstentions) to open its doors to the refugees. In 1982 Fife also agreed to help organize a system for passing illegal immigrants from church to church across the country. He educated and galvanized Presbyterians nationwide to provide initial communications and monetary donations. Presented with the immediacy of human suffering, doctors volunteered to treat torture victims, lawyers represented asylum seekers pro bono, and, church laypeople extended their hospitality to refugees.

Many churches were torn over supporting the burgeoning sanctuary movement. A very conservative Republican at Central Presbyterian in the manufacturing town of Massillon, Ohio, advocated joining the movement—"We look down on those churches in Germany that allowed the Jews to be rounded up after they knew what would happen to them"—but a forty-year member of the same church protested, "We are all Christians, how can we be considering breaking the law!"[30]

Impelled by a sense of growing urgency, Corbett continued entreating religious communities to engage in bolder forms of direct action. He made a well-received plea before the National Council of Churches to provide material support for the nascent Sanctuary Movement:

> The refugees are right here at our door pleading for help to avoid capture. Actively asserting the right to aid fugitives from terror means doing it . . . not just preaching at a government that's capturing and deporting them, not just urging legislation that might help future refugees.[31]

While continuing to use his familiarity with the Sonoran Desert to personally shepherd hundreds of Central Americans fleeing civil war to safety, Corbett began reflecting on what he saw as the injustices perpetrated by his government vis-à-vis Biblical stories. He deeply resented his government's stance on refugees, writing on Christmas Eve 1982:

> Herod's slaughter of the innocents casts the shadow of the cross on the Christmas story. I couldn't help remembering, from two weeks earlier on the Mexican-Guatemalan border, the grief in Mother Elvira's eyes as she told of just such a baby boy, nine months old, whom Guatemalan soldiers had mutilated and slowly murdered, forcing his mother to watch. Only at the risk of wounding the mind can one learn about the methodical torture of dispossessed persons that the United States is sponsoring in Latin America.[32]

Despite Corbett's somber mood on Christmas Eve, he had much to celebrate. By 1982, the new Underground Railroad had blossomed into a public Sanctuary Movement that engaged thousands of US churches.[33] With depots in Tucson, El Paso, and in the Lower Rio Grande Valley, the new Underground Railroad gave desperate refugees hope beyond mere prayer.[34]

As the movement grew, Corbett preferred taking a backseat in organizing efforts and allowing the Chicago Religious Task Force on Central America to coordinate efforts between US churches and Latin American congregations. A letter from the Ministry of the United Church of Christ noted, "We have been chastened further by an urgent plea from colleagues in the Church in El Salvador, Honduras and Nicaragua, that Christians in North America accept responsibility for attempting to stop the bitter war deepening in these countries."[35] Throughout the early 1980s, activists built the movement through a decentralized decision-making process in which power was horizontally shared among autonomous communities of faith. By 1983, a loosely structured network of more than forty-five faith communities declared themselves "public sanctuary sites" and benefited from public endorsement of more than six hundred "co-conspiring" religious organizations.[36] Church after church opened its doors to fleeing refugees, as did several synagogues. Reagan had feared a domino effect regarding Communism, but instead was faced with one regarding houses of worship declaring themselves sanctuaries.

■ ∎ ■

The monomaniacal anticommunist direction of US asylum practices was particularly pronounced in the government's treatment of Central American refugees in the 1980s. These refugees were especially problematic for the Reagan and Bush administrations, both of which adopted foreign policies that sought to protect US national security interests in the region by supporting military dictatorships.[37] Reagan's ambassador to the United Nations, Jeane Kirkpatrick, succinctly captured the administration's position. "Speaking generally, we must make it perfectly clear that we are revolted by torture and can never feel spiritual kinship with a government that engages in torture," said Kirkpatrick in an interview with *U.S. News and World Report*. "But the central goal of our foreign policy should not be the moral elevation of other nations but the preservation of a civilized conception of our own self-interest."[38]

By testifying in gruesome detail to the political repression and virtual economic slavery in their homelands, these refugees complicated the administrations' official narrative of a clear-cut battle between communism and democracy. The Reagan-Bush response to Central American fugitives was to deny they were bona fide asylum seekers by classifying them as "economic" rather than "political" fugitives.[39] They knew that legitimating fleeing Central American refugees threatened to undermine US political and economic support for regimes brutally oppressing their own populations.[40] Elliott Abrams formulated the Reagan administration's position in these words: "Legally and morally, the distinction between economic migrants and political refugees matters greatly. The United States is legally obligated and morally bound to protect refugees but not to accept for permanent residence every illegal immigrant who reaches our shores."[41] Abrams called the nascent sanctuary movement a "willful and casual violation of American law."[42]

During fiscal year 1983, the INS granted political asylum to 71 percent of applicants fleeing Ayatollah Khomeini in Iran; 62 percent fleeing from the Soviet-occupied Afghanistan; 25 percent of Polish and Ethiopian applicants fleeing Communist governments; and less than 3 percent of Salvadoran applicants.[43] The office of the United Nations High Commissioner for Refugees (UNHCR) expressed its concern that the US government failed to grant asylum to any significant number of Salvadorans, saying it represented "a negation of [US] responsibilities assumed upon its adherence to the [UN] Protocol on Refugees."

■ ● ■

In public letters, Corbett insisted "the ongoing gross violations of Salvadorans' and Guatemalans' human rights have been documented more thoroughly and convincingly than with any other first-asylum refugees who have arrived in the United States during recent decades."[44] The Roman Catholic organization Pax Christi concurred: "Murder, torture and disappearances have reached 'horrifying proportions' in Guatemala and El Salvador." Amnesty International later confirmed that the Guatemalan government was the "worst violator of human rights of any country in the world."

After intensely studying refugee law, Corbett decided that advocates of sanctuary for Central American refugees defended humane laws that US government officials insisted on violating.[45] He believed that Thoreau's immortal words spoke to modern-day sanctuary providers: "They are lovers of the law who uphold it when the government breaks it." Corbett noted that these laws included the UN Refugee Protocol and the 1980 Refugee Act that implemented the protocol. Upon submitting the protocol to the Senate for ratification, President Johnson had summarized its intent: "Foremost among the humanitarian rights which the Protocol provides is the prohibition against expulsion or return of refugees to any country in which they face persecution."[46] Sanctuary, for Corbett, was not "civil disobedience" but "civil initiative"—a way of enforcing humanitarian laws.[47]

Corbett noted that virtually all other countries that signed the UN Refugee Protocol and the Geneva Conventions recognized that Salvadorans and Guatemalans seeking asylum were bona fide refugees. Corbett concluded, "Nothing in the law permits the U.S. government to return refugees to persecution in their homeland if they have resided in or crossed other countries, nor does the fact that refugees have economic needs alter their status as refugees."[48] Members of the flourishing Sanctuary Movement, such as Reverend William Sloane Coffin, noted that Congress could retire the entire movement by doing one of two things: insist that the Refugee Act of 1980 be properly administered according to both the spirit and the letter of the law or, alternatively, pass an extended voluntary departure act, which would allow refugees to remain in country until political violence in their homelands subsided.[49]

- • -

Aware of the moral stature of religious leaders in their communities, Reagan administration officials admitted participants in the Sanctuary Movement were "well meaning," but attacked them for meddling in politics and breaking the law. In an interview on the PBS program *Frontline*, INS commissioner Alan C. Nelson noted correctly, "Many of them will admit what they are really doing is opposing the president's policy in Central America."

As Nelson noted, the Sanctuary Movement was not an apolitical act of charity, but part of a deliberate attempt to expose and remedy what participants saw as abuses of American foreign policy. In response to Reagan's interventionist agenda, specifically in reaction to the invasion of Grenada in 1983, several Nonviolent Direct Action (NVDA) movements articulated an anti-interventionist platform attacking US imperialism in the Third World, especially Central America.[50] Feminist theologian Rosemary Radford Ruether bluntly stated:

In ways that most U.S. citizens neither know nor understand, the United States, since the Second World War, has developed a permanent war economy. The purpose of this war economy is to maintain U.S. control throughout the world in defense of the Western empire and its ability to use cheap labor and resources of formerly colonized regions of the planet.[51]

The war economy, according to Ruether, pursues military escalation where it perceives its control to be threatened by counterrevolutionary movements in the Third World. "Much of the war against the Third World is carried out through surrogate armies maintained by military elites whose power the United States funds within those Third World states."[52] Commenting on the Sanctuary Movement, she said, "For the first time since the end of the Vietnam war, the United States government is faced with a major challenge to its policies of global control, a challenge spearheaded by the American religious community."[53]

Although organizers never clearly articulated their political worldview, anti-imperialist rhetoric permeated the entire movement. Dick Simpson, a sanctuary volunteer, described one of the homilies given by a Guatemalan refugee, Felipe, at a Cincinnati sanctuary church:

> Felipe told us that Christ was not just crucified 2,000 years ago, Christs are being crucified in Central America today. Instead of the Christ with whip marks, the Christs in Central America have their fingernails pulled out. Instead of the crown of thorns, the Christs of Central America have their feet cut open and have the wounds rubbed with salt and lemon. Instead of carrying a wooden cross, the Christs of Central America are being killed by the whirling crucifixes of helicopters and planes that drop napalm rockets, weapons made here in the United States. Indeed, there was a Pontius Pilate sitting in the White House who was washing his hands of the whole event. In this country [the United States] and other countries, there were the Herods who were supporting the puppet governments of Central America.[54]

On January 25, 1985, a delegation of religious and peace leaders hand-delivered a message to the office of the secretary of state announcing that 42,352 US citizens had signed a Pledge of Resistance, a contingency plan of public resistance in the event of a US invasion or military escalation in Central America.[55] Jim Wallis, editor of the progressive Christian magazine *Sojourners*, met with Craig Johnstone, then-deputy assistant secretary of state for inter-American affairs. "The domestic cost [of escalation] will be the imprisoning of tens of thousands of U.S. citizens."

Wallis warned Johnstone, "We mean what we say, and we will do what we promise."

■ • ■

Unlike in medieval Europe, the United States grants no legal right to asylum in churches. Yet, in the 1980s, the idea of sacred safe zones initially deterred immigration raids. "We're not about to send investigators into a church and start dragging people out in front of TV cameras," Bill Joyce, an INS council officer, told the *Christian Science Monitor* in August 1982. "We'll just wait them out, wait until they leave the church. This is just a political thing dreamed up by the churches to get publicity—a game to pressure the government to allow Salvadorans to stay here. If we thought it was a significant problem, then maybe we'd look at it. But there are plenty of illegal aliens out there."[56]

Although the INS wished to dismiss the Sanctuary Movement as an anemic pest, it flourished into one of the most notable grassroots movements of the decade. Between 1982 and 1992, the movement benefited from the support of more than two hundred religious orders and congregations nationwide, several universities and municipalities, and more than six hundred religious organizations, including the National Federation of Priests' Councils (representing more than 33,000 Catholic priests), all united in their support of sanctuary.[57] In total, over fifty thousand Americans participated in the movement by providing assistance or public support to asylum seekers.[58]

Many religious communities provided members of congregations to assist refugees escaping violence. One such volunteer, Dick Simpson, described his experience escorting two peasants, Felipe and Elena, fleeing Guatemala after seventeen of their coworkers were killed for teaching others to read and write:

> When we arrived [in Cincinnati], there were a hundred or more people standing outside the community Friends Meeting House singing songs and hymns, carrying banners, clapping vigorously, hugging and making everyone welcome. To be greeted by this sort of celebration in the United States when we were breaking the law and could go to jail for five years for doing so, or when Felipe and Elena could be seized by our government agents and sent back to Guatemala to be killed, was a very ecstatic experience.[59]

The movement drew heavily on the Hebrew Bible, which consistently demands particular concern and compassion for the weak, the powerless, and the dispossessed. Most emphatically, the Bible promotes protecting the immigrant, the alien, the sojourner, and the refugee.[60] There is no distinction between the foreigner and the native. Vanderbilt Divinity School Professor Paul Lim told *TIME* magazine, "In the Old Testament, God speaks of being the God of the aliens about 103 times."[61] The New Testament, he noted, features Jesus' famous criterion for the saved—"I was a stranger, and you welcomed me"—as well as, in its original Greek, an endorsement of philoxenia, the practice of warmly embracing strangers.

Sanctuary providers often evoke God's solidarity with the threatened and hounded by paraphrasing the Book of Exodus: "I have heard their cries and I have come, and I send you, not only to bring my abused people out of Egypt, but permanently to change the blind, stumbling, insensitive imperialist heart of Pharaoh."[62] In the Judeo-Christian tradition, "sanctuary" has a dual meaning: a place where a faith-based community gathers for worship, and a place of protective refuge. It is the recognition of civil order's moral limits and a divine claim on human mercy.[63] Activists often paraphrase Micah 6:8 as: "Never mind what they tell you to do: your peer, the electorate, your governmental prophets and priests. What God requires of you is the doing of justice; the love and the exercise of human compassion; and a stance, surely national as well as personal, which eschews arrogance imperiousness, and tyranny."[64]

In the Book of Numbers, sanctuaries—which include "cities of refuge"—served as safe havens for those who committed crimes and faced inappropriate, cruel, or unjust punishments.[65] Members of the Sanctuary Movement figured if Biblical cities went so far as to protect the guilty, then modern cities should at least protect the innocent.

Many Jews felt particularly drawn to the movement from a deep sense of historical consciousness. Rabbi Gerold Serotta, a founder of New Jewish Agenda, noted that Jews, "especially because of our history, should be involved in sanctuary. Where there are people fleeing oppression and danger, the Jewish community of all communities should be involved."[66] Holocaust survivor Elie Wiesel explained, "in the Jewish tradition, [sanctuary] refers to human beings . . . every human being is the dwelling of God—man or woman or child, Christian or Jewish or Buddhist. Any person, by virtue of being a son or a daughter of humanity, is a living sanctuary whom nobody has the right to invade."[67]

Skeptics who argued against sanctuary on Biblical—rather than nationalistic—grounds turned to Paul's more general advice in Romans to "let every person be subject to the governing authorities" or, from Matthews 22:21, "Render unto Caesar the things which are Caesar's, and unto God the things that are God's." Sanctuary providers dismissed unfavorable interpretations of Biblical passages. A pamphlet distributed by the Chicago Religious Task Force on Central America endowed sanctuary providers with a religious prerogative to defy Caesar:

Basta! Enough! The blood stops here at our doors! This is the time for us to claim our sacred right to invoke the name of God—to push back all the powers of encroachment and violation and profanation in the name of the One to whom we owe our ultimate allegiance. This is the time to tell Caesar and his henchmen, "No Trespassing, for the ground on which you walk is holy."[68]

Alexander Solzhenitsyn, the Russian novelist who awakened the world to the Soviet Union's Gulag through his writings, similarly noted: "When Caesar, having exacted what is Caesar's, demands still more insistently that we render unto him what is God's—that is a sacrifice we dare not make."[69]

■ ■ ■

In 1984 Jim Corbett accepted the Letelier-Moffitt Human Rights Award on behalf of the Sanctuary Movement. A year later, in January 1985, the national campaign came under direct attack by the American government, which sought to drain its funds, divert its energies into self-defense against criminal charges, and discredit it before the American public. The federal government indicted Corbett and ten others, including two Catholic priests and several religious lay workers. The activists were indicted on seventy-one counts of conspiring, encouraging, and aiding illegal aliens to enter the United States by shielding, harboring, and transporting them. Welcoming the additional media attention the indictment generated for their cause, Corbett publicly vowed to continue his work despite facing a lengthy prison term for flaunting US law.

Churches nationwide responded to the indictments by reiterating that sanctuary is a valid ministry of the church. Five days after the indictment, the movement's renewed commitment was demonstrated when volunteers from Tucson brought seven Guatemalan refugees across the Mexico-US border.[70] They traveled on foot through the rugged Sonoran Desert until chartered vehicles transported them to one of eleven Tucson sanctuary churches.[71] Church workers spent two days and nights backpacking through the countryside with the refugee family.[72] The family had lost seven relatives to Guatemalan death squads, including their own nine- and ten-year-old daughters. "We knew we were under surveillance," said the father. "We knew that leaving was the only alternative for people who are in danger of being murdered in our country. If we are sent back, there is no doubt we would be killed."[73]

By then, over seventy thousand people, four hundred faith communities, and twelve universities had declared sanctuary for Central American refugees.[74] Sanctuary communities included an interfaith and interregional network ranging from a religious order of nuns in Kansas to a monastery in Vermont to a synagogue in Chicago. The indicted activists fielded media inquires regarding their pending trial. Darlene Nicgorski, one of the indicted activists, told a reporter, "It is a sad day when the government tells the church whom it can feed, whom it can clothe, and whom it can welcome. . . . If I have done anything, I am guilty of following the gospel."[75] The US government insisted sanctuary providers were not above the law and worried that their actions would create a precedent for "harboring illegals." In response, movement leader Michael McConnell insisted, "Our goal is not to have a thousand sanctuaries. Rather, it is to eliminate the need for sanctuaries."[76]

On January 14, 1986, the defendants appeared in court and were warned not to mention the word "refugee." After a six-month trial in Tucson, the eight sanctuary providers defended their actions at the sentencing that July. John Fife, pastor of Southside Presbyterian Church, told Judge Carroll about encountering a fifteen-year-old Salvadoran orphan whose family had been killed. "The haunting thought that came to me was, if that was my boy, what would I want the church to do?" Fife said. "We had no choice. None of us ever had a choice. Our only choice was whether we wanted to sell our souls."[77]

Judge Carroll responded, "Good motive is not a defense to intentional acts of crime" and found the activists guilty of various felonies. However, he ultimately suspended the sentences and put all eight activists on probation for terms ranging from three to five years. Unfazed, Corbett promised to continue helping Central American refugees. "The work of sanctuary will continue exactly as it has," the movement's leader said immediately after the verdict was announced. "We'll stand trial as often as we have to. It'll continue as it has because the refugees and their needs actually set the agenda."[78]

— • —

In November 1985, members of Congress received a letter from Arturo Rivera y Damas—successor to assassinated archbishop of San Salvador, Oscar Romero—urging them to support a bill introduced by Massachusetts representative Joseph Moakley and Arizona senator Dennis DeConcini that would halt the deportation of Salvadorans for two years while the federal government studied the human rights situation there.[79] "To return the persecuted to the source, the origin, the cause of his suffering is an act of injustice in the eyes of Christian love," the archbishop wrote.

The bill languished on Capitol Hill, but on Good Friday, 1986, Governor Toney Anaya became one of the few politicians to support the movement by declaring New Mexico a "state of sanctuary."[80] Anaya's decision was an anomaly at a time when the federal government's approach to asylum-seekers remained punitive. Regional Immigration Commissioner Harold Ezell instructed his subordinates not only to throw back the "illegals" but also, "if you catch 'em, you ought to clean 'em and fry 'em yourself."[81] Corbett confirmed that Ezell's comments were not empty rhetoric: "[I met] a young Mexican who had had his front teeth knocked out and his ribs and an arm broken by Texas Rangers."[82]

When severe arthritis twisted Corbett's fingers and forced him into early retirement, he continued speaking out against the militarization of the US-Mexico border. He told a reporter, "One day, we will be as ashamed of borders as we are of slavery." Corbett continued working on behalf of refugees until his death in August 2001 and was never prosecuted again.

— • —

The Sanctuary Movement continued until the early 1990s, at which time the State Department and congressional leaders responded to mounting pressure to stop funding the foreign civil wars. A peace accord was signed in El Salvador in 1991 and in Guatemala in 1996. Although some sanctuary congregations began the bureaucratic process of repatriating refugees or assisting them in building news lives in North America, the movement gradually ended.

According to Sharon Nepstad, author of *Convictions of the Soul: Religion, Culture, and Agency in the Central America Solidarity Movement*, the movement's demise reflected a combination of internal tensions and external political circumstances. The humanitarian and political wings of the movement failed to reconcile their differences regarding the future of the movement, especially after peace accords were signed. The Tucson group started by Corbett and Fife saw themselves as primarily humanitarians, whereas the Chicago Religious Task Force fashioned themselves as educators on US foreign policy. Also, as civil wars ended and electoral organizing increased in Central American countries, there was less urgency for sanctuary work. According to Nepstad, US activists' attention was drawn toward other pressing political problems in the early 1990s—namely the Gulf War—so activists triaged by scaling back their work on immigration and refugee issues. Although a large number of refugees' lives no longer precariously dangled in balance as they did in the early to mid-1980s, scholars estimate that five thousand undocumented immigrants died on the US side of the border from 1985 to 2002—immigrants whose lives might have been saved had the movement not prematurely disbanded.[83]

From a social science perspective, Nepstad notes, it is very difficult to prove the Sanctuary Movement single-handedly caused government policy changes. Understandably, the US government is not likely to concede that it made changes as a direct response to what it regarded as unlawful protests. Some sanctuary providers consider the 1986 Immigration Reform and Control Act (IRCA) among the movement's successes. The first major overhaul of immigration law since the passage of the Refugee Act in 1980, IRCA contained several provisions that extended temporary worker visa programs. However, other sanctuary activists are loathe to claim IRCA among their successes, calling it a restrictive measure aimed at reducing the number of undocumented immigrants by penalizing their employers.

Putting aside broader questions of legislative successes, the movement undeniably made an immediate, visceral difference to the countless terrified refugees who found warm meals and safe lodging in an inhospitable country. Elsa de Leon, thirty-eight, who arrived with her husband in Tucson from Guatemala in 1983 succinctly captured how the movement affected her life in an interview with the *Arizona Daily Star*: "If it weren't for [Corbett] . . . we would be dead."[84]

The brilliance of the Sanctuary Movement, in Nepstad's opinion, is that it reached congregations throughout the United States in a very personal and intimate way. As churches and synagogues took in these individuals, heard their stories, and put a human face to the suffering of Central America, they became far more informed about the effects of US policy in the region. As congregational members throughout the nation grew angry at US involvement in Central America, it became increasingly difficult for politicians to get aid packages approved and other policies passed through Congress. Participation in the movement awakened many previously superficial believers to a depth of commitment that forced them to respond to their faith's demand that they struggle for social justice against war, poverty, and oppression.

Still, despite the movement's considerable successes, it ultimately failed to systemically revamp US immigration policy or change the inhumane conditions that continue to characterize INS/ICE detention facilities today. In 1996 the lack of an organized movement created a window for then-president Bill Clinton to sign into law two bills that further compromised the future of thousands of immigrants. Green card holders fleeing persecution, undocumented workers earning less than minimum wage, and immigrants detained on secret evidence all became potentially deportable. Detained immigrants awaiting deportation remained subjected to humiliation, rape, and torture while indefinitely confined in county jails and prisons with little legal recourse.

By remaining myopically focused on Central American refugees fleeing brutal regimes propped up by the US government, the Sanctuary Movement never harnessed its true potential to radically reform immigration policy. Although individual members of the movement occasionally drew parallels between the direct violence of roving paramilitaries and indirect violence of economic oppression, the movement was unable to galvanize large masses of activists after political persecution ended and economic violence continued. From the early 1990s to 2006, communities of faith remained regrettably silent on immigration reform.

— ∎ —

In 2006 the first signs of a new Sanctuary Movement emerged when millions of people participated in protests over proposed legislation known as H.R. 4437, which would have raised penalties for illegal immigration and classified anyone who assisted them as felons. Wisconsin Republican Jim Sensenbrenner's "Border Protection, Anti-Terrorism, and Illegal Immigration Control Act of 2005" (H.R. 4437) was passed by the United States House of Representatives on December 16, 2005, by a vote of 239 to 182 and mandated up to seven hundred miles of fence along the US-Mexico border at points with the highest numbers of illegal border crossings.

National protests occurred on April 10, 2006, with an estimated crowd of 500,000 in Los Angeles, around 300,000 in Chicago, and hundreds of thousands in other major cities.[85] Although initially galvanized by the particular piece of legislation, many protestors sought a comprehensive reform of the country's immigration laws that included a pathway to citizenship for all undocumented immigrants. On Ash Wednesday, 2006, Cardinal Mahony of the Archdiocese of Los Angeles warned that he would instruct his clergy and laity to ignore H.R. 4437 if it were to become law.[86] The bill languished in the Senate, which activists consider one of the successes of their protests.

In May 2007 an interfaith coalition alarmed by immigration raids—raids that detained nearly three hundred people per week in New York alone—decided to emulate the 1980s movement and officially declare a New Sanctuary Movement.[87] Congregations and religious leaders in Seattle, New York, Los Angeles, Chicago, and elsewhere protested what they saw as unjust detention and deportation laws and actions. The movement received hundreds of calls from interested congregations and participated in thirty-three phone conferences and fifteen visits.[88] As before, the new movement drew from an actual grassroots network, but it has also gained approval from larger bodies such as the United Methodist Church. "The New Sanctuary Movement offers spiritual, moral, and legal services for families in trouble, as well as the possibility of shelter," said Reverend Donna Schaper, senior minister at Manhattan's Judson Memorial Church and a sanctuary activist.[89] "We go to hearings and stand with people in solidarity as well as help educate the American public about the cruelty of our current immigration laws." When asked why she joined the movement, the elderly reverend said, "The language of hate against immigrants is appalling. Scripture is committed to the stranger, the alien. We meet God in the stranger."[90]

Sanctuary providers such as Schaper could not recall any instance in which immigration officers forcibly entered church property to seize an undocumented immigrant for deportation.[91] Nonetheless, civilian vigilantes such as the Minutemen have picketed outside of sanctuary churches, and pastors reported routinely receiving hate mail and threats of violence.[92]

Similar to the original Sanctuary Movement, the new movement fractured between those concentrating on broader policy changes and those addressing the immediate needs of undocumented immigrants. Eventually the new movement lost momentum and dwindled, but several individual religious groups remained active in assisting immigrants in safely crossing the most brutal stretches of the United States border. The Unitarian Universalist organization No More Deaths leaves water canisters in the Sonoran Desert along the Arizona-Mexico border. Over the past decade, nearly two thousand men, women, and children died while trying to cross the border into Arizona.[93] One volunteer, Dan Millis, found the body of a fourteen-year-old girl from El Salvador in the southern Arizona desert. Two days later, as he was leaving gallon-sized sealed jugs of water along the same migrant trails, he was ticketed for littering by the US Fish and Wildlife Service.[94] He insisted that humanitarian aid is not a crime.

Humane Borders, another religiously inspired organization, offers humanitarian assistance through more than one hundred emergency water stations near the US-Mexico border.[95] The organization is inspired by a literal interpretation of Isaiah 49:10: "They will neither hunger nor thirst, nor will the desert heat or the sun beat upon them. He who has compassion on them will guide them and lead them beside springs of water."

- • -

Reverend Schaper of Judson Memorial Church insists that those fleeing economic destitution have as strong a moral claim to sanctuary as those fleeing death squads a generation ago.[96] Laborers enter illegally because the immigration process makes it difficult to enter legally; however, dire economic realities—often exacerbated by US initiatives such as NAFTA—make it difficult to remain stationary, notes Schaper. Under NAFTA, unemployment and economic desperation in Mexico skyrocketed; immigration to the United States became the only hope for survival for millions of Mexicans.[97]

The US Immigration and Customs Enforcement (ICE) disagrees with Schaper that undocumented immigrants seeking a better livelihood are genuine refugees. ICE deported nearly 350,000 immigrants nationwide in September 2008, compared with about 174,000 in the same period in 2004.[98]

Amy Dalton, a human rights activist, attended the May 1 Immigrants' Rights Rally and held a colorful banner reading "People of Faith Standing Behind Families Facing Deportation." Dalton says today's activists are motivated to "take civil action when their country acts like an empire" but, unlike their predecessors, focus more on providing legal aid rather than direct shelter.[99] Dalton notes the nascent movement is more interfaith than the original one, benefiting from the support of imams such as Shaykh TA Bashir from House of Peace, but remains largely Judeo-Christian. "It's important to remember that the Judeo-Christian tradition is also historically the most responsible for many of the problems we're facing today," says Dalton, referring to "a tiny group of [right-wing religious] people with a lot of money and a large bullhorn" who declare wars in the name of God. Dalton notes that President George W. Bush consistently evoked God's name in speeches leading up to the Iraq War that began in March 2003, a war that created hundreds of thousands of Iraqi refugees. Alaa Naji, one of the 25,000 Iraqi refugees in the United States, told the *Christian Science Monitor* that refugees "never imagined that they would be struggling to survive here in America. . . . We expected more from a country that was involved in the violence that destroyed our land, homes, and loved ones."[100]

— • —

On April 23, 2010, Governor Jan Brewer of Arizona signed one of the nation's harshest bills on illegal immigration into law. The law, which proponents and critics alike said was the toughest immigration measure in generations, enables law enforcement officials to identify, prosecute, and deport illegal immigrants as well as detain anyone failing to proffer immigration documents.[101] Decrying the law as an invitation to harass and discriminate against minorities regardless of their citizenship status, defenders of immigrants' rights say the outrage over Arizona's controversial immigration law "awakened a sleeping giant." Reverend Jim Wallis denounced the new law as "a social and racial sin." He added, "This law will make it illegal to love your neighbor in Arizona, and will force us to disobey Jesus and his gospel. We will not comply."[102]

The largest protests in the recent history of the nation occurred after the Arizona bill was signed into law, including half a million protestors in Los Angeles. On May Day, a united coalition of activists marched in white as a sign of peace and waved flags from the United States, Mexico, Guatemala, and other countries. Activists participated in rallies, vigils, hunger fasts, marches, and acts of civil disobedience including linking arms and blocking oncoming traffic outside of government immigration agencies' offices. As of now, it remains uncertain if these activists will launch a robust new movement that emulates the successes of Corbett's Sanctuary Movement while simultaneously learning from its shortcomings or if these activists will simply organize against the Arizona bill and then disperse from the scene.

In July 2010 President Barack Obama announced plans for comprehensive immigration reform—reform that might include a pathway for citizenship for the twelve million undocumented immigrants currently living in fear in the United States—but stressed the need for bipartisan support. Achieving that support will inevitably depend on the ability of religious communities to resurrect a massive, interfaith movement reminiscent of the 1980s, a movement demanding that legislatures radically and humanely revise the country's moribund immigration policy.

5 JOHN DEAR

Beating Nuclear Swords into God's Plowshares

Any intelligent fool can make things bigger, more complex, and more violent. It takes a touch of genius—and a lot of courage—to move in the opposite direction.

—ALBERT EINSTEIN

We have spent years of our lives in developing ever-sweeter means of destruction; we have been doing the work of the military, and I feel it in my very bones that this was wrong. . . . We have been doing the work of the devil.

—"OPPENHEIMER," in *In the Matter of J. Robert Oppenheimer*[1]

On September 9, 1980, eight Christian pacifists carried household hammers and baby bottles filled with their own blood to the General Electric nuclear missile facility in King of Prussia, Pennsylvania. At approximately 8:50 AM, while GE workers changed shifts, the eight infiltrators flashed false identification cards and strode into the manufacturing plant, where they proceeded to locate and enter the high-security room storing golden-colored, first-strike, and ultra-accurate Mark 12A nuclear weapons. For twelve minutes, they hammered on warhead nosecones—a symbolic action that caused negligible damage—and doused various security documents with their own blood. Seeing themselves as carrying on a tradition started by Isaiah and Micah, the Bible-toting activists used hammers as symbols of spiritual rebirth. They regarded their spilt blood as a reminder of humanity's common life and shared destiny. By trespassing onto the missile plant and vandalizing property, the eight pacifists hoped to literally enact Isaiah's prophecy: *They will hammer their swords into plowshares and their spears into pruning hooks. Nation will not lift up sword against nation, and never again will they learn war.*[2]

After clanging on the warheads, the group knelt in a circle and joined hands to pray for a world free of nuclear weapons and preparation for genocide. They prayed for President Ronald Reagan to reverse his stated commitment to strengthening American military capacities and, instead, strengthen social welfare programs. They prayed for the country to remember President Dwight D. Eisenhower's 1961 farewell address, which warned that "the Military Establishment, not productive of itself, necessarily must feed on the energy, productivity, and brainpower of the country, and if it takes too much, our total strength declines." They prayed for a rejuvenated economy in which corporations no longer depended on defense contract profits to stay in business, local officials no longer relied on military facilities to brighten job prospects in their struggling communities, and congressmen no longer supported the military industrial complex to remain in office. They prayed for their complacent churches to awaken to the dangers of the Just War position—a position that sanctified war provided it met certain criteria—at the dawn of the nuclear era. They prayed that their moral witness and "experiment in truth" would inspire others to similarly challenge status quo assumptions on war planning activities. They prayed the workers at the GE plant would abandon what they regarded as the "business of genocide," instead joining them in sabotaging the nation's stockpiles of missiles before the Pentagon's policies reduced the whole world to radioactive dust.

An enraged plant manager soon stumbled upon the radical anti-nukes activists. He immediately notified the plant's security officers that religious fanatics had managed to trespass onto the plant's premises and dangerously tamper with potentially lethal weapons. The officers, in turn, notified local police, who notified the FBI, who promptly arrested the activists. Pointing to the rosary-reciting activists he feared had irrevocably compromised national security, one flabbergasted FBI agent asked the plant manager, "How did they know where to go? They couldn't have done this without a leak!"[3] An activist Jesuit priest, Daniel Berrigan, quipped, "One cannot but reflect that the myth that 'the weapons are secure' is matched by the myth that 'the weapons supply security.'"[4]

The American public reacted to the "Plowshares Eight," as they were called in the media, with a mixture of awe, confusion, and anger. At the height of the cold war, it was an article of faith for many Americans that the Soviet Union would destroy the country if not held in check by a nuclear deterrent. Few genuinely thought a country enmeshed in political conflict, proxy wars, and economic competition with the formidable Soviet Union was liable to change its nuclear strategy simply because members of the clergy smeared weapons with their blood. Similarly, the Catholic Church was not going to reevaluate its Just War position to appease a fringe pacifist movement dramatically proclaiming the Gospel message of nonviolence. Even sympathizers who questioned the wisdom of US policymakers wondered if the activists were naive for rejecting the country's retention of at least a small nuclear stockpile as a credible deterrent against foreign aggression.

Yet, the Plowshares Eight did prompt many Americans to wonder what drove these otherwise law-abiding nuns, priests, and laypersons to oppose what seemed like a pragmatic policy and risk a lifetime in prison. In a press statement released shortly after their arrests, the Plowshares Eight explained their actions:

> We commit civil disobedience at General Electric because this genocidal entity is the fifth leading producer of weaponry in the U.S. To maintain this position, GE drains $3 million a day from the public treasury, an enormous larceny against the poor. We also wish to challenge the lethal lie spun by GE through its motto, "We bring good things to life." As manufacturers of the Mark 12A reentry vehicle, GE actually prepares to bring good things to death. Through the Mark 12A, the threat of first-strike nuclear war grows more imminent. Thus GE advances the possible destruction of millions of innocent lives. In confronting GE, we choose to obey God's Law of life, rather than a corporate summons to death. Our beating of swords into plowshares is a way to enflesh this biblical call. In our action, we draw on a deep-rooted faith in Christ, who changed the course of history through his willingness to suffer rather than to kill. We are filled with hope for our world and for our children as we join in this act of resistance.[5]

Dismissing the activists as criminally ignorant of US foreign policy and dangerously irresponsible in their roguery, federal authorities culled the Pennsylvania statutes before charging each activist with over a dozen different felonies and misdemeanors. Members of the Plowshares Eight were dismayed to learn they faced up to seventy-five years behind bars, which far exceeded the maximum sentence initially anticipated. One of the activists, an experienced criminal defense lawyer named John Schuchardt, noted, "I was really shocked at the [charges of] aggravated assault, simple assault, terroristic threats, on and on and on. They just opened up the Pennsylvania statutes . . . and fired at us with five shotguns, double-barreled."[6]

Schuchardt coached his fellow cell mates on how to approach their trials as opportunities to testify to their opposition to nuclear weapons. Despite facing the prospect of spending the rest of their lives in prison, the group refused reduced sentences in exchange for pleading guilty. "Our brains reeled at the contradictions implied," Daniel Berrigan lamented. "How to plead guilty to nonviolent activity, on behalf of children, the future, the ecology, the plowshare that opens and releases life?"[7]

= • =

In March 1981 the Plowshares Eight appeared in court. The activists opened the trial by arguing their action was warranted by the "necessity defense," which holds that someone is allowed to break a law when imminent danger is present, when the normal channels of dealing with the threat are ineffective, and when the person is acting to prevent a greater harm.[8] To support their claim that General Electric's Mark 12A warheads posed an imminent danger, the defendants planned to call Robert Aldridge, an engineer who had worked on first-strike weapons; George Wald, a 1967 Nobel Prize winner in medicine; and Robert J. Lifton, a psychiatrist who had studied the effects of trauma on survivors of Hiroshima.[9] Judge Salus threw out the argument, saying nuclear weapons were not on trial so these experts' testimonies were irrelevant. The judge similarly rejected an appeal to international law when the activists proclaimed they were respecting the Nuremberg laws, which hold individuals accountable for their governments' actions and grants them the right to interfere with crimes against humanity. He clarified that the jury would determine only if the defendants had trespassed and vandalized property.

During his direct examination, Daniel Berrigan addressed the jury on what he called accomplishing "the first act of nuclear disarmament in thirty-five years"[10]:

> Years and years we spent writing letters, trying to talk to authorities, vigiling in public places, holding candles at night, holding placards by day, trying, trying, fasting, trying to clarify things to ourselves as we went, trying to speak to others. . . . We spent years within the law, trying to be that kind of person, a non-betrayer. Then we found we couldn't. And if we kept forever on this side of the line, we would die within ourselves. We couldn't look in the mirror, couldn't face those we love, had no Christian message in the world. . . . The only message I have to the world is: We are not allowed to kill innocent people. We are not allowed to be complicit in murder. We are not allowed to be silent while preparations for mass murder proceed in our name, with our money secretly. . . . [As a priest], it's terrible for me to live in a time where I have nothing to say to human beings except, "Stop killing."[11]

After two weeks of hearing the activists' testimonies, the judge remained unmoved and reiterated that weapons of mass destruction were not on trial. Regarding the activists as paranoid troublemakers shadowboxing against a threat they blew out of proportion, the judge declared his regret "at not being able to send you all to a Siberian prison camp or a Puerto Rican leper colony."[12] Unbeknownst to the judge, Berrigan had assisted lepers in Hawaii and would have welcomed the opportunity to return. A group of lepers later rebuked the judge for his insensitive comment, inviting him to "visit us and, perhaps, yourself be healed."[13]

Most of the charges against the Plowshares Eight were eventually dropped, but the group was convicted of burglary, conspiracy, and criminal mischief. They received sentences ranging from eighteen months to ten years, and the judge set bail at $250,000. The lengthy sentences and hefty bail price were designed to deter potential copycat sympathizers; nonetheless, the protest in King of Prussia emerged as the inaugural event launching the Plowshares movement.

- ∎ -

After the King of Prussia event, Daniel Berrigan issued a clarion call for every Christian to agitate for a world without warfare. Nobody answered that call more wholeheartedly than twenty-three-year-old John Dear, a Jesuit in training with shaggy blond hair combed to the side of his boyish face. Dear found Berrigan's dramatic opposition to warfare as mesmerizing as the parting of the Red Sea. When Dear first read Berrigan's impassioned plea for Christians to oppose what he regarded as an imminent nuclear holocaust, the idealistic novice priest decided: *This is what a Jesuit is supposed to be like. Here is a real Christian.* In the fall of 1981, Dear initiated a lengthy correspondence with Berrigan in which he expressed his hope to emulate the radical pacifism of the Vietnam-era outlaw priest. Over the next decade, Berrigan mentored Dear and imbued him with a self-sacrificial understanding of Christian testimony, telling him that the point of their priestly vocation was "to make our story fit into the story of Jesus, so our life makes sense in light of Jesus."[14]

By the early twenty-first century, Berrigan's protégé has emerged as a linchpin of the religious progressive community, succinctly capturing the sentiments of Christian nuclear abolitionists when he said, "Jesus is active and provocative but not harmful."[15] Personifying the tenacity of a movement driven by the "politics of moral witness" rather than the "politics of pragmatism," Dear has been arrested on seventy-five separate occasions for nonviolent acts of civil disobedience against militarism and nuclear proliferation. In 1993 Dear—who bears an uncanny resemblance to his state's former senator John Edwards—joined three Plowshare activists in North Carolina at the Seymour Johnson Air Force Base to hammer on an F-15 "Strike Eagle" nuclear fighter-bomber. Similar to other Plowshares actions, the demonstration on the base never posed any real security risk since the activists barely succeeded in chipping paint off the fighter planes, but Dear faced ten years in prison for his symbolic act. The outspoken Jesuit's persistent opposition to nuclear weapons continues to simultaneously confound Americans who believe priests should not meddle in issues of national security and invigorate "no-nukes" abolitionists who welcome his moral witness against what they regard as an imminent nuclear Armageddon.

- ■ -

John Dear was born on August 13, 1959, in the small town of Elizabeth City, North Carolina. Situated at the narrowing of the Pasquotank River, the town is perhaps best known for hosting the North Carolina Potato Festival and housing the largest United States Coast Guard Air Station on the East Coast. Until he turned seven, Dear enjoyed a genteel Southern life complete with a colonial-style estate and chocolate-colored pony named Lucky. Then, in early 1967, his family relocated to Bethesda, Maryland. Dear's father worked full-time at the National Press Club in Washington, DC, and his mother taught nursing at Johns Hopkins University. When Dear's father inherited the family newspaper chain, the upper-class Catholic family increasingly congregated around the television to follow the latest developments in Nixon's Vietnam War efforts and Martin Luther King Jr.'s civil rights campaign. An impressionable Dear absorbed images he didn't fully understand at the time, images of Dr. King's assassination and, two months later, Robert F. Kennedy's. The child grew increasingly intrigued by the arbitrariness of death and the capriciousness of a world in which a person could lose his life to a wanton act of violence.

A decade later, as an undergraduate at Duke University, a directionless Dear feared his own life was wasting away, and his thoughts remained consumed with the eternal questions of what makes life worth living or dying for. The classically handsome aspiring rock star had once hoped to relocate to Los Angeles and jam with singer-songwriters such as Jackson Browne and James Taylor at the Ash Grove, but now he felt uncertain about entering an industry that seemed so cutthroat and money driven. He struggled to reconcile the plight of Durham's impoverished residents with the privilege of his classmates at the prestigious "Gothic Wonderland" called Duke. Pondering the age-old question of theodicy, Dear grew agitated over his inability to understand how an omnipotent, benevolent God countenanced human suffering and evil. In the middle of an especially raucous beer-chugging competition at his Kappa Sigma fraternity house, Dear saw his life flash in front of him, a life full of cocktail parties and office socials, a life that was utterly boring and painfully ordinary. The more he attempted to sidetrack his preoccupation with the impermanence of life and mystery of death, the more anxious he grew that his life was without intelligent purpose, objective meaning, or intrinsic value. Dear began wallowing in moods of disillusionment and cynicism, teetering on the brink of a spiritual crisis.

Dear's bout of nihilism eventually caused him to ricochet in an opposite direction. "I couldn't bear the scope of such meaninglessness," admitted Dear years later in his autobiography, *A Persistent Peace*. "Deep down, more than anything, I craved meaning. . . . I wanted my own existence to have meaning."[16] As had so many before him, Dear ultimately found that meaning through a religious awakening. He began attending the daily noon Mass in the basement of the majestic Duke Chapel, a neo-Gothic building distinguished by its steel trusses, giant stone piers, pointed arches, ribbed vaults, and flying buttresses, which created a vast open space similar to the belly of Grand Central Station. Basking in the light streaming through the stained glass and the music emanating from the fifty-bell carillon, Dear found time to parse through his childhood religious upbringing and formulate his own understanding of faith, mortality, and life beyond college. At mass, Dear befriended a stout, garrulous Jesuit priest named Father Joe Burke. Instead of badgering Dear to join retreats or service trips, Burke simply listened to the troubled student and encouraged him to work through his conflicted feelings.

Around the same time, Dear befriended Duke's artist-in-residence, legendary jazz pianist Mary Lou Williams, who had played with Duke Ellington when she was sixteen and later dazzled Carnegie Hall with her classic *Zodiac Suite*. In 1952 Williams shocked her fans by rediscovering Catholicism, taking a hiatus from performing, and dedicating herself to contemplative prayer as well as service to the destitute. Eventually, one day while attending mass at Saint Ignatius Loyola Church, Williams met a Jesuit who convinced her to return to her music as a way to inspire people to love God and one another. She wrote and performed religious jazz sensations like *Black Christ of the Andes*, a hymn in honor of Saint Martin de Porres, and went on to regale over three thousand fans as the first jazz performer at Saint Patrick's Cathedral. The matronly woman with a penchant for black papier-mâché brooches eventually founded the Bel Canto Foundation to rehabilitate addicted musicians and encourage them to perform again.

Dear listened to Williams explain to her jazz class, "Jazz is love. You have to feel the love in the music. It will make you into a more loving person and bring joy into your life." Billed by her contemporaries as "The Lady Who Swings the Band," Williams's jubilant declaration resonated with Dear like the finer points of syncopation, and the once-jaded party animal began riding a bus each week to visit her at her home on the outskirts of Durham for private lessons.

Williams was one of two women who profoundly influenced Dear—the other was Elizabeth Ann Seton. Dear came to know Seton through her biography, *Mrs. Seton*, which was assigned in his course "History of Christianity in America." The daughter of a wealthy physician, Seton shocked her friends and relatives by trading in her life as a Manhattan socialite for the Catholic nunnery. Pronouncing her vows of poverty, chastity, and obedience, "Mother Seton" devoted herself to running a school for the poor. Dear later reflected:

> Mother Seton had helped hundreds, had influenced thousands, and through her life with Jesus and her service to suffering humanity had found purpose and meaning. That must mean that I could, too. In the midst of a busy, difficult life, she had found personal peace; there was no reason I couldn't as well. I could take the risk, as she did, and surrender myself. Finally I saw it: God existed . . . it was an all-or-nothing choice. If God exists, I should renounce my life, surrender it to God, reach out in universal love, and take off in the footsteps of Jesus.[17]

In the lives of Williams and Mother Seton, the Duke undergraduate found examples of what he regarded as an admirable belief in a benevolent caretaker who promised eternal life; an invitation to make a public commitment to that higher being; and a blueprint for living his own life with meaning.

On Ash Wednesday, February 20, 1980, Dear attended a service at Duke Chapel, where Father Burke spoke about the Lenten themes of repentance and conversion, of changing one's life and following Jesus. Dear approached the limestone altar and closed his eyes as Burke traced a cross on his forehead. At that moment, he decided he would become a Jesuit.

Dear began spending less time at the Kappa Sigma fraternity house and more time with the Catholic chaplain at the Duke Medical Center. One day while volunteering at the hospital, Dear was shocked to find the name of his former jazz teacher on his roster. Mary Lou Williams had been diagnosed with terminal cancer. Sitting at her hospital bedside between her chemotherapy treatments, Dear learned about Williams's life running a Harlem clothing center, crooning alongside Billie Holiday, and experiencing mystical visions of Saint Martin de Porres. Shortly before her death in May 1981, a week after Dear graduated from Duke, Williams whispered to her former student, "The secret of life is to love everyone."

– ▪ –

The summer before Dear entered the Jesuit novitiate in Pennsylvania, he decided to make a pilgrimage to the Holy Land. After all, Saint Ignatius and Saint Francis similarly sojourned to the birthplace of Jesus of Nazareth before devoting themselves to emulating the life of the Prince of Peace.

Arriving at the Sea of Galilee, Dear waited for divine confirmation that he had chosen the right path, but he only experienced confusion and misgivings. He suddenly grasped the full magnitude of his decision to live a celibate, ascetic life of a priest on the margins of society. Dear balked at the thought. Just as he considered returning home to pursue law school, he heard a deafening roar crack the sky. Two Israeli fighter jets soared across the sea breaking the sound barrier and heading straight toward the balcony where Dear crouched in disbelief. At the last moment, the jets soared upward and proceeded toward Lebanon, just fifteen miles north. Dear later learned that the 1982 Israeli war on Lebanon, ironically named "Operation Peace for Galilee," had begun. This was not the sign the young pilgrim had expected; at most, he had hoped for the soft whisper of the Holy Spirit or gentle hum of an angel's harp. Dumbfounded and petrified, Dear watched thousands of heavily armed soldiers march past him just moments after he had read the words "blessed are the peacemakers" on the walls of the Chapel of the Beatitudes. Deciding that God worked in mysterious ways, Dear concluded that he had received a divine sign after all.

– ▪ –

On August 18, 1982, Dear and ten other novices arrived at a forested 250-acre estate in Wenersville, Pennsylvania, for Jesuit boot camp, where they would learn to serve as foot soldiers on the frontlines of the church. The highly structured schedule included early morning prayers followed by classes on topics such as Bible exegesis, Jesuit worship, self-denial, martyrs, and missions.

Assembling in the basement lounge, Dear joined other newcomers at an informal meet-and-greet after the first session. Sitting in a circle on plush cushioned chairs, the Jesuits discussed what prompted them to enter the novitiate. Still invigorated by his recent trip to Israel and convinced of the singularity of his mission, Dear enthusiastically volunteered to go first: "Well, I want to spend my life following Jesus, serving the poor, opposing war and injustice, working for peace and justice, being poor and simple like the saints and martyrs, and really giving my life to God."[18] Dead silence followed his exuberant proclamation.

Finally, one of the novices rolled his eyes and smirked. "Oh my God! I'm going to have to live with Saint Francis over here." He stood up, beckoned the others away, and poured the group a round of stiff drinks. Baffled, Dear wondered what he had said that was so absurd, and why his dedication to emulating Jesus' example reduced him to a laughing-stock. Then, Dear remembered that Jesus had similarly experienced rejection and decided with a tinge of smug satisfaction that he was on the right path. Over the next few months, the zealous twenty-three-year-old Jesuit sought to impress God rather than his peers by pursuing cosmic companionship to offset his loneliness. Dear wrote a letter to Jesus in his journal: "Here I am: take me. Make me your faithful servant, your disciple, your companion, your friend."

— • —

As a Jesuit in training, Dear intensely studied the path to peace as envisioned by Dr. King, Dorothy Day, Thomas Merton, Gandhi, and the Berrigan brothers. More and more he saw his vocation as a call to daily meditation, Bible study, life in community, service, and active peacemaking.

In the fall of his first year, Dear befriended a fellow novice, Ed DeBerri, who told him about his own peace ministry and efforts to compile Catholic social teachings into a book. One weekend, the two novices attended a screening of *The Day After Trinity*, a documentary about J. Robert Oppenheimer and the atomic bombing of Hiroshima. Dear watched the events unfurl onscreen: the United States manufacturing the atomic bomb during World War II; the initial deployment of the bomb against the Japanese in the summer of 1945; the interplay of personal neuroses of the brilliant minds collaborating on the Manhattan Project; and the complex moral conundrums posed by the nuclear era. Dear was bewildered by the political calculations of the bomb's development and the long-term effects on mankind of the nuclear age left to be revealed.

After the screening, Sister Anne Montgomery and Elmer Maas, both of whom had participated in the Plowshares Eight action with the Berrigans, spoke to the audience about working for nuclear disarmament. They spoke passionately and convincingly about the threats of nuclear war, saying people of faith must begin the process of disarmament through direct action and nonviolent resistance. The activists explained that the first bomb, which was successfully detonated in the New Mexico desert in July 1945, portended "the beginning of the end" unless people of conscience challenged their government's policies. Audience members speculated that President Truman had dropped an atomic bomb on Hiroshima to warn Russians not to challenge the US plans to organize the postwar world. The Plowshares activists reasoned that their country would use genocidal weapons in the future to protect what they regarded as rapidly expanding worldwide corporate interests and quest for global empire. This was certain, they said, unless people of conscience disrupted business as usual. The battle cry went out to the roused mass: people of faith must begin the process of disarmament through direct action and nonviolent resistance.

Dear left the event consumed with terrifying images of first-degree burn victims poisoned by radiation exposure. He feared that nuclear accidents like the one that occurred at Three Mile Island in March 1979 were increasingly inevitable. In his mind, the nuclear doomsday clock ticked away with increasing speed.

Shortly afterward, Dear struck up a written correspondence with Daniel Berrigan after reading an article the Vietnam-era antiwar activist had written in the *National Jesuit News* about the possibility of nuclear war. Berrigan was one of the most prominent pacifist voices in the Catholic Church speaking against nuclear proliferation, and he had a profound influence on Dear. "The Christian response to imperial death-dealing is in effect a nonresponse," he wrote. "We refuse the terms of the argument. To weigh the value of lives would imply that the military solution had been grotesquely validated by Christians. There is no cause, however noble, which justifies the taking of a single human life, much less millions of them."[19]

For Dear, the possibility of a nuclear holocaust dwarfed all other evils in the world and the specter of global genocide clouded his every thought. He found himself agreeing with Father Richard McSorley, a Jesuit who taught Peace Studies at Georgetown University, who said:

> The taproot of violence in our society today is our intent to use nuclear weapons. Once we have agreed to that, all other evil is minor in comparison. Until we squarely face the question of our consent to use nuclear weapons, any hope of large-scale improvement of public mortality is doomed to failure. The nuclear weapons of Communists may destroy our bodies, but the intent to use nuclear weapons destroys our souls.[20]

On Pentecost Sunday, 1983, Dear joined McSorley at a prayer service for disarmament and civil disobedience at the US Capitol. Thousands of people gathered in the Washington National Cathedral carrying peace signs urging Congress not to vote for another proposed military budget increase. Dear watched from the opposite side of the street as over two hundred people, including McSorley, entered the rotunda singing "We Shall Overcome." The strain remained strong as police carted them off to jail. Dear's Jesuit superiors had ordered him not to risk arrest and he obeyed despite wishing to join the demonstration. Dear—who later edited McSorley's book, *It's a Sin to Build a Nuclear Weapon*—came to agree with McSorley that Jesus had encouraged civil disobedience when he turned over the moneylenders' tables in the temple.

McSorley spoke about nuclear weapons incessantly, interjecting a reference to their deadly capacities in the middle of otherwise mundane conversations. Dear came to share his fear that these weapons could, any second, vaporize humanity. He later wrote in his autobiography, *A Persistent Peace*: "I sat up in bed and resolved, there in the wee hours, to stand against war and nuclear weapons and risk prison. . . . My heart burned to share the fate of the saints and help ensure that Hiroshima would never happen again."[21]

- ∎ -

In 1984 Dear convinced a fellow Jesuit, Peter Cicchino, to join him for a prayer vigil at the Pentagon every Wednesday morning during Lent. The two novices printed out thousands of copies of leaflets expounding on the Ash Wednesday themes of repentance and conversion. They read in part: "This building which commands the machinery of war is a symbol of the sin and disorder which presently afflicts us, a disorder which denies food to the poor while spending billions of dollars on instruments of mass destruction."

That afternoon, a downcast Dear watched hordes of employees pass him without stopping; the few who took the leaflet quickly disposed of it at the nearest trash receptacle. Dear was disappointed that his Gandhian "experiment in truth telling" utterly failed, but he resolved to return the next week and calmly ask employees to consider quitting their jobs. Dear urged Cicchino to distinguish the sin from sinner and remember the people running the arms race were not vicious merchants of death, but decent ordinary people whose jobs locked them into an inherently pointless and destructive system.[22]

Returning to the riverside entrance clad in clerical black suits and white collars, Dear and Cicchino happened to run into a member of the Joint Chiefs of Staff exiting his black stretch limousine. All of a sudden, Dear started yelling, "For the love of God, go home, you evil warmonger! Stop planning the destruction of the planet!" Dear's outburst took Cicchino by surprise, and he grabbed his friend and told him to get a grip. Once Dear calmed down, he blushed and, at their reflection session that afternoon, lamented lacking the inner strength of Gandhi or King to confront his adversities nonviolently. He vowed to placate the rage boiling in his own soul and repent for his outburst by incurring a personal risk while bearing witness against what he regarded as the imminent doom of nuclear warfare.

On April 27 of that year, he returned to the Pentagon alone, sat in the middle of the doorway, and started reading from his Bible as employees awkwardly sidestepped him to get to work. Refusing to budge, Dear read from the Gospels about Jesus's crucifixion until police carted him off to a holding cell in the basement of the Pentagon. The flummoxed security guards could not understand what provoked the young Jesuit to prostrate himself on the Pentagon grounds. Dear explained he was trying to follow Jesus's example of nonviolence: "He got arrested, so I have to speak out against war and injustice and risk arrest, too." The guards scoffed at the explanation.

A judge later suspended Dear's thirty-day sentence for his act of civil disobedience, and he returned to Wernersville to profess his final vows as a Jesuit. Although his Jesuit superiors nearly dismissed him from the order for his act, both Berrigan and McSorley praised their young admirer for doing what they believed their vocation called them all to do: protest war and nuclear weapons in an effort to live out the nonviolent Gospel message.

■ ▪ ■

Over the next several years, Dear visited Catholic Worker houses, joined Pax Christi groups, volunteered at soup kitchens, and worked at homeless shelters. He distributed leaflets, marched, sang, and prayed on Capitol Hill as he protested everything from apartheid policies in South Africa to substandard schools in urban Washington, DC.

In 1985 Dear volunteered with the Jesuit Refugee Service in El Salvador at the height of political violence in the country, violence that left a hundred thousand people dead. While collaborating with the Archdiocese of San Salvador to build a refugee camp, Dear met the renowned liberation theologian Father Jon Sobrino. The soft-spoken priest reminded Dear that the Jesuit task was to risk their lives, to be on the frontiers of history, and liberate the poor from poverty and death. That August, after catching dengue fever, Dear spent his twenty-sixth birthday in a Jesuit house swaddled in damp blankets in a state of delirium. He later learned from an article in the *New York Times* that the CIA had practiced germ warfare in Nicaragua and unleashed a swarm of mosquitoes carrying the dengue virus, which only redoubled his anger at his country's reliance on brute force in light of the Gospel message of nonviolence. The discovery erased any last vestige of hope that Dear had vested in his country's policymakers.

In 1986, back in the United States, Dear finished the philosophy component of his Jesuit studies at Fordham University, where he obstructed the CIA's efforts to recruit students. He made it a point to inform his classmates that the CIA trained the contras to assassinate Nicaraguans, and he helped draft a thirty-page proposal requesting the president of Fordham to replace the ROTC with a peace studies program.

In September of that year, Dear was assigned to teach in a Jesuit high school in Scranton, Pennsylvania, where he evoked the ire of parents for teaching history from the perspective of society's most marginalized members. Instead of memorizing battle dates, Dear insisted his students understand the theology of Jesus, Buddha, and Muhammad. Instead of learning about Hitler, Dear's students learned about those who resisted him, such as members of the White Rose movement. Instead of dispassionately studying current events, the children were assigned to write letters to Winnie Mandela, Nelson Mandela's wife, offering her words of encouragement. Dear denounced what he regarded as the needless deaths of over a hundred thousand victims of the Hiroshima and Nagasaki bomb blasts, and he urged students to respond to what he regarded as the urgency of nuclear peril. He taught students that preparing for war was tantamount to highway robbery of society's poorest, and he urged them to commit themselves to pacifism and denounce the lie of militarized Christianity.

Angry parents soon flooded the school principal with phone calls, accusing Dear of brainwashing their children. Many residents of Scranton served in the military and encouraged their children to similarly pursue what they saw as an honorable career. They lambasted Dear's "supreme arrogance" for thinking that he knew better than military generals how to protect their country and that he knew better than the rest of Americans how God wanted the country to address the Soviet empire. They saw no contradiction between a strong national defense policy and worshipping the Prince of Peace, and they complained that Dear wished to radicalize their otherwise patriotic children.

Dear responded, "Jesus was nonviolent and said love your enemies, which means that no Christian can be violent in preparing to kill his enemies; Jesus blessed peacemakers, therefore we cannot be war makers." He brushed off the irate parents and continued extolling the ideas behind democratic socialism, the Bulgarian resistance movements, and his own nonfiction book that was released later that year, *Disarming the Heart: Toward a Vow of Nonviolence.*

■ ▪ ▬

Over the next decade, Dear participated in sit-ins at the Riverside Research Institute to protest nuclear proliferation; sleep-ins on the steps of Saint Patrick's Cathedral to demand housing for the poor; and die-ins on Bay Bridge to protest the Gulf War. Yet the protest that most deeply affected Dear was the March 1991 Nevada Desert Experience, in which he joined a thousand people of faith for a "Lenten Desert

Experience" to bear witness against ongoing nuclear development and conduct spirituality-based events near the Nevada Test Site.[23]

The cofounder of the Nevada Desert Experience, Father Louis Vitale, though he held a PhD in sociology from UCLA and was a former air force navigator, now donned a traditional brown monastic robe and knotted rope belt signifying vows of poverty, chastity, and obedience. Dear learned that Vitale's movement had drawn thousands of participants for mass arrests at the Nevada Test Site since organizing the first protest in 1982. "The biggest threat to the world is our nuclear arsenal," the gaunt septuagenarian Franciscan once declared. "By taking on the suffering of others, we change the world. We are willing to put our bodies where they are and suffer the consequences, be what they may."[24]

In Nevada, Dear also met the stocky, elderly Archbishop Dom Hélder Pessoa Câmara of Brazil, who once famously said, "When I feed the poor, they call me a saint; but when I ask why there are poor, they call me a communist." Câmara led the group in a Eucharist service with the reciting of Scripture and then shepherded them across the no-trespassing line and onto the nuclear weapons testing ground. Police immediately detained Dear and seventy-five others.

■ ▪ ■

In late August 1989 Dear completed his studies at the Jesuit School of Theology on "Holy Hill" in Berkeley, California. Despite frequently protesting outside nuclear facilities, he grew increasingly anxious about ongoing cold war tensions and consumed with worry that he was not doing enough to deter the possibility of a nuclear holocaust.

At a weekend Pax Christi retreat in the Bay area, Dear spoke with his old friend Daniel Berrigan about the Book of Revelation's promise of "the slight edge of life over death" and how their vocation required them to retain that edge. On Good Friday of that year, Dear attended the annual march to the Lawrence Livermore National Laboratory, where technicians assemble nuclear weapons, and used the opportunity to question Philip Berrigan about the Plowshares movement. *Are you afraid of being shot? How do you not surrender in despair when facing a lengthy prison term? How do you cope with rejection from friends and family?* Berrigan explained that Plowshares are planting seeds that God will bring to fruition in time. The movement, he said, measured its success not by immediate policy changes, but by activists' own unflinching fidelity to their religious convictions. Echoing Gandhi, he noted that nonviolence for the advancement of social justice should be practiced not because it works, but because it is right.

Many Plowshares activists from the Judeo-Christian tradition evoke the Biblical prohibition of idolatry in explaining their commitment to struggling for a nuclear-free world.[25] The nuclear idol, they argue, reflects a society that places its complete trust in military prowess rather than a nonviolent God. Elizabeth McAlister, the wife of Philip Berrigan, goes as far as lambasting the "religion of nuclearism" as a violation of the constitution's First Amendment, which states that no national religion should be established. "This national religion compels a loyalty based on our acceptance of the existence of nuclear weapons as a necessity," wrote McAlister in the *Catholic Agitator*. "We must—to be good citizens—pay for them, thank God for them."[26]

Perhaps unwittingly, Pentagon procurers exacerbated these Christians' fears of idolatry by naming weapons after ancient gods. America's first strategic missile, developed in the late 1950s, was called Jupiter. Subsequent missiles were named Thor, after the Norse god of thunder; Atlas, descendent of the sky god; Poseidon, the god of the sea; and Trident, which the ancients knew as the three-pronged spear carried by Poseidon, symbol of his earth-shaking power.[27] Christian pacifists say they refuse to worship at the altar of a false god, a pagan idol: Mars, the god of war.[28] To illustrate how people of faith should respond to idolatry, Plowshares activists often point to the example of Moses smashing a golden calf. Modern Plowshares activists see themselves following Jesus's example of putting life before the law, demonstrating divine obedience through acts of civil disobedience. They find the Old Testament replete with accounts of prophets challenging oppressive rulers, such as Isaiah 1:16–17: *Cease to do evil. Learn to do good. Search for justice. Help the oppressed.* Plowshares activists claim a divine mandate to destroy lethal weapons that drain money from social services for the country's poorest.

■ ▪ ■

Early in 1992, while ministering at Saint Aloysius parish in Washington, DC, and caring for the hungry and homeless, Dear found himself unable to refute his longtime mentor's logic. He increasingly agreed with Berrigan that eradicating the "national security state," abolishing war, and establishing a just political, economic, and social order required more frequent direct action that involved greater personal risks. "We have assumed the name of peacemakers, but we have been, by and large, unwilling to pay any significant price," Berrigan wrote in *No Bars to Manhood*. "And because we want peace with half a heart and half a life and will, the war, of course, continues, because the waging of war, by its very nature, is total—but the waging of peace, by our own cowardice is partial. . . . 'Of course, let us have the peace,' we cry, 'but at the same time let us have normalcy, let us lose nothing, let our lives stand intact.'"[29]

For Dear, the threat of a nuclear war was unimaginably costly—the instant obliteration of every living creature on earth—so, he reasoned, the cost of peacemaking must necessarily be equally costly. Although he recoiled at the thought of spending the remainder of his life in prison, his fears of an imminent nuclear Armageddon loomed larger. Dear decided he had no option left except to take a hammer to the weapons' nose-cones. "I have to confront the nation, even if everyone thinks I'm crazy," he confided to his friend Father Ed Glynn.

The summer of 1993, Dear told Berrigan he was ready to open himself to channel God's healing powers by protesting the web of violence, fear, and greed that he believed directed the nation's military policies. "I've decided to take part. I'm ready."

For the next six months, Dear and the Berrigan brothers hatched the Plowshares action, but they were careful not to reveal details to outsiders since they knew the government historically had dragnet bystanders as coconspirators and prosecuted people on the periphery who were privy to the activists' plans. Bruce Friedrich, a member of the Catholic Worker movement, and Lynn Fredriksson, a Brown alumna who directed Women Strike for Peace, later joined the Plowshares team. Together, the activists decided to target the Seymour Johnson Air Force Base in Goldsboro, North Carolina, near where Dear's family lived. Fredriksson told Dear she was uncertain about her religious beliefs and still searching for answers, so she felt uneasy when the others suggested calling their group Pax Christi. Dear asked the young woman what she believed in, and Fredriksson responded that she believed in "the spirit of life." Dear exclaimed that he believed in that spirit, too, and suggested the Plowshares name their group "Pax Christi—Spirit of Life." The friends spent countless hours reading not only the Gospels, but also secular texts such as Gene Sharp's rules of nonviolent civil disobedience. They met frequently to read the Gospels, pray for moral guidance, and study the intricacies of nuclear weapons. Over lunch meetings, the friends reflected on the value of moral witness, reviewed court transcripts from previous protests, and prepared themselves to use their court trials to air their grievances against nuclear weapons. As the day of their protest drew closer, the activists enacted skits dramatizing confrontations with potentially trigger-happy air force security patrol and began building a community of supporters to sustain them while in prison.

Dear knew that the penalty for a Plowshares action was not the same as it was for marching on Capitol Hill or trespassing onto an army base or even raiding a draft board. The increasingly anxious thirty-four-year-old realized the penalty could very well be the rest of his life. The Jesuit priest tried to fathom what it would mean to spend five, ten, or even fifteen years behind bars. As the appointed day approached, Dear began suffering debilitating nightmares. The young man saw himself caged like a feral animal, wasting away behind bars, and forgotten by the rest of the world.

Around 4 AM on December 7, 1993, Dear and his three companions hiked through woods and over fields, waded through an estuary, and arrived on the sprawling 3,400-acre premises of the Seymour Johnson Air Force Base in Goldsboro, North Carolina. Dear clutched the four-pound mason's hammer, which he had engraved with words close to his heart: "Swords into plowshares" and "Love your enemies."

Scurrying through a grove of pines, the activists effortlessly crossed a dilapidated fence line without cutting or stooping and then stepped onto the tarmac. Much to the activists' surprise, the base was teeming with activity at the early hour and, according to Dear, looked like O'Hare Airport during a holiday rush. Philip Berrigan turned to Dear and whispered, "While the world sleeps tight, the war machine barrels on in full steam." They later learned the base was in the middle of a reconnaissance exercise that coincided with the anniversary of Pearl Harbor.

Amid the whirling lights and blaring trucks, the activists stealthily approached an unmanned F-15E fighter plane but soon realized none of the hundreds of air force personnel took any notice of them. Amazed by its enormity, Dear knew the $34 million spent on the F-15E plane could have provided over seven million hot meals at the homeless shelter he ran out of his inner-city parish. Instead, the plane had helped to kill thousands of Iraqis during the Persian Gulf War and might, some day, transport bombs deadlier than the ones used on Hiroshima and Nagasaki.

Dear approached the plane with all the bravado of a knight preparing to slay a mythical griffon. He soon located the narrow radar-tracking device on the plane's underbelly. Dear described what happened next in his autobiography, *A Persistent Peace*: "At long last, by the grace of God, I will strike a blow for nuclear disarmament. I swing. *Clang*! The vibrations travel through my bones."[30] The Plowshares proceeded to pour blood in the air intakes and over the side of the plane. Working quickly, they broke the F-15's lower high-frequency antenna; dented the pitot-static probe (a vent for an air-speed indicator); and damaged the nose landing gear in two or three places, including the switch that allows the nose gear to compress on landing.[31]

A group of confused air force soldiers soon surrounded the activists. Dear quickly but calmly explained, "We are unarmed, nonviolent people and we're here to dismantle this weapon of death."

A soldier began screaming into his walkie-talkie, "This is the real world! DefCon Charlie. This is the real world! Exercises canceled!"[32] The thought of actually canceling a military exercise brought tears of joy to Dear's eyes, even as he lay face down on the manicured base lawn with hundreds of deadly weapons aimed at his head.

- ▪ -

Detained at Edenton jail, not far from Dear's birthplace, the Plowshares activists shared a moldy shower and steel toilet in a claustrophobic cell while awaiting trial. For seven months, the activists remained busy responding to media requests, answering hundreds of letters, preparing for their day in court, writing articles for peace-and-justice journals, celebrating the Eucharist, and praying daily. Although they spent every waking moment in each other's company, the activists began each new day by venting grievances, sharing doubts, and politely inquiring, "So, how was your day yesterday?"

Dear initially appreciated the monastic living conditions. Soon, however, he tired of hearing his cell mates repeat every mundane detail of their lives ad nauseam. The monotony of prison life grated at his nerves and addled his brain. He longed to swim in the ocean, relish a home-cooked meal, and enjoy a walk with his family. Time slowed down to the speed of molasses and the walls of the claustrophobic eight-by-eight cell seemed to crumble. Dear's inability to control his own life in prison, coupled with his uncertainty about the future, slowly drove him crazy. He began fervently praying for his release and realized he could not survive a sentence of multiple years without falling into despair. He wished someone had told him, "For symbolically clanging on a fighter plane, the government will lock you into a room the size of your bathroom for up to ten years." One night, lying on his wrought-iron cot, Dear suppressed an urge to yell, "My God, my God, why have you forsaken me?"

Sporting a caveman's unkempt beard and popsicle-orange jumpsuit, Dear met his family and friends intermittently. The disheveled inmate received over five thousand letters from across the world. Some letters voiced support, but others assailed him for single-handedly derailing the peace movement through histrionics devoid of tangible benefits. Rattled by the accusatory letters, Dear consoled himself by deciding that his naysayers, deep down, were threatened by his actions since they were unwilling to take similar risks. Of all the missives that Dear received in prison, the one he most cherished came from Mother Teresa, who urged him to embrace his suffering, to take it in, to hold it as a lover—to unite his suffering with Jesus on behalf of the hurting world. He tried to convince himself to accept, rather than avoid, his circumstances.

Local media as well as national newspapers such as the *New York Times* and the *Washington Post* covered the story. Seymour Johnson base spokesman Jay Barber told reporters that the activists were media-hungry mongrels whose anti-American sentiments squandered taxpayers' money.[33] "I don't think that just because [an anti-nukes activist] feels that he has an agenda that is greater than the rest of the world's, that it gives him the right to destroy someone's property," said Barber. "And I believe most taxpayers would back me up if we put it to a vote." An FBI agent, Albert P. Koehler, told the *News & Observer* that the cost of repairs to the jet had been estimated at $27,129 and questioned if the red liquid poured on the plane was really blood or corrosive chemicals.

The activists, for their part, insisted that the liquid was their own blood, a sacrificial plea to their country to cut back its defense department budget and increase spending on programs for the poor.[34] They told reporters they sacrificed both their blood and freedom during the holiday season, the "season of peace," to raise awareness of the increasing militarization of their country before it descended into a garrison state.

They sought to urge the country's best and brightest minds to develop tools of productivity, not weapons of genocide, and they pleaded with policymakers to respect the sanctity of the environment rather than pollute it with nuclear waste.

A reporter, Steve Ford, succinctly captured many Americans' reaction to the Plowshares activists: "Anyone who would risk getting shot by Air Force guards en route to jail in pursuit of a dream so colossally naive as universal disarmament must be a few bricks shy of a load."[35] Many Americans regarded the Plowshares as unpatriotic in spirit and treasonous in actions. They worried that the activists emboldened the country's formidable enemies—who, presumably, had no intention of converting their own nuclear stockpiles into farming tools—by shattering the nation's united front on questions of national security.

Sympathizers defended the activists for inhabiting the unpopular yet sacred space where actions actually overlap with beliefs; they insisted the activists were no more idealistic or eccentric than Christianity's edict to turn your cheek and love your enemy. One sympathizer, former US attorney general Ramsey Clark, offered to defend the Plowshares pro bono, but the activists decided to keep with Saint Mark's recommendation: "Do not prepare a defense, but let the Holy Spirit speak through you." They wished to use their trials to explain their actions in terms of international law, which accepts ordinary citizens' efforts to prevent preparations for genocide, and divine law, which they believed mandated adherents to protect human life. The activists refused to pay bail, sign any personal recognizance papers, broker any deal for a pretrial, or promise to abstain from staging similar protests in the future.

— ▪ —

The Plowshares could not have imagined a more unfavorable court hearing: a right-wing Reagan appointee, Terrence Boyle, presided over the trial, and the jury largely consisted of locals who each had some relationship with the Seymour Johnson Air Force Base.

At the trial's onset, the prosecutor successfully introduced a motion in limine that delineated the arguments that defendants were prohibited from making during the trial: international law, the necessity defense, the Nuremberg defense, alleged crimes committed by the US government, and divine or religious law.

More than sixty peace activists staged a "festival of hope" the night before the hearing and then, at the trial's inception, packed the small courtroom above the post office in Elizabeth City and waved signs with sayings such as "Love your enemies" and "It will be a great day when our schools get all the money they need and the air force has to hold a bake sale to buy a bomber."

When the judge truncated the activists' opening statement to the jury, they turned their backs to him and led their supporters, including the actor Martin Sheen, in reciting the Lord's Prayer and singing peace songs. Police officers soon accosted Sheen, not to arrest him but to request his autograph. The furious judge found the activists in contempt of court and sentenced half a dozen of their supporters to six months in prison each.

Seeking to deter further courtroom shenanigans, Judge Boyle ordered that each activist attend separate jury trials and instructed US Marshals to tightly monitor admission into the courtroom. The carnival of festivities relocated across the Eastern Seaboard as supporters sang and prayed while waving "no nuke" paraphernalia. During Dear's trial, the prosecutor ordered him to name the individual who drove the activists to the base. Dear initially refused to comply but eventually implicated his coconspirator: "The truth is we were driven to the Seymour Johnson Air Force Base by the Holy Spirit!" Exhausted from indulging Dear's earlier jeremiad against nuclear proliferation, the judge responded: "Strike his testimony from the record and handcuff him." Court marshals escorted Dear back to his holding cell.

On July 6, 1994, the activists were sentenced to four to fifteen months in jail but given credit for time already served. They were also sentenced to three years of supervised probation and ordered to pay $2,700 in restitution. The lenient sentence pleasantly surprised all the activists. Dear was beyond euphoric that he would not spend the remainder of his life in prison and decided that he had no immediate plans to convert nuclear weapons into farming tools. Later, he speculated that the judge was possibly influenced by the defendants' passionate testimonies, by the media attention the case generated, by the dozen Catholic priests and bishops who sat in the front row during the hearing, and by rumors of Mother Teresa's plans to visit the courtroom. Ultimately, however, Dear decided the favorable sentence was an answered prayer. "I was begging God for a miracle," said Dear. "I think God released me because I couldn't take it anymore."

As a result of his participation in the disarmament action, Dear lost his voting rights and ability to travel to countries, such as Canada and Japan, that bar ex-felons from entering. Even today, Dear remains subjected to increased scrutiny at airports. He continues agitating for peace through small acts of resistance, holding vigils outside nuclear facilities, and traveling the country lecturing.

■ ∎ ■

The Seymour Johnson Air Force Base disarmament action in which Dear participated was the fiftieth such action in the Plowshares movement. The movement began in the 1980s when there was extensive debate about the arms race, but Plowshares activism has continued for over three decades despite widespread concern about nuclear weapons dissipating at the end of the cold war.[36] Activists had hoped the end of the cold war would herald a new era in which the country downsized its military and channeled money into programs of social uplift, but this promised "peace dividend" never materialized. Since the inaugural King of Prussia protest, more than two hundred people including Dear have participated in nearly eighty Plowshares actions suffused with religious symbolism and impassioned pleas for moral renewal.[37] Today, Plowshares activists are no longer exclusively Catholic but come from across the spectrum of Christian denominations as well as from Judaism and Buddhism.[38]

Activists are ridiculed, censured, and imprisoned for repeatedly trespassing onto military bases, pouring blood on symbols of the war machine, and disturbing the peace at the Pentagon and White House.[39] Critics of the Plowshares movement denounce what they regard as the participants' disinterest in dialogue about policy alternatives and note the tedious SALT negotiations did more to reduce the stock of nuclear weapons in this world than all of the activists' splattered vials of blood.[40]

Plowshares admit their movement has far from ushered in a nuclear-free era but insist they are chipping away at the civic religion of warfare. Their supporters believe they have successfully brought national attention to their cause of nuclear abolishment through high-profile court cases featuring sympathetic participants who incur personal risks to live out what they see as their religious obligations. Evoking the Gospel promise of "greater works" to those who believe, Plowshares realize there is always a gap between faith and feasibility; they believe that the moment of speaking the Truth becomes a leap of faith that opens the world to the power of that Truth.[41] Catholic pacifist Thomas Merton captured the sentiment when he wrote: "The real hope, then, is not in something we think we can do, but in God who is making something good out of it in some way we cannot see. If we can do His will, we will be helping in this process. But we will not necessarily know all about it beforehand."[42] By suggesting Plowshares' protests have intrinsic value even if they seem devoid of wider instrumental usefulness, Merton's theology of hope prevents activists from succumbing to a crisis of confidence when faced with daunting prison sentences.

Nonetheless, Dear is similar to most participants in his lack of eagerness to partake in subsequent Plowshares actions after facing the very real possibility of spending a decade in jail. The Jesuit priest remains at the forefront of the nuclear abolition campaign through organizing vigils, marches, and protests against what he regards as the country's military-industrial complex. I recently reached Dear by phone at his home in New Mexico near the Los Alamos National Laboratory, the birthplace of the bomb, which is one of two laboratories in the United States where classified work toward the design of nuclear weapons is undertaken. I asked Dear what sustains his quest to rid the world of nukes despite little hope of reaching his goal. In a voice alternatively upbeat and somber, Dear responded:

> I know that social change only comes about through the global grass-roots movement for peace and justice . . . the only way that change has ever happened was because of the abolitionists, the suffragists, the labor movement, the civil rights movement, the antiwar movements. The key thing in those movements was that people didn't give up, they kept at it, and some people broke bad laws and accepted the consequences. . . . There's no way to measure the effectiveness of any of this, but what if these are spiritual actions, what if there really is a God, and that God is a God of peace and nonviolence, and Her commandments are: beat your swords into plowshares, love your enemies, and blessed are the peacemakers. Well, God then is doing Her part, and if some people are on the forefront of the faith and conscience movement are actually embodying and undergoing these commandments, the change is going to happen . . . nonviolence gets out of the head and unleashes something in the heart that become transformative and redemptive.[43]

One of the reasons the Plowshares movement's future remains precarious is that activists often decide they are more effective out of jail. In the years since he infiltrated the Seymour base, Dear has worked for a nuclear-free world outside the movement by, for example, urging the Smithsonian to present its exhibit on the Enola Gay—the plane used to drop the bomb on Hiroshima—in the same harsh light as the Holocaust Museum depicts gas chambers.

As a stalwart of the progressive religious community, Dear has run a family literacy program at the Sacred Heart Center, offering academic training and parenting classes for hundreds of low-income minorities. He has traveled to Belfast and launched a monthly journal, *Irish Witness*, to promote a peaceful resolution to armed conflict through active nonviolence; protested the pending execution of Billy Neal Moore on death row; and risked arrest for violating US sanctions against Iraq by distributing medical and water-purification equipment in Baghdad.

From 1998 to 2000, Dear served as the executive director of the Fellowship of Reconciliation (FOR), the largest interfaith peace group in the United States. During his tenure at FOR, Dear traveled across the world defending what he sees as the unique gifts of each of the world's religions and encouraging interfaith collaboration to address the world's myriad problems. Dear, who has authored over a dozen books with eclectic titles such as *Put Down Your Sword* and *Jesus the Rebel*, believes "all the religions have to be teaching the morality and spirituality of nonviolence, which is at the center of every religion, and everybody has to work for a new culture of nonviolence." In 2008 Archbishop Desmond Tutu nominated Dear for the Nobel Peace Prize.

-■-

At the dawn of the twenty-first century, long after the cause of nuclear abolition ceased to galvanize mass protests on Capitol Hill, the Plowshares continued to instigate "holy mischief" to raise awareness about nuclear proliferation. On a balmy Sunday morning in October 2002, Dominican sisters Carol Gilbert, Jackie Hudson, and Ardeth Platte donned white mop-up suits emblazoned with the phrases "Disarmament Specialists" and "Citizens Weapons Inspection Team." The three elderly nuns broke into a N-8 missile silo in northern Colorado to paint a cross on the structure using their own blood—"because it identifies the effects of war and portrays the essential element of life," they later testified—and to hammer at the silo.[44] They concluded with a liturgy.

When air force personnel arrived in Hummers to arrest the women at gunpoint, Sister Gilbert noted they were simply following the call of President George W. Bush to destroy all weapons of mass destruction, but they wished to start that process at home. They explained their desire to reveal the hypocrisy of the United States invading Iraq as well as expose the social injustice of their government squandering billions of dollars on weapons programs that should be invested in education and social services.[45] The nuns regarded President Bush, a self-proclaimed born-again Christian, as an opportunistic politician who sullied the name of their religion. In their action statement they affirmed: "We act in the many names of God the Compassionate, ar-Rahim: our Life, our Peace, our Healer, to transform swords into plowshares, our violence and greed into care for the whole community of earth and sky, not as masters but as servants and friends."[46]

By evoking ar-Rahim—one of the ninety-nine names of Allah that takes its root from "to feel sympathy"—the nuns followed in the footsteps of social movement leaders who embrace religious plurality, from Gandhi to the Dalai Lama to John Dear.

For their symbolic act against the Minuteman III missile silo—a silo storing a weapon ten times more lethal than the bomb that killed 150,000 people in Hiroshima—the nuns were convicted of sabotage.[47] The nuns' lawyers told the *Washington Post* that sentencing guidelines of five to ten years would constitute "one of the harshest punishments ever handed down for what amounts to a trespassing case in which the gravest damage was to a piece of chain-link fence."[48] A columnist for the *Denver Post* voiced similar dismay: "If this constitutes homeland security in post-September 11 America, the watchdog needs dentures. When they're not protesting for peace, the nuns teach in poor neighborhoods, helping the least of us. Locking them up is like locking up Mother Teresa. It's just wrong."[49]

Even after thousands of letters were sent to the court to demand leniency, the clergywomen were sentenced to two-and-a-half to three-and-a-half years, which many considered overly punitive for a symbolic act of peace.[50] Plowshares activists say the government has cracked down harder in the post-9/11 world, but that has not deterred them from protesting against nuclear weapons.

Upon the thirtieth anniversary of the Plowshares movement, the conference "Resistance for a Nuclear-Free Future," held in the vicinity of the Y-12 nuclear facility in Oak Ridge, Tennessee, drew over a dozen former Plowshares activists, as well as 180 supporters who donned tie-dyed T-shirts printed with the phrases "Blessed are the Peacemakers" and "Citizen Weapons Inspector." Cars in the parking lots featured bumper stickers declaring "Peace Takes Courage / Queremos la paz" and "Fear Built Nukes; Love Will Dismantle Them."

One event organizer joked with the audience, "I just asked someone for his cell number and he said, 'Hey, I've been out of the cell for six months!'" Another told the audience, "Please turn off your phones and, for those of you on parole, please turn off your ankle bracelets." Maryville College, a small Christian school, hosted the conference; a college representative gave the audience an overview of campus policies before adding, "I know you guys like tampering with stuff, but please don't touch the fire detectors." An audience member shouted out, "We only tamper with things that are dangerous for the world!"

Former cell mates warmly embraced one another and discussed pending appeals over sugary donuts and iced tea in the campus cafeteria. Conference attendees reminisced about marching through Central Park in 1979 along with a record million protestors at the height of the antinuclear movement. In small-group sessions, participants spoke of their continuing efforts to combat a burgeoning military budget by attending public hearings, joining advocacy boards, enlisting media, lobbying congress members, leading "faith and resistance" retreats, and engaging in nonviolent civil disobedience. Members of a youth campaign, "Think Outside the Bomb," pledged to continue the work pioneered by an earlier generation. Workshops included sessions such as "International Law and Nuclear Weapons," "Freedom Songs to Sing in Jail," and "Obama's Report Card on Nuclear Weapons."

Japanese Buddhist monks draped in saffron-colored robes joined the festivities, sporting buttons declaring "Never Again: No More Hiroshima, No More Nagasaki." Members of Raging Grannies, a peace group largely composed of septuagenarians and octogenarians, belted peace songs in Japanese and English. Banners on the wall read "Fight Cancer: No New Reactors" and "We have guided missiles and misguided men." Steve Jacobs, a member of the Catholic Worker house in Missouri, strummed on his guitar and sang, "They're building nukes on a lark / if one goes off, we'll all be glowing in the dark." Attorneys from civil rights organizations and medics from Physicians for Human Rights identified themselves to the thirty-seven participants who planned to trespass onto the Y-12 nuclear facility on the last day of the conference.

Over lunch, I tracked down Molly Rush, one of the original Plowshares activists who launched the movement. Rush, who now runs a community center named after the Catholic pacifist Thomas Merton, told me why she decided to join the Plowshares Eight thirty years ago. "I got married after high school and had six children," she explained. "Foremost in my mind was my concern that my children should grow up and live their lives, [but] I knew they couldn't in a world where a nuclear accident could occur any moment." She admitted that her family thought she was crazy when she announced her plan to illegally enter a nuclear facility and hammer on nosecones. "My brother, James, snapped, 'Why don't you hang yourself on a cross in the front yard?'"

John Schuchardt, a seventy-one-year-old lawyer and former marine corps officer who once held stocks in General Electric, told me he had decided to join the Plowshares Eight as a form of repentance: "I had a spontaneous awakening to a new reality in the 1970s that helped me recover from being a trained killer for the United States government." He continued:

I knew the United States was violating international law and the US constitution by going halfway around the world and invading Vietnam. I resigned my commission in 1965. . . . I resist nuclear weapons, fundamentally, as a simple act of repentance. It's not about effectiveness, it's not about starting a movement, it's not about looking for a media response. I'm looking for repentance in a situation for which I'm responsible for the mind-set that created Hiroshima, the Trident submarine, and the drones in Pakistan . . . the future of humanity depends on a moral about-face.

Schuchardt met his wife, Carrie, while greeting sympathizers who attended the court trial of the Plowshares Eight. Together, they founded the House of Peace in Ipswich, Massachusetts, where they currently work as foster parents for Iraqi children receiving treatment in Boston— mainly at Shriners Hospital—for burns, amputations, and depleted uranium genetic malformations caused by the 2003 Iraq War.

Other Plowshares activists told me that they regarded participating in the movement as part of their prophetic witness against nuclear weapons. Many insisted that the purity of that witness depends on a stoic detachment from results and that, they reiterated, questions of faith should not be confused with questions of feasibility.

One of the last people I speak with is Carl Kabat, a seventy-three-year-old Catholic priest who also participated in the inaugural Plowshares Eight action. "I am concerned with faithfulness, not effectiveness," explains the raspy-voiced priest. "If we destroy this planet, nothing else matters, so we must address this taproot of evil in the world." Kabat has spent eighteen years in total—a quarter of his life—in prison for protesting nuclear weapons. When I ask about the efficacy of his actions, he shrugs, "Do what you need to do, then sing and dance and leave the rest up to God."

I impolitely persist, saying that spending the prime of one's life in jail without accomplishing one's goal seems like a waste. Kabat nods thoughtfully and then mentions Franz Jägerstätter, the Austrian Catholic executed for his refusal to serve in the armies of the Third Reich. "At the time, Jägerstätter's sacrifice was uniformly regarded as foolish by his neighbors, and everyone told him that they were smarter and knew better than him. They told him that he should just follow the masses and get on with his life, especially since he had three daughters," said Kabat.

According to Kabat, the conscientious objector reached a point where radical refusal to cooperate with an immediate and enormous atrocity was not a question of political efficacy but moral witness. He notes that Jägerstätter's story was almost interred with his bones, but an American writer posthumously discovered the devout Catholic's prison journal. The journal included an entry close to Kabat's heart: "Let us love our enemies, bless those who curse us, pray for those who persecute us. For love will conquer and will endure for all eternity. And happy are they who live and die in God's love." Kabat concluded our interview by saying, "Nonviolent public resistance to evil is a constitutive element of the Gospel."

Listening to Kabat, I understood why some Americans regard Plowshares activists as monomaniacal in their focus, eerily confident in the singularity of their cause, and somewhat paranoid in their fears of an imminent nuclear holocaust. Risking a decade in jail for symbolically rendering a Biblical phrase still seems somewhat foolhardy to me, and the whole courtroom-as-social-theater strikes me as rather passé in an age when the media rarely attends Plowshares' trials. Yet I wonder if maybe these activists' fear of a nuclear catastrophe—whether that catastrophe comes in the form of another Chernobyl accident, a preemptive strike, or rogue actors obtaining access to WMDs—is really so paranoid after all. If such a catastrophe occurred, I wonder what the survivors would think of those of us who didn't resist. I wonder if they would learn about the Plowshares movement and, perhaps, find a prison journal like the one that Jägerstätter left behind. Would these survivors read such a journal and scoff at the futility of such activists? Or would they take some solace in the enduring human spirit of resistance even when faced with the bleakest chances of success? I suspect they would ponder why more people did not join the movement.

6 ROBIN HARPER

Waging Peace by Resisting War Taxes

Let them march all they want—as long as they pay their taxes.
—GENERAL ALEXANDER HAIG

If a thousand men were not to pay their tax-bills this year, that would not be a violent and bloody measure, as it would be to pay them, and enable the State to commit violence and shed innocent blood.
—HENRY DAVID THOREAU

On the evening of January 29, 2002, Robin Harper sat on a leather couch in his modest home in Wallingford, Pennsylvania, and, along with millions of Americans across the country, tuned into President George W. Bush's State of the Union speech. With a vertically hung star-spangled banner in the background, Bush described Iraq as part of an "axis of evil" and solemnly explained, "What we have found in Afghanistan confirms that, far from ending there, our war against terror is only beginning." He continued, "Iraq continues to flaunt its hostility toward America and to support terror." The furrow-browed president ended his speech with a benediction—"May God bless"—and the audience erupted into applause.

Not everyone was elated with the president's oration. When pundits started dissecting the speech and speculating on a potential US-led invasion of Iraq, seventy-three-year-old Harper turned off his television and scraped the remains of his dinner into the trash, trying to ignore the sickening sensation in his gut. Opening the windows and letting the bitter winter air inside, Harper paced across his hallway's wooden floors in his bedroom slippers. When he squeezed his grayish-blue eyes shut, he felt large, warm tears roll off his stubbly chin. Harper, a carpenter by trade, wondered why Bush repeatedly mentioned God's name in his speech when Psalm 34:14 clearly instructed people to "seek peace and pursue it."

Across the nation, American flags surfaced on car bumpers, business windows, and home mailboxes. According to a Gallup poll, three in every four Americans strongly supported attacking Iraq. Richard Perle and other political advisors claimed that Saddam Hussein worked with al Qaeda and that Iraqis would greet American occupiers as liberators. The *Weekly Standard*, the *Wall Street Journal*, and the *New York Times* were among prominent publications supporting a US-led forceful overthrow of Iraq's government. The *Washington Post* editorialized in favor of the war twenty-seven times, and published about one thousand articles and columns on the war. Coverage of antiwar movements was puny in comparison: the *Post* gave a huge antiwar protest a total of thirty-six words.[1] The Pulitzer prize winner George Will summed up public opinion when he claimed that Saddam Hussein "has anthrax, he loves biological weapons, he has terrorist training camps, including 747s to practice on" and posed immediate danger to America. President Bush declared in subsequent addresses to the nation: "Iraq is part of a war on terror. It's a country that trains terrorists; it's a country that can arm terrorists. Saddam Hussein and his weapons are a direct threat to this country."

Harper thought he was too old and too tired to witness yet another war. In his lifetime, he had lost compatriots to World War II and the Korean, Vietnam, and Persian Gulf wars. In 1945 he had watched in horror as his country dropped the world's first atomic bomb and reduced thousands of people to mere dust, leaving thousands more suffering the aftermath of radiation poisoning. Harper's mind was seared with images of howling men whose flayed skin dangled from their skeletons like raw meat on an animal's bone at a butcher's shop. In college, Harper watched classmates leave home for Korea as starry-eyed young soldiers and return as vacant-eyed, bitter men with bluish-purple stumps in place of arms and legs. During the Vietnam War, Harper's thirty-year-old neighbor managed to escape the muggy jungles of camouflaged guerrillas, but not the memories he carried back to his picket-fenced Philadelphia suburb. One sunny afternoon when the neighborhood lawns smelled of freshly cut grass, the man shot himself dead.

Harper, a devout Quaker, believed that war was not only destructive, but also ungodly. Immediately after the September 11, 2001, attacks on the Twin Towers in New York City, Harper felt strangely calm while much of the nation experienced intensifying anger. While Harper understood the human desire to seek revenge, he regarded the desire as a devilish temptation. And, if Bush insisted on evoking God's name, Harper would have preferred the swashbuckling president to focus on the Bible's actual words regarding temptation in 1 Corinthians 10:13: *No temptation has seized you except what is common to man. God is Faithful; He will not let you be tempted beyond what you can bear. But when you are tempted, he will also provide a way out so you can stand up under it.*

Frustrated by his president's cavalier use of God's name, Harper opened his Bible, for comfort, to Matthew 5:38–42, a passage he already knew by heart:

> Ye have heard that it hath been said, "An eye for an eye, and a tooth for a tooth." But I say unto you that ye resist not evil; but whosoever shall smite thee on thy right cheek, turn to him the other also. And if any man will sue thee at the law, and take away thy coat, let him have thy cloak also. And whosoever shall compel thee to go a mile, go with him twain. Give to him that asketh thee, and from him that would borrow of thee turn not thou away.

From Harper's lifetime study of the Bible, he felt that Jesus had favored social justice, peace, and compassion rather than injustice, war, and cruelty. Harper doubted that the Biblical commandment to "turn the other cheek" meant that his government should use fighter planes to drop deadly toxins on people in a distant land. And Harper reasoned that the Biblical injunction to "resist evil" could not be interpreted to justify attacking a city already ravaged by years of bombing campaigns and economic sanctions. From Harper's understanding of the Bible, cycles of violence were intolerable because, according to Matthew 26:52, "he who lives by the sword dies by the sword." If warfare is your way of life, it will be your way of death. *How true this has proved throughout history,* he thought. *We armed Saddam Hussein in the Iran–Iraq War, and we armed Osama Bin Laden in the struggle against the Soviet Union.* Timothy McVeigh, the most notorious domestic terrorist in US history, credited his experience in the Gulf War for reducing him to a monster.

Harper was convinced that Jesus would have urged diplomacy and kinship in the face of violence and hatred. After all, had not the Holy Son triumphed over his own temptation to avenge wrongdoings and settle scores when he died on the cross for his love of mankind? And, as it says in Colossians 3:14, "Love is what binds us together."

My government is evoking God's name to do the devil's work, Harper thought sadly. *It is the ultimate blasphemy.*[2]

■ ■ ■

Three days after September 11, Congress voted to take military action against Afghanistan. The bill passed overwhelmingly with a vote of 98–0 in the Senate and 420–1 in the House. The only lawmaker in either chamber of Congress to vote against the use of force in the so-called War on Terror was Democrat Barbara Lee. As the lone voice in the wilderness, Lee spoke with courage and strength against more violence, and she did so by evoking a God of compassion and restraint:

> I rise today really with a very heavy heart, one that is filled with sorrow for the families and the loved ones who were killed and injured this week. September 11 changed the world. This unspeakable act forced me to rely on my moral compass, my conscience, and my God. Military action will not prevent further acts of international terrorism against the United States. Some of us must say, let's step back for a moment; let's pause just for a minute and think through the implications of our actions today so that this does not spiral out of control.

Nonetheless, three weeks after the vote, the United States invaded Afghanistan. Then, in October 2002, the US Senate passed the Joint Resolution to Authorize the Use of United States Armed Forces Against Iraq. In the speech Bush addressed to a joint session of Congress a week after the attack, he repeated the word "God" three times and, in the months leading up to the Baghdad bombings, continued to evoke God's name over a dozen more.

The country's commander in chief stunned Harper and his Quaker community by warping their Lord and Savior, Jesus Christ, into a warmonger. They held letter-writing campaigns beseeching their elected officials to renounce military intervention. At Sunday "urgent action" meetings, they organized countless candlelight vigils, peace marches, and nonviolent demonstrations against the imminent war. As the battle drums resounded louder, the Quaker community searched for newer, bolder ways to register its growing grief over the president's plans.

Since 1958, Harper had withheld support—passively and actively— for what he regarded as his government's sacrilegious reliance on brute force. Now, taking the Sermon on the Mount as his guiding principle, Harper urged his fellow Quakers to join him in withholding support for violence by refusing to pay for cluster bombs and fighter jets. In April 2002 Harper shared with his community a cordial letter he had written to the IRS accompanying his form 1040:

To the Person Who Examines My Tax Return,

How are you today? Thank you for reviewing my tax return and reading this letter.

My return shows $0.00 for IRS, although my income tax amounts to $4,613 (see Line 42). . . . This year I have paid out my full tax share to groups working for economic and social justice, the nonviolent resolution of conflicts and war, and a safer and greener environment (noted on Line 67 and detailed on the attached sheet).

Because of my Quaker religious beliefs, I cannot put one dime of my federal tax into United States warmaking and its military machine. The use of weapons against other human beings and the deliberate taking of sacred human life, for any reason whatsoever, is totally contrary to the spirit of God and the dictates of my conscience.

The First Amendment of our Constitution guarantees me the right to practice my religion freely, and I choose not to kill, or pay others to take human life. Not in my name, and not with my money!!! Not in Iraq, not in any other country the Bush warriors plan to attack.

It is just plain wrong to go out and invade and conquer a sovereign nation and its people who are not directly threatening us. I refuse to support my country when it acts as a rogue nation, substituting might for right.

We must identify and then work to eliminate the causes of violence and hatred, whether in our hearts, our homes, our cities, or elsewhere in the world. Then, and only then, will we tame the spirals of violence.

Please understand that my open, conscientious refusal as a taxpayer to pay for war and war preparation, and to redirect my tax payments to programs which affirm life, is the most responsible and faithful way I know to pay my full tax share and at the same time hold true to my deepest beliefs.

This is my way to disarm my taxes and work for a more peaceful planet. I hope you understand . . . and will find your own way to work for peace.

There is ever so much more I could say, but thank you again for reading my letter.

Sincerely,
Robin Harper

Harper told his brethren he had read over his letter to make sure it was respectful and honest. As a religious peace activist who believed anger and hatred were counterproductive emotions, Harper had participated in Vietnam antiwar protests but refused to join chants such as *hey, hey, LBJ, how many kids did you kill today?* Quakers believe that heightening one's ability to empathize requires demonstrating good-will toward everyone—including those who have temporarily lost their moral compass.

Harper regarded the act of redirecting his taxes to peaceful efforts an act of allegiance to Christ's life teachings of peace, compassion, and honesty. He wrote on the envelope: "The spirit-spark in me calls me to shout YES to life as well as NO to war."

— ▪ —

Harper first wrote papers to his draft board announcing his commitment to pacifism when he was a student at Cornell University in the 1950s studying sociology, psychology, and anthropology. Having applied for conscientious objector status during the Korean War, Harper used an oil lamp to write his own Peace Testimony—the stand generally taken by members of the Religious Society of Friends (Quakers) against participation in war and against military service as combatants. In 1960 Harper decided to profess his commitment to peace in a letter to President Dwight Eisenhower, various cabinet officers, and a number of congresspersons:

I renounce all war and will never support or sanction another;
I shall do what I can to oppose preparations for war;

I shall strive to make my daily life more loving, more nonviolent and
more truthful in thought, word and deed;
I shall devote my resources to creating conditions of peace

Harper was acutely aware of Quakers' long tradition of refusing to
contribute to government militarism on religious grounds. At the beginning of the French and Indian War in 1755, John Woolman and a number
of other prominent Quakers refused to pay the tax levied by the Pennsylvania colony primarily for war purposes. Throughout history, from
the Mexican War of 1846 to the Vietnam War of 1964 to the Iraq War of
2003, Quakers have argued that paying for war violates their freedom of
religion.

Harper's college roommate, still clad in camouflage and sweaty from
ROTC training, found the letter sitting on their dormitory desk and was
livid to learn Harper refused to fight for their country. He confronted
Harper and suggested Quakerism ("Quack-erism") was for cowards. The
two men talked through the night. Harper patiently explained that he
grew up attending Sunday school at the Quaker-affiliated Swarthmore
College, where he learned that every person is born with a divine spark
of God and to extinguish that spark was morally repugnant.

Harper traced his pacifism to the Quaker Peace Testimony of 1660,
when twelve Quakers including George Fox, one of the founders of the
Religious Society of Friends, presented King Charles II of England with
"A Declaration from the harmless and innocent people of God, called
Quakers":

Our principle is, and our practices have always been, to seek peace and
ensue it and to follow after righteousness and the knowledge of God,
seeking the good and welfare, and doing that which tends to the peace of
all. . . . All bloody principles and practices, we, as to our own particulars,
do utterly deny, with all outward wars and strife and fightings with outward weapons, for any end or under any pretence whatsoever. And this
is our testimony to the whole world. . . . And as for the kingdoms of the
world, we cannot covet them, much less can we fight for them . . . and
that they may all come to witness the prophet's words, who said, "Nation
shall not lift up sword against nation, neither shall they learn war any
more."

Harper told his roommate that he used the Quaker Peace Testimony to make decisions in his life—including his decision not to participate in the Korean War.

Listening attentively, Harper's roommate asked many questions about Quakerism. Who are Quakers? Are they concerned only with their own salvation? What do they believe? Harper explained that his religion is an active, involved community of Christians living in the modern world. The Quaker faith is comprised of people committed to traditional testimonies of pacifism, social equality, integrity, and simplicity. While, even today, there is no singular creed characterizing Quakerism, the movement is marked by beliefs inspired by the life and lessons of George Fox, such as that the light of God is in everyone; each person can have a personal relationship with God; one's relationship with God is nurtured by worship based on concentrated listening in silence; and, the nature of God is love.[3] Harper stressed that Quakers believe each person needs to find his or her own truth, so Quakers should only share, rather than impose, their worldview on others. While many Quakers pray regularly and rely heavily on the Bible, Harper said he considered all of life an act of prayer and a testament to peace.

The two men had several discussions throughout college about the validity of violence to achieve a goal. By the end of the year, Harper's roommate followed his lead and applied for conscientious objector status. He ultimately decided to pursue a career in medicine instead of the military.

■ ● ■

Writer Henry David Thoreau and freedom fighter Mahatma Gandhi inspire many modern-day war-tax resisters. Thoreau refused to finance slavery and the Mexican-American War in 1847 by withholding his poll tax and was sent to jail for a night. When Sheriff Samuel Staples told Thoreau he was free to leave the next morning, Thoreau refused to go, arguing that he had the right to remain in jail and register his repulsion of slavery. Staples finally had to put him out. Thoreau later published "Civil Disobedience," which became Mahatma Gandhi's blueprint for emancipation in his successful campaign to free India from the British Empire. The British salt tax, one of many economic atrocities used to generate revenue to support British rule, was the focal point of Gandhi's nonviolent political protest.[4] The British monopoly on the salt tax in India dictated that the sale or production of salt by anyone but the British government was a criminal offense punishable by law. On March 2, 1930, Gandhi wrote to the viceroy, Lord Irwin:

> [If] my letter makes no appeal to your heart, on the eleventh day of this month I shall proceed with such co-workers of the ashram as I can take, to disregard the provisions of the Salt Laws. I regard this tax to be the most iniquitous of all from the poor man's standpoint. As the Independence movement is essentially for the poorest in the land, the beginning will be made with this evil.[5]

Interestingly enough, it was Reginald Reynolds—an English Quaker who joined Gandhi's ashram—who hand delivered Gandhi's letter, with its proclamation of civil disobedience, to Lord Irwin.[6] Reynolds wrote, "My taking of this letter was, in fact, intended to be symbolic of the fact that this was not merely a struggle between Indians and the British," signifying that Quakers often join movements even when they have nothing personally at stake.[7] Gandhi also found support among Quakers such as Horace Alexander, Agatha Harrison, and Muriel Lester.[8]

On March 12, 1930, Gandhi and approximately seventy-eight followers set out, on foot, for a twenty-three-day journey to the coastal village of Dandi, some 240 miles from their starting point in Sabarmati, to gain support for their resistance to the salt tax. On April 6 Gandhi picked up salt lying on the seashore to claim the commodity that no Indian could legally produce—salt.[9] Upon arriving at the seashore he spoke to a reporter: "God be thanked for what may be termed the happy ending of the first stage in this, for me at least, the final struggle of freedom." The effects of the Salt March were felt across India. Thousands of people made salt, bought illegal salt, and resisted the salt tax. Gandhi was tossed in prison but continued to work toward Indian independence, which was achieved in August 1947.

- ∎ -

When Harper was a sophomore in Swarthmore High School during World War II, every classroom was encouraged to purchase war stamps and collectively build toward buying a bond, but Harper's homeroom repeatedly failed to reach a 100-percent percent participation rate. The young Quaker did not want his money used to support bloodshed. One of Harper's classmates who knew of his dovish disposition accosted him with a raised fist after school and demanded to know, "If there was a German coming down Chester Road in Swarthmore and you had a gun, what would you do?" Harper paused before calmly answering, "I wouldn't shoot him." Bracing himself for blows that never came, Harper tried to defend his position. The student remained unconvinced and accused him of being a German sympathizer.

Harper's classmates were enraged by his unwillingness to bag a Nazi. After all, World War II was debatably the most popular war the United States had ever fought. Never had a greater proportion of the country participated in a war: eighteen million served in the armed forces (including four of President Franklin Roosevelt's own sons), ten million fought overseas; twenty-five million workers gave regularly for war bonds.[10] It was a war against an enemy of unthinkable moral depravity. Hitler was extending xenophobia, totalitarianism, homophobia, racism, and militarism beyond what an already beleaguered world had ever experienced.

Harper certainly did not contest these facts, yet he remained unconvinced that legitimating violence by participating in war would, in the long run, contribute to a world where all forms of violence were unthinkable. Harper urged his classmates not to buy war bonds but instead support German Quakers on a confidential list of "trusted Friends"—men and women willing to risk their lives to help victims of Nazism by organizing mass meals and matching refugees with sponsor families abroad.[11]

Harper also encouraged his friends to question their own government's horrifying treatment of African Americans, given its stated commitment to advance the right of people everywhere to life, liberty, and the pursuit of happiness. He continued to take the unpopular stance that there must be some way to create a world in which saving one person does not require killing another. His sincere, unassuming tone won him some admirers but few cohorts. When the war ended in 1945, Harper spent a portion of his savings, twenty-five dollars, buying a US peace bond to show that he had nothing against his country, only against war.

During the Korean War, Harper completed two years of civilian alternative service, working in a self-help housing project where he met his future wife, Marlies, a German survivor of World War II who was equally opposed to using violence to create a peaceful world. In the following years, Harper and his wife took part in countless peace vigils, demonstrations, and lobbying efforts against weapons of mass destruction, the arms race, and wars both hot and cold.

While earning a taxable income to support his growing family, he learned that more than half of his federal income tax was spent to build and test nuclear weapons and fund US military programs. Harper decided he could not support this on religious principles, so in 1958 he made two life-changing decisions: First, as a conscientious objector to all war, he decided to refuse to send any income taxes to the IRS unless the commissioner assured him that his money would not pay for war. Second, he would re-channel his yearly federal income tax into contributions that would help to establish conditions for peace. For Harper, these conditions included abolishing nuclear weapons and working toward the elimination of all other weapons of war.

— • —

Over the years, Harper has carefully calculated his tax liability and redirected thousands of dollars toward the American Friends Service Committee, Greenpeace, and the National Resources Defense Council. He filed returns separately from his wife, showing zero taxes owed after deduction. His alternative payments are equal to the full tax figure. To ensure transparency, photocopies of all the checks to humanitarian organizations accompany his letters of conscience to the IRS. His wife, who was employed at a bridal shop, continued to work in order to ensure that their three children's welfare would not be jeopardized in case he was detained for his actions.

Emphasizing that war tax resisters are not anarchists who resent government involvement, Harper believes that refusing to pay for war is a religious prerogative that should be protected by the First Amendment. However, according to Peter Goldberger, a criminal defense lawyer near Philadelphia who has represented a dozen war tax resisters, there are currently no constitutional, federal, or tax laws that protect conscientious objectors. However, unlike millionaire tax evaders, war tax resisters rarely receive any jail time. "The IRS doesn't have the resources to enforce the law and their priorities are going after those with a lot of money," Goldberger says. "These people are not wealthy or greedy." He added that the IRS is wary of pressing charges because "the publicity these cases generate makes conscientious tax resisters sympathetic. They're not tax cheats."

Goldberger, who was a draft counselor in 1968, says the law has never interpreted the First Amendment—the right to religious freedom—as a reason not to pay taxes. "There is absolute freedom to believe, but there is not absolute freedom to act," he explains. A pacifist himself and an observant Jew, Goldberger says his only advice to clients is to follow the law whenever possible unless God absolutely forbids it, in which case they should still be prepared to face the consequences.

- ∎ -

The Providence Friends Meeting House in Media, Pennsylvania, founded in 1684, is one of the oldest Quaker houses of worship. Outside, a large plywood sign welcomes newcomers with a quote by Christian socialist A. J. Muste: "There is no way to peace, peace is the way." Inside the modest meeting room, large wooden benches are positioned in a circle. In mid-April 1975 a newcomer asked Harper when the service would begin. Harper explained with a wry smile, "Service begins when the worship ends." During the hour of silence that constitutes a Quaker service, Harper was moved to speak: "It is a sin to build nuclear weapons; it is a sin to buy, build, and deploy nuclear weapons; and it is beyond the pale a sin to voluntarily pay for nuclear weapons!" Harper's strident advocacy of war tax resistance upset the executive clerk presiding over the service. He reprimanded Harper and told him to refrain from instructing other Quakers on what to do with their taxes. Harper apologized and agreed that conscientious tax resistance is an intensely personal religious act.

Quakers, as a community, encourage war tax resisters, but some believe that this form of civil disobedience is futile and a misuse of community attention because so few people are willing to have their assets seized. Also, the Quaker belief in a simple, modest lifestyle rarely puts them in the top tax brackets, so their contribution to government spending is often negligible. Harper agrees that war tax resistance is not a matter of efficacy so much as principle. Self-employed, Harper admits that his tax liability is so low that it will have almost no effect on the government's overall military spending. Yet he doesn't regard war tax resistance as a "noble failure" any more than he regards the work of early Quaker abolitionists as a failure despite their inability to make headway in their time. Harper is less concerned about questions of efficiency than spiritual consistency—he regards resisting war taxes as his sacred duty because it is part of his Quaker obligation not to comply with violence in any form. He adds that most movements begin with a small number of dedicated people hammering away at what often appears to be a hopeless situation. "In my observation of the human condition, you never know when you're going to make a difference actually work and change the system, the tipping point," said Harper. He agrees with South African scholar Albie Sachs's famous observation: "All revolutions are impossible until they happen, then they become inevitable."

— ∎ —

Conscientious objectors within pacifist communities represent the cerebral wing of the antiwar movement—protesters who take their campaigns from the streets into the solitude of their homes and the privacy of their bank accounts. Tax resisters say their ranks are increasing as discontent over the war in Iraq grows, but there is no definite way of verifying their claim. The US Treasury Department doesn't track the reasons people refuse to pay their taxes, so whether the number of war tax resisters is swelling or stagnant is difficult to determine.

One soft-spoken but fiery-eyed peace activist, Ed Hedemann, has not paid any federal income tax since 1970 and says he owes the government $70,000—a sum worth several cluster bombs at $14,000 each and dozens of $9 hand grenades. Instead, Hedemann donated the money to Global Exchange, American Friends Service Committee, and other humanitarian efforts. The sixty-two-year-old pacifist says he sleeps better knowing his tax dollars are redirected to peaceful causes. "I run a risk of getting in trouble for not paying my taxes, but not as big a risk as the people of Iraq will suffer if I do pay," said Hedemann, a freelance photographer and writer in Brooklyn, New York. The author of *War Tax Resistance: A Guide to Withholding Your Support from the Military*, he helped found the National War Tax Resistance Coordinating Committee (NWTRCC) in 1982 to provide information and support to people considering war tax resistance. Not religious himself, Hedemann says that pacifist religious communities such as the Quakers make up the majority of modern war tax resisters.

The Internal Revenue Service does not recognize antiwar sentiment as a legitimate reason to withhold taxes. IRS spokesman Eric Smith said,

"No law, including the Internal Revenue Code, permits a taxpayer to avoid or evade tax obligations on the grounds that the taxpayer does not agree with the government's use of the taxes collected." But that doesn't mean the tax man is quick to haul protesters off to jail. Conscientious tax resisters usually receive generic letters from the IRS demanding payment for back taxes, penalties, and interest. Hedemann says he's received such letters for years but has had an IRS representative knock on his door only half a dozen times in his life. "Once, I tried telling him about the federal pie chart and where his money was going, but he didn't seem interested," Hedemann reminisced, chuckling good-naturedly.

The committee estimates that 51 percent of 2008 federal taxes will go toward the military this year; the US Office of Management and Budget puts the number closer to 21 percent. The National Priorities Project estimates the federal government in 2008 spent 37.3 cents of each income tax dollar on military-related spending (military and military-related debt) and only 2.8 cents on environment, energy, and science-related spending combined.[12]

The National War Tax Resistance Coordinating Committee urges people to protest the war by refusing to pay whatever they can: from a dollar to their entire federal income tax bill. "If enough people participated, you could really cripple the government," said Hedemann, who estimates that at least 2 percent of taxpayers would need to become resisters. The IRS isn't anxious to confirm such estimates; in fact, they won't even acknowledge the existence of war tax resisters. After repeated phone calls, Bruce Friedland, an IRS spokesman, declined to comment on how many tax-withholding citizens it would take to put a crimp in military actions.

Although modern-day war tax resisters note that their tradition goes back to the American Revolution, they agree it hasn't been a widely publicized or popular form of pacifism recently. "Even at the height of the antiwar protests during the Vietnam War, tax objection wasn't the main form of resistance," said Dennis Dalton, a Barnard College politics professor who is best known for his courses on nonviolence and for giving the federal portion of his tax bill to nonprofits. "But if tax resistance could be achieved on a large scale, it would be the most effective form of resisting a government that is waging an unjust war."

Hedemann was prosecuted eight years ago for refusing to divulge financial information to IRS investigators. Goldberger, who has represented both Hedemann and Harper in court, successfully argued that complying with the government would violate his client's Fifth Amendment right not to self-incriminate. The antiwar activist is so dedicated to his cause that he lives on the brink of poverty: he doesn't own a home, car, or bank account for fear the IRS will seize his assets. "I don't want to finance this country's war-making machine," Hedemann said.

In the past sixty years, there were only forty-five IRS court actions against war tax resisters, Goldberger said. Most resisters have been hauled into court either for not cooperating with the government by refusing to hand over records or, during the height of Vietnam War protests in the early 1970s, because they fraudulently altered their W-4 forms. According to the War Resistance League, since World War II only about thirty people have been jailed for reasons related to war tax resistance itself. The IRS's primary interest is to get the money, not jail the resister.

– · –

Until 1970, Harper had only cursorily interacted with the IRS through letters. However, that year the IRS billed him for $32,500 in alleged taxes, penalties, and interest for tax years 1958 to 1967. At a four-hour conference with an IRS agent, Harper established complete agreement on the figures owed and complete disagreement that he should pay the IRS if they used any portion of his money for military purposes. Telling the IRS representative that he could not in good conscience pay for warfare, Harper offered to write a check to a humanitarian agency for the allotted sum in the representative's presence. The officer in the adjacent cubicle overheard Harper and yelled, "You should go to prison, and I'll see if we can arrange that!" Harper smiled as if a friendly passerby had commented on the weather. Opening his briefcase, he pulled out a photo of a child with grotesque birth defects from exposure to poisonous chemicals used during the Vietnam War. Harper explained to the officer that he didn't want to monetarily contribute to such suffering and, perhaps, he wasn't the one who deserved jail time. With forced calm, Harper pointed to the child's distended neck that was propped up by a metal bar to prevent her trachea from collapsing. He explained, "Sir, I'm afraid this is why I can't give you my money." The man rolled his eyes, obviously unmoved.

When Harper returned home, he prayed for the tax collector to find inner peace.

- ∎ -

Harper had ended his self-employment in 1966 and, in 1972, used the W-4 resistance method to stop withholding, claiming a "war crimes" deduction, accompanied by a letter of explanation, when filing his 1040 form. Because of somewhat esoteric Pennsylvania laws, Harper and his wife's joint bank account and other assets were immune from seizure. When summoned by the IRS, Harper has gone but without records. He doesn't cooperate with the collection process.

In 1973, with the guidance of his sympathetic lawyer, John Egnal, Harper took the IRS into US Tax Court. Congress created the Tax Court to provide a judicial forum through which affected persons could dispute tax deficiencies determined by the Commissioner of Internal Revenue before they paid dispute amounts.[13] This was the first war tax resistance hearing of the Vietnam War era and the only case that involved a decade of war tax refusal. The case was decided in favor of the government, and the court dismissed the issues of First Amendment. In 1975 the IRS took Harper into district court to enforce the summons. The judge issued a carefully reasoned fifteen-page opinion (*U.S. v. Harper*) ruling that Harper did not have to comply on Fifth Amendment grounds: the right not to incriminate oneself.

In a 1977 court action, Harper's case was transferred from jurisdiction of the IRS to the Justice Department. And in August 1981, the Justice Department subpoenaed his financial records and ordered him to testify. A month later, Harper and his lawyer filed a motion to quash the subpoena on First and Fifth Amendment grounds. After two preliminary hearings before a federal magistrate and a full hearing before a district judge, at which Harper gave lengthy testimony, the IRS failed to file a final brief and abruptly withdrew the subpoena. However, the IRS initiated a second summary judgment action in 1983 and succeeded in transferring an additional alleged liability of $22,000 to Justice Department jurisdiction, thus circumventing the statute of limitations on collection. Further, Harper lost his challenge of the $500 "frivolous" penalty for his 1982 tax return.

In 1983 the IRS placed a levy on Harper's salary for the alleged liability of $17,000. Harper promptly reduced his salary to the legal level under which taxes are not paid (at that time $75 a week plus $25 for each of his three dependent children), thus thwarting collection. Harper was relieved that his family was spared an additional financial burden, and he also insists that he was willing to serve jail time to stay true to his faith.

— • —

Harper, a member of the War Tax Concerns Support Committee of Philadelphia Yearly Meeting, frequently speaks at Quaker events on how to withhold money from the government. At town hall meetings, Harper urges his brethren to "speak truth to power"—a central Quaker credo—by sending the IRS letters similar to his own explaining their reasons for protesting state-sanctioned killing. Unlike people who evade taxes to increase their wealth, Harper welcomes publicity and answers questions with gusto. "For me, a Quaker, conscientious objection to war cannot be compartmentalized," explained Harper in his husky baritone voice to a weekly meeting of Quakers. "Conscripting my money for war is as abhorrent as conscripting my person for fighting."

Harper routinely delivers a public lecture titled "What Happens When an Irresistible Force [IRS] Meets an Immovable Object [Conscientious War Tax Refuser]—The Give and Take of a Fifty-Year Saga." He asks auditoriums full of otherwise law-abiding Quakers, "What would you do if I came in to your office tomorrow with a cup in my hand, asking for contributions to enable me to buy guns and kill a group of people I don't like?" Many Quakers agree with Harper's logic, but some worry that withholding taxes means less money for social services. Harper explains that the taxes paid to the government cannot be earmarked for non-military spending, so redirecting taxes to charitable organizations is more consistent with Quaker beliefs. Others wonder if disobeying the law will lead to social disintegration and chaos. Harper insists that Quakers who refuse paying war taxes seek to build community through responsible use of their resisted money, not a society in which chaos reigns. He explains that, historically, civil disobedience has not led to people running amok in the streets, disobeying all laws. In fact, Harper says, it is those who prepare for war that contribute to a breakdown of the just social order by violating international laws.

According to Harper, resisting taxes out of a religious commitment to pacifism is very different from objecting to taxation out of distrust for government or disdain for welfare programs. He points out that there's a conscientious objector status available to draft resisters because America, at least in theory, respects religious plurality.

- ■ -

On August 3, 2000, the Harpers were interrogated by a no-nonsense, hard-edged tax auditor from the Pennsylvania IRS headquarters. He began with a litany of accusations: tax evaders like the Harpers are cheats, freeloaders, and menaces. He also warned that he had successfully locked up many tax protestors and, he added with a little swagger in his voice, some of them were armed and dangerous.

The auditor cautioned the Harpers that he had no patience for white-collar criminals' intricate scams or anarchists' revolutionary fervor. Harper explained that he and his wife were neither unscrupulous millionaires nor antigovernment rebels, but simply people abiding by the dictates of their faith. Quakers, he explained, are pacifists who do not want to support violence in any form. The auditor's shoulders relaxed a little, but his scowl remained. He told the Harpers that his own father had fought in the Korean War and returned home tormented by post-traumatic stress disorder, but that didn't mean he was going to break the law and pretend he knew better than his government.

Marlies patiently listened to the auditor's argument before respect-fully disagreeing. She said that each person must obey the dictates of her conscience—and religion—before obeying the law of man. Marlies recollected growing up in Nazi Germany and explained that good people blindly following the law enabled the Third Reich to carry out its bloody madness.

Out of the two hundred Quakers in Nazi Berlin, twenty-five suffered for their opposition to the Third Reich. [14] Quakers who listed themselves on a docket of "trusted friends" soon lost their jobs and pensions and were eventually tortured in prisons or concentration camps. [15] Yet the community refused to cower despite the hopelessness of their situation. Instead, they developed an intricate code system that involved respond-ing to "Heil Hitler" with "Gruess Gott" ("Greet God") to identify other Quakers working to hide away persecuted minorities and secure sponsor-families for potential refugees. These Quakers concealed their work not only from colleagues, but also from their children for fear of being discovered and killed. [16] Other Christian conscientious objectors to Nazi terror included Polish priest Maximilian Kolbe, who provided shelter for thousands of Jews in his friary. After the German gestapo arrested him, he sacrificed his life to save a fellow prisoner in Auschwitz. Franz

Jägerstätter, a Catholic conscientious objector to the Third Reich, similarly chose death over forsaking his religious principles. Two devout Christian siblings, Hans and Sophie Scholl, joined the White Rose group, which clandestinely published and circulated a series of six leaflets detailing Nazi atrocities. The Scholls wanted to ensure that Germans could never claim that they didn't know what was happening in their name. In a leaflet that the Scholls hoped would incite their fellow citizens against the Nazi regime, they wrote: *We will not be silent. We are your guilty conscience. The White Rose will not leave you in peace!* The members of the White Rose were caught and beheaded after their sixth leaflet was published.

Marlies, who was aware of Christian resistance to Nazism, knew these stories of heroism were the exceptions, and most Germans did not risk similar personal harm to prevent the Holocaust. Drawing a parallel with her husband's war tax refusal, Marlies pointed out how ordinary Germans' complacency and income taxes enabled the Third Reich to carry out its "legal" atrocities. The angry auditor found the analogy dishonest. After all, America was not under the Third Reich's tyranny, he argued. Marlies agreed, but noted that violence has the same outcome for a victim whether she dies from aerial bombs or noxious gases. "Violence causes deaths and only God should decide when someone dies," she explained.

The auditor pointed out that violence sometimes prevents further deaths and, he insisted, violence is often the lesser of two evils. Marlies said she respected his views, but Quakerism urged people to work toward eradicating all forms of violence—not by using even more violence, but by sacrificing their own personal welfare to help other people. "Only then can we hope to create a world rid of all forms of violence," concluded Marlies.

The auditor demanded, "What would have happened if there was no Second World War? How many more people would have died?"

Marlies replied, "Isn't the better question: what would have happened if ordinary Germans had refused to participate in the war machine or risked their own lives to save others? What if every German had emulated the heroic actions of Kolbe, Jägerstätter, and the Scholls? How many more people would have survived?"

The auditor told Harper that his wife's views were extremist and alarming.

Harper assured the auditor that, in a culture of violence, his wife's views were indeed extreme—and he fully shared them. After more than three hours of discussion, well past the auditor's normal lunchtime, the exhausted tax collector shook the Harpers' hands, smiled without malice, and said hearing their beliefs made him question his own views.

- ▪ -

Many members of the Society of Friends (Quakers), the Church of the Brethren, and the Mennonite Church—the historic peace churches—believe that paying war taxes is equivalent to participating in war, which violates the teachings of Jesus. A small number of Catholics are also among those objecting to military spending on religious grounds. Karl Meyer, a self-employed carpenter in Nashville, Tennessee, said, "If I send $1,000 to DC, I doubt ten cents would go to direct services." But, he said, "If I send it to the Catholic Worker community, the whole $1,000 will go to the hungry and poor. The logic is crushing and overwhelming."[17] Meyer has successfully resisted payment of almost all federal income tax claimed from him since 1960. The energetic activist has been arrested over fifty times while protesting, among other things, the cold war, the Vietnam War, the wars in El Salvador and Nicaragua, the death penalty, and, in 2001, UN sanctions against Iraq. Meyer has served the better part of a year in a federal penitentiary for refusing to pay his income tax, and his FBI file described him in 1960 as a "pacifist with a martyr complex."[18] The radicalism embodied by Meyer and his wider Catholic Worker community is not the radicalism of Marx and Lenin but of Jesus and the Sermon on the Mount. "Let us affirm," Meyer wrote in the *Catholic Worker* newspaper in 1969, "that it would be very practicable for us to get together in our own resistance movement to prevent the conscription of our money by the military and to create a Fund for Mankind."

Determined doves such as Harper, Hedemann, Goldberger, and Meyer believe their cause is catching the eye of war-weary Americans. Hedemann points to the rising number of hits on the National War Tax Resistance Coordinating Committee's website after January 2007, when President Bush proposed a troop surge in Iraq.

Harper hopes that one day every 1040 tax form will have a statement inquiring "Do you wish to have your money go toward peace efforts?" He is one of many war tax resisters who support the National Campaign for a Peace Tax Fund. The not-for-profit organization based in Washington, D.C, is lobbying for a "peace alternative" for taxpayers by advocating the passage of the Religious Freedom Peace Tax Fund Bill (currently H.R. 1921). If enacted, this law would recognize the rights of citizens whose religion does not permit physical or financial participation in any war. Federal taxes of designated conscientious objectors would be placed in a non-military trust fund, enabling these citizens to be free from spiritual hypocrisy. Daniel Longwing, who works for the Peace Tax Fund, says a lot of legislatures assume that war tax resisters are trying to get out of paying their taxes, so the Peace Tax Fund proves that people want to pay the amount they owe if the dollars go toward peaceful causes.

7 JOSEPH LAND

Living in the Clouds
to Save the Redwoods

God has cared for these trees, saved them from drought, disease, avalanches, and a thousand straining, leveling tempests and floods. But he cannot save them from fools.

—JOHN MUIR, *founder of the Sierra Club*[1]

I am the Lord's humble servant. I am Allah's disciple, the [Hindu] floaty thing's Gopher boy. There has been a miracle here . . . it has rained.

—TIMOTHY TREADWELL, *Grizzly Man*[2]

In August 1996 a waifish twenty-two-year-old bartender named Julia Butterfly Hill barely survived a car crash when a drunk driver rammed her Honda hatchback from behind, embedding her car's steering wheel deep within her skull. After a year of intensive therapy, Hill gradually recovered her verbal and motor skills but was no longer content serving drinks, paying bills, and living an ordinary life. The young woman with silky brown hair and a ballerina's lithe body later told the *Washington Post*: "The steering wheel in my head, both figuratively and literally, steered me in a new direction in my life."[3] Hill, the daughter of an itinerant preacher, embarked on a spiritual quest that eventually led her to Humboldt County, California, where a nascent environmental movement was protesting the destruction of the redwood forests. Learning that Pacific Lumber Company loggers intended to clear-cut the forest, Hill experienced what she regarded as a religious calling to join the tree-sitters in occupying the redwoods and refusing to descend in hopes of preventing loggers from felling the ancient trees.

Far surpassing veteran tree-sitters in her zeal, Hill spent a record 738 days perched on a six-by-six-foot platform in a 180-foot tree she named "Luna." While living in her six-hundred-year-old towering abode, Hill benefited from an expansive team of supporters on the ground that provided her with food and other necessities. Capturing world attention, the barefoot nymph clung to her hoary conifer through wretched windstorms, telling friends that she had stopped washing the soles of her feet since the tree's sap anchored her more securely to its trunk. She persisted even when lumber crews harassed her from the forest floor and heckled her from helicopters whirring above.

Hill's sympathizers christened her the goddess of the forest, the sole protector of a pristine wilderness. However, her critics labeled her a foolhardy troublemaker they accused of trespassing on private property and forcing corporations to waste money on hiring tree extractors. They blamed her for impeding free-market commerce, putting loggers out of business, and recklessly endangering her own life in a quest for stardom.

In 1999 Pacific Lumber Company and Hill reached an agreement in which the company would safeguard Luna and other trees within a two-hundred-foot buffer zone in exchange for Hill's descent. The young environmentalist viewed the agreement as a victory, yet she feared that unsustainable logging practices would continue decimating the redwood population. She knew that less than 5 percent of the roughly two million acres of original forest that had spanned California and Oregon 150 years ago remained intact. After vacating the ancient redwood, Hill later wrote about her experience in *Legacy of Luna*, which the publishing company printed on 100-percent postconsumer recycled paper with soy-based ink and chlorine-free processing. "Luna is only one tree. We will save her, but we will lose others. The more we stand up and demand change, though, the more things will improve," she wrote.[4]

Years later and some two thousand miles away, a devout Baptist named Joseph Land read Hill's words and vowed to continue her campaign of environmental civil disobedience. The teenager lived on the outskirts of Detroit and was an unlikely successor to the tree-sit movement: as a sickly child who routinely suffered ear infections, Land actually used to loathe the outdoors. Even as a young adult, he much preferred playing video games to camping excursions and cared so little about environmentalism that he rarely even bothered to recycle. Yet, in October 2004, he decided to spend two years living among the redwoods and revitalizing the tree-sit movement after experiencing what he called a "religious awakening." The limber young man with mahogany-brown dreadlocks later explained, "God spoke to me not in a booming voice but a soft whisper and said, 'I want you to go stay in the forest until I tell you what to do next.'"

The Baptist's religious beliefs actually irked many veteran tree-sitters who gravitated to Wicca or other pagan traditions over Christianity, a religion they viewed as partly culpable for ongoing environmental destruction given its emphasis on human "dominion over God's creation." Land's activism also angered the head of Pacific Lumber Company, who resented tree-sitters' alleged contempt for private property and the livelihood of their loggers. However, Land's surprising leadership role in the tree-sit movement ultimately helped protect large swathes of the forest and renew debate within churches on the responsibility of Christians to demonstrate "good stewardship" of the environment.

■ ▪ ■

Raised in a conservative blue-collar Baptist household in Rochester, Michigan, Land first heard about the redwoods from a high school friend who had visited California during spring break of their senior year. The impressionable adolescent was intrigued to learn that the gigantic trees sprouted from seeds no bigger than tomatoes, yet reached three hundred feet in height and 1,500 years in age. While further researching the ancient redwoods, Land found photos online and marveled at their wide, sinewy bark that twirled skyward as if they were illustrations in a Dr. Seuss book. The more the lonely teenager read about the redwoods, the more the trees took on mythic proportions in his mind and formed a fairy-tale world far removed from the blandness of suburbia.

Land increasingly found refuge in books about the redwoods, which he devoured with the same fervor that his friends consumed comic books and traded baseball cards. He often imagined traipsing between the redwoods' expansive canopies like a yellow-cheeked chipmunk. The high school misfit regarded these trees as magical relics of a bygone era containing the ancient wisdom of a forgotten people. Land learned that these arboreal titans ensured the purity of coho salmons' aqueous habitats and provided refuge to countless forest species, including rare mountain lions. For millennia, the Tolowa, Yurok, and Chilula tribes, among others, lived within the redwood labyrinth, eating salmon, elk, and tan oak acorns.[5] They carved long canoes from logs that naturally fell to the ground like gifts from the Gods above. Then the gold rush of 1849 nearly destroyed the two-thousand-year-old forest. After World War II and the housing boom, Caterpillar tractors commandeered the unstable soils of the redwood forests and further jeopardized the future of the forests.[6] Now, Land learned, overzealous logging companies that engaged in unsustainable clear-cutting practices were endangering the few remaining redwoods.

Although redwoods fascinated Land, he never believed he would see one in person. Shortly after graduating from high school, the directionless teenager took a job at a local Burger King, where he flipped greasy meat patties and listened to his coworkers obsess over dead-end relationships. Land increasingly felt suffocated living at home with his extremely pious grandparents and his divorcé father, who worked the graveyard shift fitting pipes for the Ford automobile company. Despite attending church regularly and trying to lead a "rapture-ready" life free of sin, Land felt hollow inside. He dreamed of escaping his conservative blue-collar Baptist household and discovering what he regarded as the unadulterated utopia of Humboldt Redwoods State Park in California, which housed the largest contiguous block of old-growth redwood forest—some ten thousand acres—left on earth.

— • —

In late 2002 one of Land's friends casually mentioned that he planned to take a road trip to northern California and needed someone to split gas money. Viewing the trip as the ticket out of his doldrums, twenty-year-old Land jumped at the opportunity to leave the dreary northern cold for the promise of the Golden State. En route, the friends stopped in Eugene, Oregon, and camped on park benches. Land stayed up all night fantasizing about frolicking through the emerald streams and playing among epiphytic ferns.

Driving down Highway 101, Land kept scanning the landscape for the renowned trees that had captured his imagination for years, but none were in sight. His friend nonchalantly explained that very few redwoods remained even in the so-called Redwood Range because logging companies cut the trees for their bark. He further explained that the redwood's straight-grained, rot-resistant wood is rich in compounds called tannin polyphenols, which deter bugs and decay-causing fungi, making it perfect for furniture.[7] Given that the redwoods produce more desirable and more mildew-resistant wood as they age, loggers covet the last remaining two-thousand-year-old trees.[8] Driving along the highway, Land's friend explained that merely 180 redwoods taller than 350 feet remained in the world, of which 130 grew in Humboldt County. Land was upset to hear that even these few surviving redwoods in protected areas remained at risk, but he felt powerless to deter overzealous loggers.

The Michigan transplant moved into a communal house in Arcata, the largest city near Humboldt Redwoods State Park, and worked odd jobs, such as making wet suits for kayakers and delivering beer for a brewery. Yet his mind remained fixated on the mammoth trees that he worried faced extinction. One night at a house party, a local activist suggested Land help save the majestic trees by participating in "direct action" such as tree-sits. Land was fascinated by the activist's stories of living in a redwood and subsisting on a diet of tofu and quinoa, but he explained he was afraid of heights and uncertain he could survive in the wilderness for such long periods of time. Privately, though, Land began wondering if maybe he could put aside his fears and live in the canopy of the majestic trees.

Shortly afterward, Land picked up a hitchhiker needing a ride to the adjacent town of Eureka. He soon discovered his travel companion was a tree-sitter, and Land asked him questions about the philosophy and genesis of the tree-sit movement. The veteran activist explained that, for generations, the Pacific Lumber Company had operated under a sustained-yield plan, which meant that they could never cut more than the forest renewed annually. It had also followed a policy of no clear-cuts, which ensured sustainable quality timber and reliable jobs with the company. Then, in 1985, Texas-based Maxxam Corporation acquired the previous landlord, Pacific Lumber, and financed the takeover with high-yield junk bonds. The new CEO, Charles Hurwitz, inherited roughly 70 percent of the remaining old redwoods in private hands and emerged as a veritable Darth Vader for the tree-sitters.[9] Hurwitz broke up the company, liquidated its assets, and replaced workers' pension funds with an annuity from a subpar insurance carrier. Evoking the ire of environmentalists, Hurwitz also aggressively pursued a profit-driven business model by tripling the annual amount of timber harvested from the company's holdings. A cadre of infuriated environmentalists responded by taking their protests off the streets and into the canopies of trees. These tree-sitters regarded Hurwitz's attempt to cut the largest remaining block of old growth on private land, known as the Headwaters Forest, as deliberate ecocide.[10]

The hitchhiker told Land that tree-sitting is occasionally employed as a long-term resistance strategy—with activists occupying trees for years at a time—and, at other times, tree-sitting is a short-term stalling tactic to prevent logging while lawyers fight protracted court trials to secure long-term victories. Tree-sitters, he related, were routinely fined for trespassing on private land, for violating closure orders or camping limits, or for erecting illegal structures. By bearing these formidable risks and making the loggers' job more difficult, tree-sitters often dissuaded logging companies from cutting ancient old growth forest for months at a time.

Pacific Lumber, for its part, blamed environmentalists for dogmatically pursuing an environmental agenda that decreased production and forced the company to lay off workers in an already depressed local economy. Tom Herman, a former resource manager of Pacific Lumber, later told NPR that Hurwitz simply took a moribund company and did what every other California timber company had done decades earlier. "You know, we [are] a corporation, and the corporation [is] set up to grow and harvest trees to make money," said Herman. "So I'm not ashamed to say, 'Yeah, that's our motivation.'"[11] Loggers frequently denounced the violent tactics of pioneering tree sitters who, in the 1980s, spiked trees with nails and sprayed latrine-drips in their direction. Calling the activists "environmental terrorists," company officials condemned tree-sitters for trying to superimpose their concept of sustainable logging on a private company.

\- ∎ ∎

After getting laid off from his brewery job in October 2004, Land decided to join the tree-sitters for a week. Organizers trained Land on how to safely scale the redwoods by fastening climbing ropes, tying sturdy knots, and utilizing protective gear. Land learned how to distinguish between sturdy climbing branches—the thick, strong, and living ones covered in leatherleaf ferns—from the weak, brittle, and decaying ones.

Yet Land felt uncertain about his commitment to the tree-sit movement, especially after witnessing activists strewing empty beer cans and marijuana butts on the forest floor. The night after he arrived, Land decided he would rather admire the beauty of the redwoods from afar than join the movement. So Land set off for Arcata on foot, hauling his six-pound backpack in the near darkness and following the stars for direction. After walking over five miles uphill, Land grew exhausted and stopped at the side of the road. It was there, he insists, that he saw the distinct shadow of an ancient redwood, though no redwood was in sight. Land said he swiveled around, trying to determine if the moonlight had silhouetted a tree from behind. He said he also rubbed his eyes to make sure he was not hallucinating. "Then I heard God talking to me," Land solemnly explained. "I heard Him say that He wanted me to return to the forest."

According to Land, the barely audible voice gave him seven days to sell his worldly possessions and relocate to the forest permanently. "I didn't want to return, but I was scared, so I sold all my possessions—including five hundred DVDs—and bought camping gear, hiking boots, climbing ropes, woolen thermals, and a waterproof tent," said Land. Most tree-sitters joined the movement out of a desire to protect the redwoods; instead, Land says he joined out of a desire to connect more fully with the higher being beckoning him to the redwoods. The gangly young man remembered that God spoke in mysterious ways in the Hebrew Bible, such as through a burning bush to Moses, and decided he must heed the calling, however strange it appeared.

Although many of his fellow tree-sitters regarded his vision as a bizarre mirage, a possible result of dehydration, Land was certainly not the first Christian mystic to venture outdoors due to supernatural communion with a higher being. Saint Francis of Assisi claimed to have experienced a vision in which Christ called him to repair his church. The patron saint of ecology sold all his worldly possessions and began administering to the poor, kissing the hands of lepers, taking refuge in the natural world, and offering benedictions to flocks of birds. Saint Thomas Aquinas declared nature as the quintessential source of knowledge about God. And, in 1867, John Muir walked one thousand miles from Indiana to Florida, delighting in what he called "God's big show."

He later founded the Sierra Club and established Yosemite National Park. Devout environmentalists from Saint Augustine to John Wesley to Thomas Berry have, time and again, found God's essence in rugged cliffs, cascading waterfalls, and ornate flowers.

In more recent years, environmentalists of various religious stripes have focused their attention on preserving the world's ancient redwoods. On January 26, 1997, the Jewish "New Year of the Trees," Tu B'Shvat, 250 celebrants gathered in Humboldt County, California. After enjoying a traditional meal honoring God for blessing humans with trees, ninety people walked over a boundary line into a six-thousand-acre section of old-growth redwoods, owned by Maxxam Corporation, that were marked to be chopped down. In defiance of Maxxam's order, the protestors, wearing traditional Jewish prayer shawls, planted redwood seedlings in a denuded stream bank. These "Redwood Rabbis" had long argued that the corporation's willingness to destroy the forest violated Jewish ethics.[12] Jewish eco-theologians emphasized the Old Testament injunction "do not destroy" in Deuteronomy 20:19–20 and the Talmud's warning that those who waste are on their way to idol worship, since wasting indicates a profound loss of self-control.[13]

■ ● ■

In the autumn of 2004, Land attended an eight-hour workshop in non-violence training that prepared him for officially participating in the tree-sit movement. Organizers explained that they rotated tree-sitters, making sure someone constantly monitored loggers' activities at any given moment. They explained how a sophisticated network of grass-roots environmentalists supported tree-sitters by providing food, water, and other supplies to the redwoods' human shields. Sympathetic hikers often tied food crates and water jugs to haul lines for the tree-sitters to pull into the tree. The organizers emphasized "freecycling" and explained they acquired much of their food from local soup kitchens or Dumpster diving. Other local sympathizers supported tree-sitters with monetary donations used to pay for walkie-talkies, climbing gear, and headlamps. Organizers explained that tree-sitters were not compensated for their service in dollars and cents, but through surreal sunsets over the bay, mist rolling down the hills in the distance, and songbirds serenading them in the morning.

During the educational component of the workshop, Land learned that loggers were part of a complex web of cause and effect, a system that predicated their livelihood on the continued destruction of Fern Gully forest. As a Christian, Land appreciated the movement's distinction between the sin and the sinner as well as its efforts to engage—rather than demonize—adversaries. In a marked shift from the violent tactics used by tree-sitters in the 1980s, organizers voiced their commitment to protecting the safety of both participants and loggers attempting to extract them. During workshops, participants read the writings of Henry David Thoreau, Dr. Martin Luther King Jr., and Mahatma Gandhi. Land learned to engage loggers by maintaining eye contact, encouraging constructive conversations, and reclaiming the moral high ground by expressing genuine concern for the loggers' lives and livelihood.

During a role-play session, Land and a fellow tree-sitter alternated impersonating an irate logger to prepare for possible confrontations. Following the script, his friend yelled, "You dirty tree-hugging hippie, you're going to cost me my job!" Land responded according to his lines: "I know you think tree-sitters are trying to take away your job, but I care about you and your family's well-being. I am worried that cutting down these endangered redwoods is not the best way to remain in the logging business, and we could both benefit from sustainable logging practices. You might be surprised to learn that I'm actually pro-logging. I just don't want you to cut down the last old-growth redwoods."

During his training, Land learned that Pacific Lumber Company in Humboldt County first hired tree-sit extractors in the late 1990s. As the tree-sit movement expanded, so did the team of extractors that aimed to nip the movement in the bud. Extractors hired by private logging companies often benefited from the support of public law enforcement agents. Land learned that just the previous year—on March 17, 2003—more than thirty police enforced an illegal road closure of a public road to assist loggers in removing two longtime tree-sitters from old-growth redwoods. Land also knew that dozens of tree-sitters had been forcefully removed from the forest throughout the years and fined for trespassing, particularly in the Freshwater area east of Eureka, California.

Veteran tree-sitters said their commitment to nonviolence was unequivocal despite the loggers' history of brutality. In 1990 a mysterious pipe bomb was planted in the car of high-profile activist Judi Bari, who had organized a series of protests against clear-cutting the redwoods.

Packed with nails for shrapnel effect, the bomb shattered Bari's pelvis and almost killed the eco-activist. Nobody was ever charged with the crime. Again in 1998, David "Gypsy" Chain and other environmentalists hiked to a tract where they believed loggers were illegally constructing roads during the marbled murrelets' nesting season. They worried that the loggers' illicit activity was discouraging the endangered web-footed seabirds from nesting in the western hemlock and red huckleberry of old-growth forests. One logger, caught on videotape, cursed the activists, saying he wished he'd brought his gun. Then, he felled a redwood in their direction. The tree struck Chain in the head and killed him instantly. The logger was never charged.[14]

After learning about these incidents and overhearing that two environmental activists had been killed as recently as 2002 during a tree-sit, Land hesitated. Having always feared heights, he was terrified that a livid tree extractor might yank him out of a redwood and send him spiraling downward. Land imagined teetering on an unstable limb, losing his balance, and plummeting to his death. Despite serious doubts, however, Land remained mesmerized by the possibility of saving the last remaining redwoods. He knew tree sitting was not merely a symbolic gesture, but also a movement with a growing record of success.

— : —

The first recorded tree-sit action occurred in 1978 in New Zealand and led to the protection of what is now the Pureora Forest Park. In May 20, 1985, Mikal Jakubal launched the North American tree-sit movement by ascending a Douglas fir in an area of the Middle Santiam region of Willamette National Forest that was in the process of being clear-cut. Although Jakubal's efforts were quickly stymied, the organization Earth First endorsed his tactic and launched a group tree-sit during the summer of 1985 in Fall Creek Oregon. The team draped banners over the trees announcing "Closed: No Logging" and "Ecotopia Is Rising." During the six-year occupation, activists built a veritable tree village composed of seven houses with five occupants each; the houses were roped together with traverses 200 feet high and spanning up to 125 feet between platforms. Tree-sitters equipped this environmentally sustainable, self-sufficient tree village with composting toilets, solar and wind power, eco-friendly communication wires, individual rappel lines, hydroponic sprout farms, and cargo lines connecting support teams on the ground with tree-sitters in the canopies. From February 1998 to November 2003, more than one thousand activists occupied the trees at various times. As a direct result of the tree-sitters' Fall Creek campaign, the forest remains uncut today. .

— • —

In the autumn of 2004, Land tied a Prusik cord to his climbing harness and another cord with a webbing loop to each of his feet. As if learning to walk anew, he slowly but steadily scaled the trunk of a redwood. Land rested on a tarp-covered platform roped to a thick branch about fifty feet above the forest floor and then continued upward until reaching a doughnut-shaped platform where fellow tree-sitters gathered to play music, share stories, and cook on a communal fifteen-dollar Coleman propane stove. They offered Land some boiled mushrooms, wild chard, and stinging nettle, which he gratefully accepted. When Land bashfully mentioned he needed use the toilet, a veteran tree-sitter laughed and passed him an empty milk jug.

That evening, nestled in the embrace of the majestic tree, Land felt completely at peace. Then, in the middle of the night, a windstorm nearly knocked him from the tree and shattered his romanticized ideas of nesting in a redwood. Unable to grab his safety harness, Land began panicking. In desperation, he closed his eyes, sang every hymn he knew, and told himself his fears were evil spirits he must cast away. Land also remembered Hill's message in *Legacy of Luna*: she survived an El Niño storm not by resisting the wind, but by mimicking the behavior of the tree's sturdiest branches. Hill knew that branches that broke were the ones that stubbornly resisted the changing winds, whereas the ones that survived were those that swayed and bended with the storm. Land stopped hyperventilating, relaxed his body, and patiently waited for the turbulent clouds to pass. Deciding God was testing his resolve, Land remembered the words of Isaiah 58:14: if you delight God, he's going to put you in a high place. He spent the rest of the weekend reading the Bible, writing in his journal, and playing with yellow-cheeked chipmunks while contemplating how to lead a meaningful life. The weekend retreat seamlessly merged into a weeklong trip. Land came to understand what Anne Frank must have meant when she wrote, "The best remedy for those who are afraid, lonely, or unhappy is to go outside, somewhere where they can be quite alone with the heavens, nature, and God."[15]

■ ■ ■

Land's faith was enriched by the fellow tree-sitters he met who came from beyond the Judeo-Christian belief systems he was familiar with, from Wiccan, Buddhist, and Native American religious traditions. One such tree-sitter, Tai Chi, explained to Land that Buddhists did not share the Judeo-Christian notion of nature as God's creation and environmentalism as humans' obligation to a higher deity. Tai Chi noted that the conquest of nature makes us profoundly dissatisfied with life, according to Buddhist beliefs, which locate human misery in the desire to possess and consume. Ecologically minded Buddhists focus on how environmental degradation negatively impacts spiritual health. Tai Chi told Land that he aspired to apply essential Buddhist tenets of mindfulness and interdependence to the ecological crisis.

While living in the redwoods, Land also acquired a deeper appreciation for Native American traditions that stressed the symbiotic relationship among all living creatures. He continued consulting the Bible for guidance, but he came to regard the Earth itself as an ancillary Holy Book. While the Bible stressed caring for God's creations, the Earth showed Land the practicality of such an edict: disrespect for the rivers and animals was foolish because he needed water to drink and animals for companionship. While Christianity stressed heavenly salvation, Land learned from Native friends that honoring Mother Earth provided a type of salvation in itself. One of the tree-sitters, Whisper, told Land that Natives who over-hunted buffalo in the past were left struggling to survive; their only salvation was to restore respect for Mother Earth. He came to better appreciate the Native American proverb, "Treat the earth well: it was not given to you by your parents, it was loaned to you by your children." Land spent many happy hours balancing on his redwood's sinewy limbs reading books on indigenous worldviews that expressed the intimate relationship of the individual person, her native society, and the larger community of life—including nature and animals.

Although Land never abandoned his deep Christian beliefs, he found Native traditions' emphasis on the interconnectivity of all life compatible with his own spiritual development. He eventually came to agree with Reverend Rich Cizik, who once famously declared, "I don't think God is going to ask us how He created the earth, but He will ask us what we did with what He created."[16]

— • —

Leafing through the Bible, Land found countless references that echoed the secular ethos motivating tree-sitters: protecting the common good, preserving a delicate ecosystem, and respecting all critters no matter how big or small. Land's slowly evolving understanding of "ecojustice"— a prophetic vision of a social order in which both nature and people are treated respectfully and lovingly—seemed indistinguishable from the vision of Earth First, a secular nonprofit that helped organize tree-sits.

Slowly, Land formed his own connections between a life of senseless consumption and environmental degradation that had led to a feeling of spiritual decay. For much of Land's life, religion had been an abstraction, a family obligation that involved saying grace before meals and attending church on Sunday mornings. The God of his youth was angry and domineering, demanding allegiance and shunning difference. Land was taught that God's command to Adam in Genesis 1:28—"Fill the earth and master it"—was a divine license to dominate the Earth however man saw fit.

Only after Land began his independent religious inquiry did he come to reinterpret the creation story as God endowing the Earth to humans as a sacred gift in need of protection. But Land's father had little tolerance for hippie idealism and chastised his son for wasting his life. A church-going pipe fitter in Michigan, Land's father viewed environmentalism in much the same light as the conservative pundit Ann Coulter:

The ethic of conservation is the explicit abnegation of man's dominion over the Earth. The lower species are here for our use. God said so: Go forth, be fruitful, multiply, and rape the planet—it's yours. That's our job: drilling, mining, and stripping. . . . Big gas-guzzling cars with phones and CD players and wet bars—that's the Biblical view.[17]

Land, struggling to explain his dedication to the redwoods, told his father that he understood the Bible to instruct people to behave as good stewards of the Earth. Quoting Leviticus 25:23, Land told his father the Earth does not belong permanently to its human inhabitants, but is on loan: *The land must not be sold permanently, because the land is mine and you are but aliens and my tenants.* Land's father dismissed his son's "holier than thou" attitude, told him to get a job, and abruptly ended the conversation.

Hurt by his father's dismissive attitude, Land reminded himself that God's people were the "radicals" of their times and were often misunderstood by their families and peers. According to Land, Jesus urged his followers to live by a different set of rules altogether and hold themselves apart as peculiar people.

— • —

Land spent two entire years living in a redwood he named "Libertall" and survived primarily on a diet of tofu, quinoa, nuts, and berries. While living in Fern Gully forest, the lonely mystic came to attribute to the towering redwood all the qualities he had hoped to find in friends while growing up as a socially awkward teenager in suburban Michigan. He regarded the tree as a constant companion, patient listener, and trusty confidant. Endowing Libertall with feminine qualities, Land saw himself as her brave protector, often whispering to her that he would not forsake her in her hour of need. The idea of a logger felling his majestic beauty brought tears to Land's eyes. To him, it was as if the logger's chainsaw would spew not sawdust, but blood.

Land says that he prayed one day for a Bible and it miraculously appeared. Evangelists did routinely place Bibles at the bases of trees, but it is more likely they hoped activists would spend less time protecting trees and more time saving souls. Spending entire days in solitude, Land immersed himself in the Bible, seeing divine signs in every obscure sentence. Psalm 24:1—*the Earth is the Lord's*—convinced Land of the righteousness of his cause. The young Baptist nodded emphatically while rereading Deuteronomy 20:19 and its proscription against axing down trees. He came to cast himself in the tradition of Biblical prophets who warned against excessively exploiting the earth: *Woe unto them that join house to house, that lay field to field, till there be no place, that they may be placed alone in the midst of the earth* (Isaiah 5:8). Land concluded all trees needed protection—*for as the days of a tree, so will be the days of my people; my chosen ones will long enjoy the works of their hand* (Isaiah 65:22). Land saw himself aligned with the angels who had advised God to *destroy those who destroy the earth* (Revelations 11:18), but vowed to nonviolently "destroy" people's ability to deface God's artwork through civil disobedience because he understood the message of the Gospel—when read as a whole rather than in snippets—as one of compassion for adversaries. Desperate to find meaning in life and not fade into the ordinary masses, Land stylized himself as God's peaceful warrior on a crusade against loggers.

Many of Land's fellow tree-sitters regarded him as a religious zealot and wondered why he needed to justify his commitment to Fern Gully forest by parsing through dry text written by dead men instead of simply protecting the redwoods out of concern for the environment. Yet, they came to regard Land fondly since he posed no threat, rarely proselytized, and contributed productively to the movement. He helped equip the redwoods with a rain-catch system, which transported water 40 feet down to a running tap at the platform, and he installed a solar panel at 207 feet in a tree named Watsi.

Land's calm and reasoned suggestions resonated with his comrades and helped reinforce group solidarity in the middle of the forest. Among the half-dozen tree-sitters in the village, Land emerged as a natural leader by the end of his first year. Drawing on his Christian ethos, he successfully convinced his fellow tree-sitters to broaden their understanding of nonviolence by abandoning the practices of digging trenches to trap loggers' trucks, or even hurling expletives. Whenever a veteran tree-sitter left, Land interviewed potential new recruits by inquiring about their commitment to nonviolent civil disobedience. He explained to novice tree-sitters that violence was not limited to something as extreme as punching a logger, but could be much subtler, such as harboring hostile feelings. Land believed Jesus saw nonviolence not as a tactic, but as a way of life that informed his every thought and action. Although Land happily shared his religious beliefs when friends inquired, he realized that framing environmental degradation as sacrilegious, sinful, and an offense against God jolted secular activists wary of religious conservatives who volleyed the term "sin" haphazardly.

Land encouraged new tree-sitters to tread softly, respect the forest critters, and take a holistic approach to protecting the entire forest. Observing the forest's many creatures—from its largest Roosevelt elk to its smallest wandering salamander—Land came to agree with Christian novelist C. S. Lewis that denying rights to animals merely because they lack the same level of rational thought that fully formed humans exhibit means also denying rights to the mentally handicapped, the senile, and other classes of humans.[18] The Fern Gully tree-sit soon emerged as a paragon within the wider tree-sit movement.

— • —

On February 15, 2005, Land learned that a fellow forest defender named Dorothy Stang had paid the ultimate price for protecting Brazil's rainforests and its people from illegal exploitation by logging firms and ranchers. The seventy-four-year-old American nun read passages from the Bible to her killer—a Brazilian rancher named Vitalmiro Bastos de Moura—right before he shot her six times in the head, throat, and body at close range. Prosecutors said Moura had ordered Stang's death because she blocked him and another rancher from taking over land the government had given to small farmers. Moura was convicted in April 2010 and sentenced to thirty years in prison.[19] The murder of Sister Dorothy outraged environmental and human rights activists, who say she dedicated over thirty years of her life to helping the area's landless peasants by confronting businesses responsible for plundering 20 percent of the rainforest's 1.6 million square miles.[20] When Land heard about Stang's murder, he thought, "So *that's* what Jesus was talking about."

Reminded of the dangers they faced, Land used walkie-talkies to keep in close contact with the half-dozen tree-sitters scattered across Fern Gully. Together, they spent countless days planning and rehearsing for their inevitable encounter with loggers. A few months later, the day that Land calls his "day of reckoning" arrived.

In August 2005 Land tossed and turned in his sleeping bag as light bathed Fern Gully forest. The groggy twenty-three-year-old lowered himself from the tree's canopy to the forest floor and felt tremors in the moist soil like those of an earthquake. Treading barefoot, Land ventured deeper into the forest to investigate. He noticed that the huckleberry thickets surrounding the narrow deer trail connecting the forest to the outside world had been slashed haphazardly. When Land saw a fifteen-foot road bulldozed into the heart of Fern Gully, he knew Maxxam Inc., the Houston-based lumber company plotting to level the largest remaining block of old growth redwoods, had sent tree extractors into the forest.

Afraid to leave Libertall unattended lest loggers descend in the thick of night, Land quickly returned to his perch. He slept fitfully that night, fearing even the slightest creak or groan was a prelude to whirring chain-saws. At daybreak, Land watched intense sunlight flood the damp forest floor and heard marbled murrelets frantically fluttering their wings. A baby nocturnal flying squirrel that had nestled in the bottom of Land's sleeping bag surfaced for air, her beady eyes darting questioningly. Rubbing the sleep from his own eyes, Land crouched on his five-by-five perch constructed from recycled plywood and fastened to one of Libertall's sturdy branches approximately 180 feet off the ground. He turned to his favorite Biblical passage, Psalms 1:3, and reread it while waiting for loggers to descend: *And he shall be like a tree planted by the rivers of water, that bringeth forth his fruit in his season; his leaf also shall not wither; and whatsoever he doeth shall prosper.*

Aware that loggers would soon locate his hideout, he used climbing ropes to lower himself into his dream catcher—a hammock-style bed that he fashioned from a net of nylon parachute cords woven through the hefty branches of the five-hundred-year-old redwood he called home. Now, with a clear view of the forest floor, Land saw he had a visitor waiting for him at Libertall's base.

"Hello," hollered Land.

"Hello, young man," said the heavyset man with peppered hair.

"How are you, Sir?"

"Do you know who I am?"

"No, Sir."

"I'm Richard Bettes, head of Maxxam security."

After a long pause, Land inquired, "What did you have for breakfast, Sir?"

"Bacon and eggs. You know, I'm watching my figure."

"Would you like some coffee?"

"Coffee? No, we know what you hippies are up to."

"Excuse me, Sir?"

"We know all about your tricks. We know how you keep jugs full of urine and buckets full or excrement just for occasions like this."

"Sir, I know some past tree-sitters have done horrible things, but I'm a Christian and I believe in nonviolence. Even if you were my worst enemy, I would never mix urine in your coffee."

"Young man, do you know you're trespassing?"

"Sir, you don't own these trees because these trees belong to God."

"We're tired of the games y'all play and we're going to call in the federal marshals once and for all. What do you think about that?"

"Well, Sir, I must admit that doesn't sound too great . . . but I'm willing to risk my life to protect God's last remaining redwoods, and federal marshals don't scare me."

"I'll be back soon, and when I return, I hope you're out of that tree."

"Sir, I know what I'm doing is illegal, but please think about what you're doing. If you're saying you want to come out here and cut one or two trees that's OK, but if you're saying you want to come out here and destroy everything, then no, you may not—"

"I'll be back soon," interrupted Bettes. "I'm going to pay a visit to your friends on the other side of the forest."

Bettes bushwhacked his way around Libertall and disappeared as suddenly as he had appeared. Standing in the center of his dream catcher, Land rested his palms—calloused from scaling the redwood—at Libertall's ruddy trunk and hugged her with his sinewy arms as if she were a damsel in distress.

Soon, Bettes would return with an arborist who would attempt to yank Land down to earth and a logger who would try to quickly chop down Libertall before the tree-sit movement had a chance to deploy a new human shield. Land felt as calm as silent water despite knowing the decision he now had to make could determine whether he and Libertall survived. Although Land was prepared to sacrifice his own life to protect the tree, he did not aspire to martyrdom. He brainstormed ways to protect himself against the loggers while not betraying the tree he increasingly regarded as his friend, confidant, and even lover.

- ∎ -

During the eight-hour workshop Land attended before joining the tree-sit movement, he memorized several nonviolent strategies to deter loggers. Now, with the loggers rapidly approaching, one strategy Land considered was tying his body to Libertall with heavy chains, but he knew loggers often carried saws to break these defenses. He considered another strategy that involved precariously balancing his body at the tip of Libertall to create an uneven weight distribution, but he knew an arborist could use a rope as a lasso and yank him down. After praying for guidance, Land hoisted his climb line, bucket of food, gallon of water, sleeping bag, camcorder, and Bible to the traverse connecting Libertall to her neighboring redwood. Earlier, Land and another tree-sitter had created a system of wooden bridges connecting thirty-three of the nearby redwoods, including Libertall. Chopping one could potentially cause all of them to collapse in a domino effect; therefore, they had created a conundrum for the loggers. By standing on the traverses, the tree-sitters dissuaded loggers from axing any single tree in fear of chaotically felling all the trees simultaneously and endangering themselves.

Land ventured thirty feet out onto the 150-foot-high traverse and waited, his finger on the camcorder's record button. He intended to film his encounter with the arborist and the loggers in case they recklessly endangered his life and later conveniently attributed his death to suicide. Waiting for the loggers, Land used his walkie-talkie to warn the remaining tree-sitters at the other end of the three-acre Fern Gully forest about Bettes's imminent return. Their static-laden voices warbled back a confirmation. The tree-sitters informed Land that they, too, had ventured onto the traverses connecting the trees. If the loggers chose to cut the intertwined traverses, they would be deliberately killing the tree-sitters.

Land remained in communication with the tree-sitters and reviewed what they had learned in their tree-sit workshop a year earlier: nonviolent communication helps transform alleged enemies into partners in a common enterprise. Inspired by his Christian faith, Land encouraged the tree-sitters not to resort to hatred but instead extend compassion to their adversaries. He reminded them that nonviolent civil disobedience challenges the cyclical nature of violence, allows people to redeem their self-respect, and transforms relations between conflicting parties in a way that makes "peace with justice" more feasible and sustainable. Land concluded with a silent prayer that God would give the tree-sitters courage to follow their convictions.

An hour later, a tree-sitter who went by the nickname "Shag" announced to Land via walkie-talkie that loggers had arrived on the other end of Fern Gully. Praying silently, Land waited and listened. Moments later, Shag informed him that the loggers were slashing the ropes of their dream catchers and tree platforms. Hearing wood and metal crash hundreds of feet downward, Land cringed. He feared the loggers were irreparably damaging the delicate forest floor.

Shag's voice emanated from the walkie-talkie loudly but calmly as he addressed the loggers: "I don't mean to be rude, but we spent a lot of time building this eco-village and keeping the forest clean. If you must cut our platforms, could you please lower them gently?"

Silence ensued.

The next thing Land heard was an excited whisper: "I think the loggers heard us because they're lowering the platforms with ropes now."

Half an hour passed in silence. Then Land heard a logger try to coax Shag and the other tree-sitters off the traverse. The tree-sitters politely refused. Shag told Land they were playing a waiting game with the logger. Two more hours passed, but nobody budged.

Over the walkie-talkie, Land heard Shag grumble to another tree-sitter, "Man, I'm hungry." Then, to Land's amusement, he heard Shag exclaim, "Aw, thanks, I can't believe I caught that!" A logger had tossed Shag an apple.

In the late afternoon, Land heard his earthen utensils and bowls crashing to the ground. An arborist had discovered his dream catcher at eighty feet and destroyed everything, including the delicate sorrel and sword ferns at the base of his tree. Then, to Land's surprise, the arborist rappelled back down. Land realized his second hideout, the platform at 180 feet, remained undetected.

On the tree adjacent to Libertall, another arborist appeared at the foot of the traverse. Land greeted him and offered the arborist a cup of soy milk. The arborist politely declined and locked eyes with Land. Remembering what he learned in the tree-sit workshop, Land held the logger's line of sight without flinching. In the heart of Fern Gully forest, the two men precariously balanced in the redwood canopy and waited to see who would make the next move.

Breaking the silence, Land introduced himself.

"I'm Land; nice to meet you!" he hollered.

The logger returned the greeting and flashed a smile. "Say, could I convince you come off that traverse for a moment?"

Land laughed good-humoredly. "No, Sir, I'm afraid not."

The logger nodded. "All right. Well, just so you know, I'm not going to cut your traverse . . . but, I was just wondering, what type of knot did you tie?"

Stranded on the 150-foot high traverse, Land feared the logger might inadvertently kill him if he tampered with the knot. He paused.

"Well," said Land as calmly as if he were discussing a crossword puzzle with a stranger he had just met at a coffee shop, "that's a rewoven figure-eight knot around the tree trunk, and it's backed up by twelve half hitches and a barrel knot."

The arborist scratched his head and nodded. "Interesting. I see from the warning you put at the base of the tree that cutting any of these redwoods would make all of them collapse because of the traverses, right?"

"Yes, we had a friend in the movement acquire the timber harvest plan. She helped us determine the best strategy for protecting the last remaining redwoods."

"How did you get a copy of the timber harvest plan?"

"Oh, it's really simple, the plan was submitted for approval to the California Department of Forestry and we filed for access under the Freedom of Information Act."

"So you kids really know what you're doing, huh?"

"Well, we're determined to save the last swath of old-growth redwoods."

Land and the arborist spoke for twenty minutes across the traverse in a conversation marked by mutual respect. Land explained the tree-sitters' devotion to protecting the last ancient stretch of redwoods. He noted that clear-cutting the redwoods would remove the vegetative matter that holds the ground in place and absorbs the heavy seasonal rains. Land explained that clear-cutting would also wash out the formerly rich forest alluvium into Freshwater Creek, a creek that was already struggling to host its native salmon population and that was categorized as an impaired waterway under the Clean Water Act. Land also noted that destabilizing the slope where Fern Gully sat would pose a risk of landslides for the homes and elementary school below.

When Land stated that he wasn't against logging, the arborist scoffed in disbelief. Land reiterated his support of loggers, insisting he only disapproved of company practices that contributed to the disappearance of the old-growth forest. Land told the arborist that corporations such as Maxxam were contributing to the destruction of the remaining coastal redwoods, Douglas fir, and Sitka spruce. If these trees vanished, explained Land, so would endangered spotted owls and marbled murrelets. He told the logger about the year he had spent in the canopy of the trees observing the delicate equilibrium of insects, arachnids, mosses, lichens, and animals. Land shared his fears with the arborist that this ecosystem, which had existed for millennia, would disappear overnight if corporations such as Maxxam had their way.

The arborist listened attentively. "I respect that, kid," he said, heaving loudly. "I respect that you know what you're doing, but I have a job to keep and a family to feed."

Land assured the arborist that he understood his difficult position. This surprised the arborist, who had long resented self-righteous tree-sitters for demonizing loggers. Land said he would not have joined the tree-sit movement if it were not compatible with his religious principles, and he vocally lamented the vitriol spewed by past activists who were not organized under a nonviolent ideology at the time. Land told the arborist that contemporary tree-sitters aspired to catalyze political change by demonstrating the same honesty, compassion, and courage as Martin Luther King Jr. and Gandhi. The arborist laughed, "You got high hopes, kid."

Realizing that Land had no intention of venturing off the traverse, the arborist decided to leave: "Have it your way, kid, but I can't promise corporate won't send someone else up here soon." On his descent, the arborist heeded Land's request to lower his tree-sit platform gently rather than dislodge it with one violent swoop, as was customary, so it did not damage the forest ecosystem below.

When the arborist left, Land realized his second dream catcher was still intact and Libertall remained unscathed. He was almost certain the arborist had seen both dream catchers and was confused as to why he had not destroyed the second one.

Land concluded that, by some small miracle, the arborist had deliberately chosen to disobey corporate orders. He was elated at the thought of having changed the mind of his so-called adversary by staying true to the principles of his faith.

— ◦ —

Land was the only tree-sitter who still had a dream catcher, and he remained in Fern Gully forest even after the loggers left. Shag and the other tree-sitters retired from the forest, as their homes and supplies had been destroyed. Land decided to remain among the redwoods, spurred by his profound sense of duty toward Libertall, until the movement replenished Fern Gully with new recruits. Land did not blame the other tree-sitters for feeling exhausted after a year in the forest; however, he felt buoyed by his faith and peaceful with his decision to remain.

Three days later, Land was violently woken from his slumber by the sound of machinery. He scaled down Libertall's trunk and perched on her lowest branch, from which he witnessed massive metal plates swooshing back and forth like guillotine blades swinging in opposite directions. The machine methodically tore up the recently plowed dirt road that bisected Fern Gully and would have allowed caterpillar tractors and Maxxam loggers to access the redwoods. That evening, Land descended from Libertall to survey the damage. The machine had lacerated the forest floor and left ripples of dirt five feet deep. Land's ankles sank into the brackish, ruddy water as he treaded barefoot past heaps of burgundy-colored soil towering above his head. When Land informed others in the movement of what had happened, they explained Maxxam was probably "winterizing" the road in anticipation of coming rain. Land breathed a sigh of relief. He knew the loggers could not access the forest without a smooth road and, despite the destruction wreaked on the forest floor, he felt the redwoods were safer than before.

Drawing strength from Colossians 1:16—*For by Him all things were created: things in heaven and on earth*—Land remained in the forest for another year. He continued to care for God's creation and remained committed to protecting his forest friends. Spiritually at peace, the tree-sitter felt revitalized each day Libertall remained standing.

Land realized the Bible is open to interpretation but decided there is only one true message that is communicated when read in its entirety: have respect for all God's creations. The more Land read the Bible, the more he came to believe that following the words of Jesus would lead to an overnight revolution. According to Land, that revolution would put environmental protection above corporate profit. Whenever secular tree-sitters pointed out that right-wing Christians had stymied efforts to curb global warming, Land nodded sadly in agreement before adding that countless secular groups, such as the Advancement of Sound Science Coalition, were also waging a war on science—their leader was not God, but Philip Morris, and their constituents were not churchgoers, but Exxon Mobil.[21]

- ■ -

The twenty-year-long campaign to save the redwoods of Fern Gully forest—spearheaded by Julia Butterfly Hill and sustained by Joseph Land—won a major victory on July 29, 2008. A US bankruptcy judge filed a final order paving the way for Mendocino Redwood Company (MRC) to wrest control of the Pacific Lumber Company in Humboldt County, California, from Maxxam, Inc., of Texas. The president and chief forester of MRC, Mike Jani, assured the activists that, under his company's policies, the trees would not be axed. Shortly afterward, "Do Not Cut" flagging marked the surviving redwoods, including Hill's Luna and Land's Libertall. Jani publicly promised to revive the practice of selective cutting, never cutting more than 70 percent of a stand of timber or cutting more from its forests than would grow in a year. According to *National Geographic*, the company has already implemented this approach on 230,000 acres of heavily logged redwood forest in Mendocino County. MRC also stabilized logging roads, reestablished sustainable standards, and made a practice of limiting cutting quotas to only a half of the overall volume of timber grown on its property each year through a variety of selection techniques. By doing this, the company heeded the tree-sitters' request to sacrifice greater short-term profits for long-term investment in the forest.[22]

Land rejoiced upon learning that MRC accepted the tree-sitters' terms, but he did not wish to leave Libertall or stop reading environmental tracts to nocturnal flying squirrels. Yet history has shown that nature rarely treats its sentimental lovers kindly: In April 1992 a twenty-four-year-old idealist named Chris McCandless gave up everything—including his trust fund and ties to a seemingly stable family—to trek across Alaska's barren wilderness; four months later, a moose hunter discovered his decomposed body. In October 2003 a grizzly bear enthusiast named Timothy Treadwell videotaped his professions of love for wild animals before a bear devoured him alive. That same month, a seven-year-old male tiger named Montecore bit the neck of his trainer, Roy Horn of Siegfried & Roy. In September 2006 the Australian conservationist Steve Irwin was fatally pierced through the chest by a stingray while filming in the Great Barrier Reef. And Land was ultimately forced to vacate Libertall after developing painful kidney stones that required immediate medical attention. After spending two years residing in the canopy of a redwood that he regarded as his forest princess, Land explained somewhat sheepishly, "She kicked me out."

- ▪ -

Even today, it remains unclear why a steering wheel lodged in the skull of a young woman or the silhouette of an phantom redwood compelled two environmentalists to spend years living in the canopies of towering redwoods. "The question is not whether God exists," the journalist Chris Hedges writes in *I Don't Believe in Atheists*. "It is whether we contemplate or are utterly indifferent to the transcendent, that which cannot be measured or quantified, that which lies beyond the reach of rational deduction. We all encounter this aspect of existence, in love, beauty, alienation, loneliness, suffering, good, evil and the reality of death."[23]

While some may look upon the redwoods and see Earth Mother or God's artwork or aesthetic evolution, others see only valuable timber for the commercial market. Both Hill and Land experienced something indescribably divine and exquisite in the presence of these ancient trees, something they wished to preserve for posterity. It might be that they briefly encountered the spiritual world, or perhaps they imagined voices and visions where none existed. Perhaps they hoped that climbing the trees would bring them closer to the celestial heavens, or hoped preserving the trees would allow future generations to experience a sliver of heaven here on earth. In the end, though, Hill's and Land's reasons for taking up residence in primeval redwoods are, perhaps, no more unclear than the reasons that generation after generation of Americans—from the earliest native tribes to contemporary environmental activists—have marveled at these stately trees and experienced an unprecedented sense of grace and serenity in their midst.

8 SUEZANN BOSLER

Modern-Day Abolitionists Against the Death Penalty

O, vengeance!
Why, what an ass am I! This is most brave,
That I, the son of a dear father murdered
Prompted to my revenge by heaven and hell
Must like a whore unpack my heart with words,
and fall a-cursing like a very drab.
A scullion! Fie upon't! Foh!
— HAMLET, ACT II, SCENE II

The role of the religious community is to reconcile what seems irreconcilable: love for death row inmates and their human dignity and love for murder victims and their dignity and compassion for the hurt of their family members. Our spiritual energy can unite and combine what ideology alone can never bring together.
— SISTER HELEN PREJEAN, author of *Dead Man Walking*

On December 22, 1986, SueZann Bosler was getting ready to wrap Christmas presents she'd purchased at the Swap Shop, a large flea market in Fort Lauderdale, Florida. The petite twenty-four-year-old hairdresser with shoulder-length, chestnut-brown hair had just stepped out of her shower when she heard the doorbell ring. Bosler was accustomed to unannounced guests stopping by her family's modest, pastel-pink First Church of the Brethren parsonage in Opa-locka, Florida. Parishioners visited her father at all hours of the day seeking food, shelter, clothing, and spiritual guidance.[1]

Family friends often wondered why SueZann's father, fifty-three-year-old Reverend Billy Bosler, chose to work in the low-income, high-crime suburb where gunshot blasts and ambulance sirens constantly pierced the night silence. The reverend, sharing his grandfather's devotion to principles of simplicity and pacifism, explained plainly, "These are God's people and I love them. We Christians must show God's acceptance, not just talk about it."[2] Reverend Bosler had led a peripatetic life ministering to the poor; however, he decided to settle down after relocating his family from western Michigan to Opa-locka in 1978. Despite frequent robberies at the church and perpetual scuffles on its doorsteps, the toothy-grinned reverend assured parishioners: "There is no place I'd rather be! I plan to be here till the Lord calls me elsewhere."[3]

On the afternoon of December 22, moments after Reverend Bosler opened the door, SueZann heard a series of guttural groans followed by a sickening thud. Racing to investigate, she found an intruder stabbing her father. SueZann screamed and ran toward them, flailing her arms at the hulking assailant. Her father collapsed on the floor and the assailant redirected his wrath at her. SueZann turned to flee, but the intruder gouged his knife into her back three times and three more into the side of her head. He continued until she crumpled onto the floor, stabbing her with such malice that he chipped the tiles under her body. When he finally stopped and proceeded to ransack the parsonage, SueZann held her breath and feigned death. Darkness descended as warm blood trickled down her face and coagulated on her eyelids.

When the man finally left, SueZann forced herself to find a phone, dial 911, and give the dispatcher her address before blacking out completely. Detective Hank Ray Jr. later testified that he had never seen a crime scene as gruesome as the Bosler's blood-splattered home.[4] Viscous streams of fresh blood ran from the living room's lime-green carpet to the terrazzo patio floor.

After a helicopter med-evacuated SueZann to Jackson Memorial Hospital, emergency ward personnel spent the remainder of the day fighting to save her life. They removed hundreds of pieces of shattered bone, the entire left side of her skull, and two pieces of her brain. Each time SueZann regained consciousness she asked about her father, but no one dared tell her that Reverend Bosler had died before the ambulance even arrived.

The coroner's report revealed that Reverend Bosler sustained no fewer than twenty-four stab wounds before dying. A particularly fierce blow to his stomach penetrated five-and-a-half inches and perforated his lower three ribs, puncturing his liver and flooding blood into his right chest cavity. Another fatal blow had punctured the left lobe of his lung and likewise inundated his left chest cavity.[5]

Three days later—on Christmas morning—SueZann fully regained consciousness. Doctors explained that she would need to wear a plastic cap with padding on her head for the next eight months to protect her scarred brain tissue. She was instructed to sleep with her head propped at a 90-degree angle to prevent swelling. While SueZann accepted her weakened physical condition, she could not fathom what she heard next: her father was dead. Ripping medical tubes out of her body and being restrained by the ICU nurses, she screamed that she no longer wanted to live.

■ ∙ ■

Bosler spent a month hospitalized under constant supervision, and doctors informed her mother that she might need a live-in caretaker for the rest of her life. Once discharged, Bosler and her mother rented a studio apartment near the hospital so her intensive physical, occupational, and speech therapy could continue, as could her routine neurological and psychological examinations. Since Bosler was without health insurance, her congregation established a fund on her behalf and raised enough money to cover one-third of her mounting medical bills.

For the next year and a half, Bosler sleepwalked through a life that no longer felt worth living. The once perky and talkative young woman now struggled to find simple words to express her feelings, words that seemed to float through her head just beyond the grasp of her tongue. Sometimes, in the middle of a conversation, Bosler would struggle to remember a simple word and grow so frustrated that she stopped talking altogether. Other times, she had trouble remembering what had happened a few hours earlier since her medication impaired her short-term memory. However, the details of her father's murder remained painfully clear. Bosler remembered her father's contorted face as he lay on the ground, struggling to inhale air that stopped short of his punctured lungs. She remembered hearing her keys clatter on the kitchen tiles as the short, stocky intruder emptied her purse. She remembered watching the intruder wrap his wounded hand with floral linens he'd stripped from her parents' bed before dashing out of the parish.

The loss of her father remained with her like a phantom limb, and she spent evenings leafing through old family albums showcasing photos of birthday parties and church socials. Bosler struggled to remember the smallest details about her father, from the crow's-feet at the corners of his eyes to the way his chin protruded slightly. As the days seamlessly merged into weeks and then months, the young woman gradually regained her speech and motor facilities well enough to live independently, but she frequently experienced debilitating panic attacks.

— ▪ —

In 1987 Bosler found a reason to live from the most unexpected of sources. James Bernard Campbell, the twenty-year-old gardener who had viciously attacked Bosler's father, faced capital punishment despite the late Reverend Bosler's outspoken opposition to the death penalty. Growing up, Bosler had often discussed the death penalty with her father, specifically his religious opposition to what he called state-sanctioned murder. Influenced by the Church of the Brethren, a historic peace church, Reverend Bosler explained to his daughter that only God should determine when someone must die, and he often structured his sermons around Jesus's commandment to love their enemies.

As a child, Bosler had accepted her father's religious opposition to the death penalty because the issue seemed uncomplicated in the abstract. Now, she couldn't help wondering if society would benefit from one less killer on the prowl. Bosler did not have an ounce of compassion for the heavyset man who had murdered her father for all of thirty-one dollars. She fantasized about locking him in a room and pummeling him with a baseball bat, or even using her bare fists to punch out each of his gold teeth. Bosler knew killing Campbell would not bring her father back, but she wondered if it would bring her some comfort or closure.

In calmer moments, Bosler was ashamed of her lust for revenge—not because she cared an iota about Campbell, but because she feared his execution would profane the memory of her father. Reverend Bosler had clearly explained his opposition to the death penalty to his daughter: "Why kill people who kill people to show us that killing is wrong?" In church, Bosler often referred to the Sermon on the Mount, in which Jesus advocated transcending the endless cycle of violence—morally corrosive to both victim and aggressor—by extending compassion to adversaries.

Tormented by her indecision and lonelier than ever, Bosler prayed for guidance and began asking herself the same question her father once asked himself in moments of doubt: "What would Jesus do?" Bosler decided that she knew the answer when she reread Mathew 5:38: *You have heard that it was said, "an eye for an eye and a tooth for a tooth." But I say to you, do not set yourself in violent or revengeful resistance against an evildoer. But if any one strikes you on the right cheek, turn the other also.* She spent several more weeks trying to convince herself that the Biblical injunction directly applied to her own life. Finally, she decided that if she really believed in the New Testament message of love, hope, and compassion for the outcast, indigent, and prisoner, she must speak out in favor of preserving Campbell's life.

By late 1987, as the state prepared to execute Campbell, Bosler began organizing a massive campaign to spare the life of her father's murderer. She asked members of her family's congregation to flood Judge Alfonso Sepe with letters explaining the community's long-standing religious opposition to the death penalty. They noted that Christianity emphasizes the mercy of God—"Be ye merciful, even as your Father is merciful" (Luke 6:36); they advised against begrudging wrongdoers (Matthew 5:21 ff); and they explained they sought peace with those who wished them harm (Matthew 5:21 ff). They begged the judge to honor the late reverend's wishes by showing mercy to his killer.

As Christians, they realized that parts of the Bible seemed to advocate capital punishment, especially Genesis 9:4–6, which unequivocally states: *Whoever sheds the blood of man, by man shall his blood be shed; for God made man in his own image.* However, as the late reverend's congregants explained to the judge, they believed the Prince of Peace had rendered anachronistic the mentality of "an eye for an eye" by teaching that only she without sin should cast the first stone. They pleaded with the judge to favor a God of redemption who calls his followers to be merciful.

On January 4, 1988, more than a year after SueZann Bosler's father's murder, Campbell's first trial took place, and national media descended to hear Bosler recount every terrifying detail of the day her father was murdered. But then she did something that baffled the jurors. Locking eyes with her father's killer, Bosler declared: "I believe in the value of all human life, and that includes James Bernard Campbell's." For Bosler, the verbal affirmation was as much for her benefit as for that of the vacant-eyed man sitting in front of her. She told the jury about her past conversations with her father concerning the death penalty and concluded, "It's not right to take a life, no matter what."

The jury returned with its recommendation of nine to three in favor of death. Under Florida law, the judge could either accept or reject the jury's recommendation within the following months. In the interlude, Bosler continued vocally opposing the death penalty and utilizing the media to convey her message to a broader audience. On April 13, 1988, the *Miami Herald* reported that Bosler met with a group of eleven local clergymen and shared her ongoing struggle to recognize the humanity of her would-be murderer. "I do not hate him at all," she said. "But right now I do not love him. I have not forgiven him totally. I have prayed for him. . . . I don't know everything about life and death, but I am learning more."[6] Whenever feelings of bitterness and revenge overwhelmed Bosler, she prayed, *Our Father, forgive us our trespasses as we forgive those who trespass against us.*

Staring in the mirror, Bosler instructed herself to genuinely forgive Campbell, but she felt nothing but sadness and exhaustion. She remembered that her father once gave her a heart-shaped locket with a single mustard seed inside and told her the seed would grow into a plant strong enough to move mountains. Reverend Bosler drew a parallel to the mustard seed and faith in God, saying that both were capable of accomplishing the seemingly impossible.

■ ▪ ■

While the Church of the Brethren community largely supported Bosler's faith-based opposition to the death penalty, the long-winded and slightly incoherent young woman felt increasingly defensive when explaining her views to strangers. Beyond her church community, most people believe it is not a sign of weakness when a bereaved family member seeks retribution, but a sign of strength—a sign that someone so loved the victim that he is willing to struggle at a personal cost to avenge the most immoral act imaginable: the unjustified killing of another human being.

From the earliest Greek tragedies to contemporary Hollywood block-busters, avenging a father's death is regarded as a heroic calling, if not a sacred duty. To many, the essence of being a human is that one does not seek an unattainable ideal, that one is sometimes willing to seek worldly revenge to testify to the intense love felt for a victim, and that one does not push theoretical convictions over loyalty to kin. For supporters of the death penalty, the delicate social order requires that a person who claims another's life must forsake his own life. The very fabric of a community is held together by a social contract that protects a person's rights only so long as he respects the rights of others.

The idea that a daughter would actively seek mercy for her father's killer struck even Bosler's own grandmother, eighty-three-year-old Nora Dickerson, as unnatural and upsetting. In the months between the jury's recommendation and the judge's final decision, Dickerson announced to the media that she sought the death penalty against her son's murderer and pleaded with the judge to "put [Campbell] in a position where he will never be able to do this to anyone else." For Dickerson, Bosler's decision to advocate against the death penalty was noble in the abstract, but potentially fatal in practice. She couldn't help wondering if Campbell would murder another mother's son.

The Son of God may have turned his cheek to his enemy, but Dickerson wondered why her own grieving granddaughter felt compelled to suppress a sense of hatred that was only instinctual. Dickerson, who considered herself a law-abiding American as well as a practicing Christian, interpreted Matthew 22:21—*Render therefore unto Caesar the things that are Caesar's and unto God the things that are God's*—to mean Jesus sanctioned the state authorities' prerogative to determine how to punish criminals. Pitting Old Testament retribution against New Testament forgiveness, Dickerson also noted the dozens of Biblical passages from Exodus, Leviticus, and Numbers that establish that Mosaic Law sanctions the use of capital punishment for particularly repugnant crimes.

For Dickerson and other supporters of the death penalty, the exceptionally heinous and gruesome nature of certain crimes warrants capital punishment because, they argue, the severity of the punishment lends dignity to the lives of victims by setting apart their murderers from, say, petty thieves. Dickerson feared that punishing Campbell the same way a recidivating car thief is punished would degrade the value of her son's life. She might have accepted losing her only son as "the will of God" if her son had died in an airplane crash or after sudden illness, but she could not accept losing her son due to the intentional actions of another human being. She wanted to know why the murderer should fare better than his victim. Watching Campbell pay his debt on the electric chair, she hoped, would offer her family some catharsis and closure after their years of excruciating agony. In Dickerson's mind, the law of moral proportionality—severest punishment for severest crime—required that Campbell die.

When the court reconvened in May, Judge Sepe ultimately agreed with Dickerson by upholding the jury's recommendation and sentencing Campbell to death by electric chair. Judge Sepe wrote that the defendant was capable of distinguishing between right and wrong but had an "evil mind" and that science had yet to learn how to "predict, uncover, or cure" that evil.[7] The head prosecutor, Michael Band, praised Judge Sepe's decision, told the *Miami Herald* that he had never represented a victim who wished for her would-be murderer to receive clemency, and noted that the state of Florida "cannot be as charitable as SueZann."

Exceedingly frustrated with a judicial system that paid lip service to "victims' rights" but ignored her pleas, Bosler concluded that each courtroom actor seemed predominantly interested in advancing his own career by winning the death sentence in this highly publicized case. Judge Sepe's decision and attorney Band's comments only redoubled Bosler's commitment to overturning Campbell's death sentence, and she filed an appeal.

Reading the Bible each night after the unfavorable ruling, Bosler grew increasingly certain that God would not want Campbell to die. She saw the cross as the universal symbol of mercy and believed Christ had sacrificed himself so neither she nor Campbell would have to serve the sentences they deserved as sinners but might instead have eternal life. Bosler decided that a person's religious convictions mattered most when they were tested in the crucible of life, and she continued strategizing how to get Campbell off death row.

When the Church of the Brethren asked Bosler to speak at its annual conference, Bosler used the opportunity to thank her community for the love and support they showered on her in the wake of her father's murder. She told the crowd of several hundred people that her faith kept her anchored to a world that would otherwise seem unbearably lonely and asked the audience to pray for Campbell. Bosler explained that her father's values sustained her during moments of despair and, by extending God's protection to Campbell, she kept alive her father's memory. She used the remainder of her speech to reiterate her belief that Jesus advocated mercy and repentance. She reminded congregants that the Apostle Paul directly opposed taking a life as retribution for a life in Romans 12:19, which most New Testament scholars believe echoes wider Biblical teachings against retaliation: *Beloved, never avenge yourselves, but leave it to the wrath of God.* She spoke of the Biblical episode where Jesus addressed the scribes and the Pharisees accusing a woman of adultery—*"He who is without sin among you, let him cast the first stone"* (John 8:3–11)—to illustrate her belief that Jesus favored forgiveness and humility over retribution and self-righteousness.

A few months after Judge Sepe's ruling, Bosler embraced another opportunity to share her views with a sympathetic audience when Oprah Winfrey invited her to fly to Chicago and appear on an episode of her television show called "Forgiving the Unforgivable." On the show, Bosler met a clean-shaven conservative Baptist named Bill Pelke, who spoke of experiencing a spiritual transformation while grieving for his murdered grandmother. He initially supported the death penalty for the fifteen-year-old gang ringleader, Paula Cooper, who stabbed his grandmother to death with a twelve-inch-long butcher knife. Ultimately, he decided that his grandmother, who taught Bible classes, would have forgiven the emotionally disturbed teenager. "My grandmother died a martyr for Jesus Christ, who forgave his enemies," Pelke once told his hometown *Post-Tribune* newspaper in Gary, Indiana. "My grandmother would want us to do the same. Christian principles mandate forgiveness." Just as Bosler's grandmother disagreed with her anti–death penalty activism, Pelke's father told the *Post-Tribune* reporter, "I believe my son is one of the so-called new breed who doesn't believe people should have to pay their debts."[8]

After the show, Bosler and Pelke immediately bonded over their similar experiences of suddenly losing a loved one to a violent crime, taking the unpopular position of opposing the death penalty for the murderer, and watching their families fracture during a time of tragedy. They confided that they still struggled to reconcile their great personal suffering with their religious beliefs. Sharing feelings of isolation, rejection, and confusion, Bosler and Pelke worked with other victims' family members who opposed the death penalty to establish an organization called

Survivors of Loss Against Capital Executions (SOLACE). They hoped the organization would address the concerns of pro–death penalty advocates who accused anti–death penalty advocates of privileging the criminals' wishes over those of the victims.

— • —

Over the following years, Bosler used the intense media spotlight that her case generated to broadcast the new organization, which later merged with Murder Victims' Families for Reconciliation (MVFR). Finally finding a distraction from her father's murder, Bosler spent every spare moment recruiting, training, preparing, and mobilizing victims to get involved in jurisprudential campaigns. MVFR developed strategies with other state-focused death penalty abolition groups and empowered family members against the death penalty to testify in front of legislatures. The organization formed alliances with various victims' groups and partnered with policymakers, prosecutors, defense attorneys, law enforcement, media, and victims' advocates supporting alternatives to the death penalty.[9] MVFR also supported the efforts of the Friends Committee to Abolish the Death Penalty in drawing up a "Declaration of Life" for individuals to notarize and attach to their wills. The declaration directs prosecutors, in the case that a signatory is murdered, not to seek the death penalty for the suspected murderer.[10]

MVFR assisted Pelke in launching an international crusade on Cooper's behalf and helped garner the support of several prominent Roman Catholic groups as well as progressive political organizations. Cooper's attorney, William Touchette, even sought intervention from Pope John Paul II to draw the wider Catholic community's attention to his client's case. Touchette traveled to the pope's residence and made a personal appeal on Cooper's behalf on Italian television talk shows. Since Italy has no death penalty, many Italians viewed the imminent execution of the young American woman as barbarous and took up her cause. In 1986 anti–death penalty activists demonstrated outside the US embassy in Rome holding signs that read "The death penalty equals barbarity" and "For whom the bell tolls."[11] A year later, the Vatican radio broadcast an extensive interview with then eighteen-year-old Cooper, which increased outcry against her conviction. Eventually, the pope added his name to a petition, signed by approximately two million Italians, urging clemency for Cooper. On July 13, 1989, the Supreme Court commuted Cooper's sentence from death to sixty years. When a reporter called Pelke for a response, he exclaimed, "Praise the Lord!"

Meanwhile, Bosler embarked on a national speaking tour on behalf of MVFR. The tour was a crash course for Bosler, who quickly learned how Americans viewed the death penalty and larger questions of justice, forgiveness, and redemption. While the historic peace churches—Church of the Brethren, the Mennonites (including Amish), and the Religious Society of Friends (Quakers)—had opposed the death penalty for over a century, the majority of larger religious bodies in North America had only recently adopted an abolitionist position.[12]

Secular opponents of capital punishment note that statistics about recidivism, deterrence, racial disparity, and poorly trained public defenders undermine the alleged benefits and assumed fairness of the punishment. They observe that a person's race, class, and home state, as well as the victim's race and the local district attorney's competency, determine if he or she will receive the death penalty. Groups such as Amnesty International argue that the death penalty disregards mental illness, costs innocent lives, and diverts limited resources from genuine crime control. According to Amnesty International, 95 percent of death row inmates cannot afford their own attorney. The location of the crime, plea bargaining, and pure chance all affect the probability that an inmate will receive the death penalty, which essentially reduces the process to a lottery.[13] Abolitionists argue that an evolving standard of decency renders the death penalty a violation of a person's constitutional right not to be subjected to cruel punishment, and they tend to agree with Justice William Brennan's comparison of electrocution to "disemboweling while alive, drawing and quartering, public dissection, burning alive at the stake, crucifixion, and breaking at the wheel."[14]

Religious abolitionists concur with secular activists that the death penalty is capriciously applied with unsatisfactory results, but they add a theological paradigm for understanding why racism, classism, and bloodlust offend their sense of justice, retribution, mercy, reconciliation, and equality before God.

Opinion surveys confirm that religion continues to influence how people gauge the morality of capital punishment. A 2001 poll conducted by the Pew Forum on Religion and Public Life found (in line with other surveys) that religion is the second most important factor (right after the media) in determining people's beliefs about the death penalty. Interestingly, among those who opposed the death penalty for murders, 42 percent cited religion as their most important influence, while only 15 percent of those who favored the death penalty said the same.

In 1965, only thirty countries had definitively outlawed the death penalty, whereas by March 2010 Amnesty International estimated 95 countries have done so. Among the largest and most outspoken anti–death penalty activists responsible for this progress have been the historic Churches of Peace and the Roman Catholic community.[15] Executions have continued in the United States despite the actions of these religious groups, but the number of crimes for which the death penalty can be prescribed are much more limited due to these groups' efforts.[16]

During her extensive travels, Bosler carried a Bible inscribed with Campbell's name and encouraged audience members to write messages of concern for her father's killer.[17] For Bosler, campaigning against the death penalty was part of her spiritual journey to forgiveness, but she struggled to understand the forces compelling her commitment. On one occasion, after sharing her experience with a large audience, a cop at the back of the room asked her a question that took her off guard. "SueZann, if there had been a gun on the table when you were going through that situation, would you have picked it up and shot James Campbell?" Bosler didn't know what to say. She had never asked herself that question and felt acutely uncomfortable. What if she could have saved her father's life at the expense of Campbell's? Did she truly value the sanctity of life or was her anti–death penalty activism simply a way to fill a lacuna in her life? Exhaling deeply, Bosler finally responded, "You know what? I bet I would have. I have normal human instincts." Bosler went on to explain that her faith called her to move beyond those primordial instincts now that her father was dead and could not be brought back by purely vengeful violence.

■ ● ■

In May 1990 members of MVFR joined two hundred anti–death penalty activists for a 325-mile "Pilgrimage of Life" from the maximum-security prison in Starke, Florida, to the gravesite of Dr. Martin Luther King Jr. in Atlanta, Georgia. The assassinated Baptist minister had famously declared, "Returning violence for violence multiplies violence, adding deeper darkness to a night already devoid of stars. . . . Hate cannot drive out hate: only love can do that." At the march's inception, attorneys, students, ex-convicts, professors, and activists gathered in a circle to read off the names of all the people on death row in Florida and Georgia and then set off to "ignite the consciences of the religious community around the problems of the death penalty."

The spokesperson for the group, Sister Helen Prejean, has been one of the most renowned and passionate defenders of the "consistent ethic of life." In 1971 the worldwide synod of bishops had declared justice a "constitutive" part of the Christian gospel in the spirit of earlier "social encyclicals." In 1980 Prejean's religious community, the Sisters of Saint Joseph of Medaille, echoed the call and made a formal commitment to "stand on the side of the poor."[18] According to Roman Catholics such as Prejean, Jesus preached good news to the poor, and an essential part of that good news was that they were to be poor no longer. As part of this reform movement, Prejean spent years living and working at Saint Thomas Housing Project for low-income African American residents in New Orleans. While working at Saint Thomas, Prejean came to understand racism and poverty as forms of "structural violence" that caused people to suffer gratuitously. She regarded failing schools, racial profiling, and lack of job opportunities as responsible for cyclical, intergenerational poverty. The death penalty, Prejean believed, was meted out exclusively to those already subjected to structural violence. She agreed with the sentiment often heard on the streets: "capital punishment" meant "them without the capital get the punishment."

Prejean opposed the death penalty because she believed Jesus called people to go beyond vengeance, saying *I desire mercy and not sacrifice* (Matthew 9:9–13). She read the Bible as well as the works of Gandhi, Alice Walker, Albert Camus, Dorothy Day, and Martin Luther King Jr. to better understand how to comfort the suffering, indigent, and imprisoned. She was particularly moved by a passage from Camus's "Reflections on the Guillotine" in which a Russian man about to be hanged by the czar's executioners repulses the priest who comes forward to offer a blessing: "Go away and commit no sacrilege."[19] Camus comments on Christians:

> The unbeliever cannot keep from thinking that men who have set at the center of their faith the staggering victim of a judicial error ought at least to hesitate before committing legal murder. Believers might also be reminded that Emperor Julian, before his conversion, did not want to

give official offices to Christians because they systematically refused to pronounce death sentences or to have anything to do with them. For five centuries Christians therefore believed that the strict moral teaching of their master forbade killing.[20]

Yet Prejean was aware that the swath of violence cut by Christians across the centuries is long, wide, and bloody: inquisitions, crusades, witch burnings, persecutions of Jewish "Christ killers," and support for capital punishment.[21] For Prejean, the problem, therefore, is one of human interpretation of religious texts, not religion itself. She writes in *Dead Man Walking*:

One intractable problem, however, is that divine vengeance (barring natural disasters, so-called acts of God) can only be interpreted and exacted by human beings. *Very* human beings. I can't accept that. First, I can't accept that God has fits of rage and goes about trucking in retaliation. Second, I can't accept that any group of human beings is trustworthy enough to mete out so ultimate and irreversible a punishment as death. And, third, I can't accept that it's permissible to kill people provided you "prepare" them with good spiritual counsel to "meet their maker."[22]

When a friend at the Prison Coalition asked Prejean, in January 1982, to serve as a pen pal for a death row inmate, Prejean remembered Jesus' words to His followers: *Whatever you did for the least of these brothers of mine, you did for me.* The nun's internationally acclaimed books, *Dead Man Walking* (the basis for an Oscar-winning film) and *The Death of Innocents*, are autobiographical accounts of the time she spent ministering to death row inmates. Fifteen years after beginning her crusade, the Roman Catholic sister has witnessed five executions in Louisiana and continues to educate the public about what she sees as the self-defeating pathologies of hatred spawned by the death penalty.

As a supporter of the organization that Bosler and Pelke helped spearhead, MVFR, Prejean counsels inmates on death row as well as families of murder victims. "Jesus forgave his executioners and showed us the way of compassion, as do all religious traditions," Prejean told the Democratic Interfaith Gathering. "All religions teach that life is sacred, and Jesus—and all religious leaders—showed preferential love for the least of us, the vulnerable."[23]

- • -

On June 14, 1990, the Supreme Court of Florida issued an opinion revers-ing Judge Sepe's earlier ruling that Campbell simply "had an evil mind" and granted another sentencing on grounds that the judge unduly ignored mitigating circumstances in Campbell's life. In *Campbell v. Flor-ida*, the court noted:

> Evidence of impaired capacity was extensive and unrefuted—Campbell's IQ was in the retarded range; he had poor reasoning skills; his abilities were on a third-grade level; he suffered from chronic drug and alcohol abuse; and he was subjected to a borderline personality disorder. We note that he attempted suicide while in jail and was placed on Thorazine, a high-potency antipsychotic drug.[24]

When Bosler heard the news, she was ecstatic that the last half decade of her life was not spent working in vain, but she did not look forward to going through another sentencing hearing and reliving each ghoulish detail of her father's murder. "It would have been so much less traumatic and drawn out if the state simply dropped the death penalty and gave Campbell a life sentence without parole," said Bosler in a phone interview.

This time, the case was assigned to Judge Leonard Glick. In the days leading up to the trial, Bosler remembered Jesus's call to visit those who are incarcerated—*I was in prison, and you came to visit me* (e.g., Luke 4:16–21, Matthew 25:31–46)—but Campbell repeatedly rebuffed her overtures.

Five and half years after her father's murder, Bosler took the stand for the second time and once again faced Campbell in court. She raised her right hand, reiterated her opposition to the death penalty, told Campbell that she and her father forgave him, and explained to the jury that her growing role in the anti–death penalty movement was a religious call-ing that helped her find inner peace. "I forgive you, James Campbell, whether you accept it or not." Bosler said she experienced a subtle float-ing sensation after voicing her forgiveness and, for the first time, genu-inely felt no anger toward Campbell. When Nora Dickerson, the slain reverend's mother, took the stand, she made her wishes equally clear:

> Since the murder, I have had two strokes and severe cases of shingles. . . . These strung-out court episodes are taking further toll on us as well

as on SueZann, our granddaughter. She will never be whole because of the repeated stabbings and attempted murder resulting in the loss of her retentive memory.

Because of Campbell's history of criminal recidivism and the fact he was free on early release from prison and on parole for a previous trial before he heinously stabbed my son the Reverend Bill Bosler to death and injured SueZann for life, I plead with you, Judge, to retain the original death penalty for James Campbell so he can never, never hurt anyone else as we have been hurt. Thank you.[25]

The lead prosecutor, Michael Band, used his closing remarks to remind the jury: "The death penalty is a message sent to certain members of our society who choose not to follow the rules. It's only for one crime, the crime of first-degree murder. It is for those who choose to violate the sacredness and sanctity of human life."[26]

The jury adjourned and soon returned with its verdict: ten to two in favor of the death penalty. Judge Glick upheld the verdict and sentenced Campbell to death by electric chair.

Bosler realized with some alarm that she felt more animosity toward the lead prosecutor than her would-be murderer. "The state attorney's office lied to my grandmother by telling her that James [Campbell] would kill me when he got out of prison so he needed to receive the death penalty," said Bosler. "They tried to pit us against each other to get the death penalty they so desperately wanted to win in this case." Although Bosler questioned how long her stamina would last in the fight for Campbell's life, she decided to appeal the decision yet again.

— ∎ —

Viewing anti–death penalty activism as her lifetime religious calling, Bosler joined her old friend Bill Pelke and helped organize a "Journey of Hope" in 1993 to spread their message of "hope in the power of forgiveness and hope in the possibility of a world without violence."[27] Together, they spoke to anyone who would listen and arranged educational events at schools, churches, synagogues, mosques, universities, and civic groups. Death row inmates' family members joined murder victims' family members in touring the country in a *Abolition Movin'* bus for seventeen days speaking to 175 different groups. The Journey formed an Abolitionist Action Committee to organize a four-day fast and vigil outside the Supreme Court to mourn the anniversary of the July 2, 1976, *Gregg v. Georgia* decision that allowed states to pass death-penalty statues again. Drawing members of the Catholic Worker community and Amnesty International, organizers decided to hold a similar fast annually until the Supreme Court again abolished the death penalty.

While waiting for the court to grant a new sentencing trial, Bosler traveled internationally on behalf of the Journey and often appeared as a guest speaker for the Church of the Brethren's program "On Earth Peace." In 1994 she further publicized her mission to save Campbell's life when she joined other survivors of violent crimes, including members of Murder Victims Families for Reconciliation (MVFR), on the Discovery Channel's documentary *From Fury to Forgiveness*. The television magazine program *48 Hours* also produced an hour-long segment on Bosler's campaign.

Eventually, on June 27, 1996, the Florida Supreme Court overturned the verdict in *Florida v. Campbell* and returned the case for resentencing, citing misconduct by the prosecutor.

- ■ -

Ten years after the murder of Bosler's father, on June 9, 1997, Dade County Circuit Judge Marc Schumacher and a third jury convened to retry the case. What was in question was not the conviction, but the possibility of life imprisonment or capital punishment. Bosler was in court yet again to persuade the jury to reject imposing the death penalty on her father's murderer. She wanted the jury to understand that Campbell's death would not bring her father back to life. She wanted the jury to hear the words of her father's favorite hymn: *Let there be peace on earth and let it begin with me.*

Bosler's growing prominence in the abolitionist movement drew the attention of renowned anti–death penalty attorney Melodee Smith. Smith was an ordained minister in the United Church of Christ who regarded her work on death penalty cases as part of her ministry. Smith contacted Bosler through a mutual friend and offered her expertise, which Bosler gratefully accepted. Smith instructed her to retain eye contact when addressing jurors, remain calm when fielding the prosecutor's questions, and steady her voice during her closing remarks so as not to sound overly emotional.

At the trial's inception, Smith told reporters, "The death penalty is a hate crime, used primarily against the poor and in a racist way. . . . I believe the support for it, especially by politicians, is just a veneer, an exercise in political demagogy."[28]

On the opening day of the trial, Judge Schumacher strictly forbade Bosler from mentioning any opinion regarding capital punishment while under oath. Bosler suspected the judge was pandering to a bloodthirsty public by citing a seldom-evoked Florida Supreme Court ruling that a victim may not sway jurors by suggesting the type of penalty an offender should receive.

When Assistant State Attorney Michael Band presented graphic testimony and photographs of the murder, Bosler refused to allow her facial expression to betray the pain she experienced remembering each detail. Calling Bosler to testify, Band asked if she were employed. Bosler replied that she had several jobs. Then, she paused. Defiantly avoiding Band's gaze, Bosler addressed the jurors, "For over ten years, since my father's murder, my main job has been working to *abolish* the death penalty."

Bosler had stated a fact, not an opinion, but the rankled judge dismissed the jury and hissed at Bosler that she was under court order not to say "even one word about the death penalty or anything that has to do with the death penalty." The judge continued, "If you violate the order, and I will find you in direct criminal contempt, and you face six months in a Dade County jail with a $500 fine."

Bosler nodded solemnly in agreement but knew she had successfully flaunted the judge's orders by communicating her opposition to the death penalty to the jurors. Nothing the judge could say now would erase her opposition from the official record.

For the remainder of the trial, she did not cooperate with the state attorneys except for terse, clinical answers to their questions. The atmosphere changed when the defense counsel, Reemberto Diaz, questioned her. He attempted to give her an opportunity to speak freely about her opposition to capital punishment but was prevented by a series of objections from the assistant state attorney, which were sustained by the judge.

Diaz returned to his chair but paused before sitting down. He announced, "I have one more question." Pointing to Campbell, he asked Bosler, "Do you hate this man?" She immediately responded, "No." Seconds later, state attorneys leapt to their feet, shouting objections, which were loudly sustained by the judge.

- · -

Until the trial's third day, Bosler had never fully understood why Campbell rejected her offers to visit him in jail. Now, she listened to the defense counsel call a number of witnesses who testified that Campbell had suffered extreme abuse from both his parents as a young child and was forcibly and repeatedly removed by Child Protective Services. Two psychologists testified that Campbell was severely beaten by his mother with extension cords, water hoses, and pool cues.[29] One witness described how his mother spat in James's face in crowded areas to publicly humiliate the child. After unsuccessfully trying to kill himself by drinking bleach at age nine, Campbell ran away from home. He arrived at his aunt's house with bluish-purple welts across his body and blood dripping from his ear.[30] The young boy turned to alcohol and crack cocaine abuse, and psychologists confirmed that Campbell now read at a third-grade level, suffered from mental retardation, and had a borderline personality disorder. A witness testified that Campbell watched his mother stab his stepfather much in the same way he would later stab Reverend Bosler and SueZann.

Campbell exemplified what researcher Craig Haney called the "profile" of capital defendants. After twenty years of compiling histories of people on death row, Haney noted: "The nexus between poverty, childhood abuse and neglect, social and emotional dysfunction, alcohol and drug abuse, and crime is so tight in the lives of many capital defendants as to form a kind of social historical 'profile'."[31] Although the media depicted murderers like Campbell as inherently evil, Bosler suspected that Campbell was mimicking the violence that had plagued his childhood. She did not condone Campbell's crime or completely absolve him of human agency but understood that he was a product of terrifying circumstances. The problem, thought Bosler, did not begin with the crime, but the causes of crime: the violence of poverty, neglect, and abuse. She concluded that Campbell did not truly understand what he was doing when he repeatedly plunged a knife into her father's chest, and she wondered if she would have made similarly destructive decisions if her life were full of pain and suffering. She decided that she knew only one thing for certain: Campbell was a child of God and, when he bled all over her house, his blood was the same color as her own. For Bosler, the most significant difference between Campbell and herself is that he murdered a man, while she refused to do so by denouncing capital punishment.

For Bosler, the proverb from the Gospel of Matthew echoed loudly: *Those who live by the sword will die by the sword.* She believed humanity's only hope lay in rejecting the sword or, in this case, the electric chair. During her lonely decade as a crusader against the death penalty, Bosler found solace in Gandhi's axiom: "An eye for an eye makes the whole world blind." She explained to sympathizers and skeptics alike that the death penalty cheapened the sacredness of all human life.

The jury adjourned for its deliberations on Friday the thirteenth. After three hours of conversing with supportive friends and nervously pacing the courtroom halls, Bosler was told the jury had returned with a verdict. The hour Bosler had anticipated for over a decade had finally arrived. She studied the jurors' faces as they entered the courtroom, making eye contact with a few. Whatever the outcome, Bosler vowed to continue fighting for the abolition of the death penalty. She silently prayed for good news as the bailiff handed the judge a piece of paper. The courtroom was silent.

Judge Schumacher cleared his throat and looked askance. Then, he announced the verdict: eight to four in favor of life, not death. The judge imposed a life sentence on Campbell with a mandatory minimum of twenty-five years without parole, to be served consecutively with his three other life sentences from the same case.[32] Band, the lead prosecutor, accepted the jury's decision as final and later admitted, "It's easier to discuss the death penalty at home than looking at a human being twelve feet away when your decision may alter his life."[33]

An exhausted but elated Bosler was invited to address the jurors. Holding the Bible she brought for Campbell, she said:

Thank you for giving life and not death to James Bernard Campbell. No matter how mad I could be at James Bernard Campbell, I still don't believe in the death penalty for this man. I'm so overwhelmed. This is the happiest moment of the past ten and a half years for me. I can't thank you enough. I have worked hard for his life to be spared. Now I can go on with my own life. And I thank you very much for that.[34]

Walking out of the courtroom for the last time, she turned to the jurors and said, "God bless you all."

Several jurors hugged each other and offered one another tissues to dab their tears. One juror told a reporter that the sentence was "a fair, humane decision" while another admitted, "If something like that happened to me, I don't think I could forgive."[35]

Today, Bosler serves on the board of directors of Journey of Hope. She remains an active member of MVFR, which grew into a national organization with 4,500 interfaith supporters, of which 800 identify themselves as family members of murder victims, all of whom oppose the death penalty in all cases.[36]

9 CHARLOTTE KEYS

Ecojustice Warriors Against Pollution

I don't want to flee, nor do I want to abandon the battle of these farmers who live without any protection in the forest. They have the sacrosanct right to aspire to a better life on land where they can live and work with dignity while respecting the environment.
                    —DOROTHY STANG, *ecojustice activist murdered in 2005*

Our struggle is not easy. Those who oppose our cause are rich and powerful and they have many allies in high places. We are poor. Our allies are few. But we have something the rich do not own. We have our own bodies and spirits and the justice of our cause as our weapons.
                    —CÉSAR CHÁVEZ, *union organizer of United Farm Workers*

On a muggy morning in March 1977, a lanky fourteen-year-old girl with knobby knees, tightly coiled hair, and smooth ebony skin challenged her cousins to a race. The long-legged ninth grader, Charlotte Keys, ran on Columbia High School's track team in rural Mississippi and planned to spend her spring break conditioning for the upcoming season. As Keys sprinted past her cousins on the patchy yellow lawn outside their weatherworn ranch, a terrifying sonic blast pierced her eardrums, a boom as loud as cannon fire in a war zone. Moments later, the ground beneath her feet hiccupped and she felt her legs buckle underneath her weight. Lying prostrate with shock, Keys choked for fresh air and her nostrils burned from the stench of toxic waste. Her chest constricted painfully as she struggled to breathe and her head felt light and airy, as if clouded with fumes from paint thinner. As she propped herself on her scabby elbows, Keys watched black smoke consume the pale azure sky. *Oh God,* she began to silently pray, *please get me out of here, God.*

Blinded by the acrid smoke, Keys heard but could not see the sirens wailing through the heart of Columbia as a man on a bullhorn yelled in the distance, "Do not run in the direction of the wind! Get out of here!" Keys was unable to see her own hand in front of her face, much less discern which way the wind was blowing, but guessed the explosion had originated in the east where the Reichhold Chemical Company plant was located. She and other children in Columbia had grown up playing amid the heaps of scrap metal that the plant burned in evening hours, creating massive bonfires that glittered against the dark night sky like summer fireflies. Now, pulling her sweat-drenched shirt over her nose and gasping for air, Keys raced two miles away from the plant toward Highway 13 on the other end of Columbia's parameters. The smell of burnt rubber and festering sewage followed her no matter how fast she ran. At last, Keys's aunt spotted the gangly, heaving girl amid the exodus of hysterical Columbia residents and instructed her to squeeze into the family car.

Once reunited with her family and friends at a highway rest stop, Keys kept asking what had happened. Nobody knew for certain. Eventually, she learned that the deafening blast from Reichhold Chemical Company had resonated for nearly fifteen miles, reduced nearby windowpanes to spiderwebbed glass, and sent residents of Columbia hurling through their trailers and fearing for their lives. The eighty-one-acre Reichhold site had burned to the ground as quickly as a straw hut, and the explosion knocked over people half a mile away. Neither Keys nor any of the other 775 residents in her mostly African American community had any idea what, exactly, the chemical plant manufactured, let alone what had caused it to internally combust.

In the evening, a police officer announced that everything was under control and evacuees should return to their homes. When confused residents asked the officer what happened and how he could guarantee that a subsequent explosion would not occur, he apologized that he had no further information. Keys was eager to resume her spring break plans

and welcomed the news, but her mother, Corrine Alford, clucked dis-
approvingly and worried about an aftershock. Sitting at the rest stop,
Alford, an evangelical preacher, expressed her doubts that the municipality had contained the noxious gases.

The stench and fogginess hung like a funeral shroud over the city of
Columbia for three weeks. Keys listened to her neighbors chatter incessantly about the explosion and felt frustrated that every explanation
seemed equally plausible. She overheard churchwomen speculate that
the explosion resulted from a failed attempt to dispose of wood chips
with dynamite. She listened to her parents argue whether or not the
blankets of billowing smoke from the factory's burning heaps of trash
had accidentally ignited an electric cable. At school, she refused to laugh
when classmates accused each other of detonating the neighborhood
stink bomb.

In the wake of the blast, word spread through Columbia that a fifty-
year-old gardener named Virgie Peavy, whose house shared a fence with
the chemical plant, had fallen ill and shed layers of charred, flaky skin
pocked with tiny black bumps. A few weeks later Keys's mother told her
the gardener, who had once brought homegrown corn to church socials,
had inexplicably died in her sleep. Terrified, Keys began examining her
own body much more closely and stood in front of a full-length mirror
each night, craning her neck to see if her skin had similarly morphed into
something resembling phyllo dough.

After Peavy's mysterious death, congregants flooded the Environmental Protection Agency with angry phone calls demanding it deploy
a team to investigate the Reichhold blast. In early 1978 the EPA obliged
and sent a team of environmental specialists to Columbia. According to
Keys, the EPA team was predominantly composed of white men who
spoke dispassionately through their teeth in measured tones. Keys says
her community viewed the EPA representatives with increasing suspi-
cion, especially after they encircled the incinerated factory's premises
with a permeable cyclone fence that did nothing to prevent diffusion of
the noisome toxins.

Keys remembers her mother wondering out loud why the government officials encouraged the residents of Columbia to resume their
everyday lives but insisted that their own employees wear Hazmat suits
equipped with oxygen supplies providing filtered, uncontaminated air.
Keys and her friends joked that everyone should get a free "moon suit"

but continued playing near the site largely unperturbed. After surveying the area, the EPA team insisted the air quality no longer posed any serious health hazards and departed as suddenly as it had arrived.

- ∎ -

Keys was born in the economically depressed town of Columbia, which is nestled on the flat, eastern bank of the Pearl River just north of New Orleans and south of Jackson, Mississippi. The loquacious child with a ready smile grew up attending Bible classes and Sunday services as well as participating in choir revivals, national provincials, and church councils. Keys's mother founded the Apostolic Pentecostal Church in town and presided as the pastor of the one-room building with a splotchy white facade and missing roof shingles. Over the years, the modest church came to sustain the residents of Columbia by organizing sports days for children, social forums for parents, and a community resource center for unemployed residents in need of job assistance, food stamps, and spiritual guidance. Keys was enraptured by her mother's talent for preaching with all the gusto of a hellfire-and-brimstone preacher while still communicating a message of the universalism of humankind, the Biblical promise of divine hope, and the social gospel of human betterment. In this boarded-up and run-down rural Mississippi Delta town where foreclosure signs were more commonplace than mailboxes and a quarter of the residents subsisted below the poverty line, the Apostolic Pentecostal Church emerged as one of the few local institutions offering residents economic relief by encouraging members to pool resources and share expertise.

Keys's earliest memories revolved around the church social hour, a time when congregants shared their concerns about soaring gas prices and dim job prospects. However, in the years following the Reichhold Company explosion, Keys noticed the subject of her community's complaints perceptibly shifted. Now every conversation seemed to involve a litany of health afflictions: asthma, ulcers, skin rashes. Residents in houses and trailers near the abandoned Reichhold site often complained of breathing difficulties, nosebleeds, and persistent migraines. Keys was confused about why her neighbors all seemed to suffer from similar ailments and wondered if her own excruciating migraines, which left her temples throbbing and eyes watering, had anything to do with the Reichhold blast.

-·-

For sixty years, Keys's impoverished community had attracted pollution-producing companies the same way affluent neighborhoods attracted upscale retail stores. Before Reichhold began producing chemicals on the plant's premises, a wood preservative company spewed pentachlorophenol into the air. When the wind blew from the north, residents inhaled sawdust saturated with chemical resins that burned their throats and laced their lungs.

In 1975, Reichhold Company, a subsidiary of Dai Nippon Ink and Chemicals in Japan, moved into Columbia without notifying employees or nearby residents that it produced noxious chemicals—chemicals that Keys would later discover included carcinogenic dioxins and other active ingredients in the potentially lethal Agent Orange defoliant. Even after an inspector from the Occupational Safety and Health Administration (OSHA) determined that the plant operated in Columbia without an official permit, it remained in commission because Keys's community lacked the political clout and financial resources to take Reichhold to court.

After the blast, Reichhold closed shop and interred its byproducts—over 4,600 rusty barrels of toxic sludge—in the county landfills. The barrels of chemical waste soon corroded, cracked, and seeped into the town's soil and drinking reservoir. Children in the local school wheezed through classes and emerged from the community swimming pool itching so furiously that their skin bled, scabbed, and bled again.

For nearly a decade after the blast, residents of Columbia continued badgering the EPA with health complaints that they blamed on the Reichhold explosion. They wanted to know why the fish population in Jingling Creek mysteriously disappeared; why an estimated two hundred cattle on nearby ranches keeled over for no apparent reason; and why the toxins in the soil singed off the soles of their shoes. They complained that the surface of Pearl River was streaked with gasoline rainbows that caused the murky water to catch fire in the summertime, startling children playing and wading.

In October 1986, almost a decade after the blast, the EPA returned to Columbia to further examine the community's claims of environmental poisoning. This time, the EPA closely examined the charred skeleton of the abandoned Reichhold plant and discovered thousands of barrels of chemical cocktails, which they later determined included a toxic alphabet soup of everything from acetone, benzene, and pentachlorophenol to toluene, xylenes, and zinc.[1] The EPA also discovered that Reichhold had dumped phenols, grease, and oil into the creek without a permit. Although the EPA did not bring in a team of health experts, officials again assured Columbia residents that the noxious gases once emitted by the factory no longer posed health risks. The EPA added Columbia to the national priorities list for Superfund hazardous waste sites and promised residents that it would clean up the mess by removing the abandoned barrels of chemicals. Keys couldn't help wondering, *how clean is clean? Is it clean enough just for low-income people?*

In early 1987, shortly after the EPA report was issued, a cadre of lawyers from a variety of competing firms in Houston and New Orleans appeared unannounced in Columbia and offered residents a take-it-or-leave-it deal: they would press for personal injury and property damage settlements from Reichhold on behalf of the residents in exchange for 45 percent commission for their work. The lawyers convinced one-third of the town's residents to press charges and sign contingency fee contracts. In an article published in the *National Law Journal*, titled "Getting Victimized by the Legal System," Marcia Coyle and Claudia MacLachlan described the difficulties that Columbia residents faced: "[Residents] complain that besides paying excessive fees they never received copies of their contracts, never received promised medical examinations, and never knew what [their lawyers] were doing on their behalf."[2] Keys remembered her family feeling uncomfortable around the mainly white, upper-class team of lawyers who condescendingly suggested that "eating too much fast-food might explain the community's health problems." Back in 1987, Janice Kennedy went further, telling the *National Law Journal*, "We were talked to like we were illiterate, stupid dogs."

Residents of Columbia did not receive word from the lawyers for fifteen years. Although the community regarded the attorneys as carpetbaggers attempting to bilk them, it remains unclear if these attorneys acted unethically since, as the *National Law Journal* noted, tort cases involving toxic materials are extremely expensive to bring to court, and 30 to 50 percent for fees is not uncommon.

A federal judge eventually approved a $500,000 class action settlement for punitive damages. The lawyers returned to Columbia and explained they would parcel out the settlement among 3,400 people who lived near the plant. Each resident, on average, would receive $163, although some would receive several thousand.

Lawyers encouraged residents to accept the offer, saying that Reichhold could go bankrupt that year and leave residents empty-handed. However, that year, Reichhold recorded sales over $1 billion and a company spokesman told the *Times-Picayune* that Reichhold was doing quite well.[3] The company says it eventually paid $63 million after the Columbia factory explosion, but the community saw little of this money since $30 million was earmarked for cleanup efforts and another $30 million was spent in lawsuits.

Reichhold community liaison Alec Van Ryan told *Chemical Week* that the company aggressively pursued community involvement in Columbia, guaranteed local real estate values, and spent millions of dollars cleaning up the site. Ryan added that Reichhold's responsibilities do not extend to fulfilling the wish lists of low-income residents. "There's some terrible poverty and abhorrent living conditions in the South, but to say that the site is responsible for them is a leap that is not supported by the facts."[4]

— • —

Back in the late 1980s, as a senior at Columbia High School with aspirations to join the ministry, Keys's mind wandered away from the Reichhold explosion and toward more immediate concerns such as going to the prom, passing exams, and helping her mother compose Sunday sermons. One day during chemistry lab, however, Keys was reminded of the blast when she noticed a scrawny classmate with off-kilter glasses select a translucent solution—instead of an opaque solution as instructed in their lab manual—to titrate the cool blue liquid in his glass beaker. Keys remembered that her teacher, Mr. Noole, stressed the importance of following lab instructions carefully when handling volatile substances, and she wondered with morbid curiosity what would happen when her classmate poured the wrong solution into his beaker. As soon as the oblivious boy mixed the solutions, the pale blue liquid fizzled and crackled like Pop Rocks candy before shattering the beaker with a sharp blast. The murky chemical solution seeped out of the cracked glass and let off a sulfuric stench. Keys realized that a chemical explosion of much greater proportions must have reduced the Reichhold plant to ashes years earlier, and she wondered what chemicals were involved.

After graduating from high school, Keys attended Pearl River Community College, where she earned an associate degree in secretarial sciences, and, in January 1989, she took a job as the deputy chancery clerk at the Marion County courthouse. Close to home, she remained active in her mother's church and grew increasingly alarmed by congregants' persistent complaints of chronic nausea, vomiting, diarrhea, sweaty hands, cold feet, and sensitivity to sharp light. Keys also noticed an increase in lupus, tumors, cysts, and a peculiar whitish skin irritation among her friends and neighbors.

Keys soon emerged as the community's de facto counselor, thanks to her knack for finding a spiritual message relevant to any situation. Dozens of residents complained to Keys of severe stomach knots after years of drinking the tap water in Columbia, and a few even reported internal bleeding. Lorraine Powell, a buxom woman with gold-plated teeth and plastic aviator glasses, told Keys that her daughter died from toxemia shortly after giving birth and that her sister was recently diagnosed with terminal cancer. She confided to Keys that, shortly after the explosion, the figs on her trees withered and the hogs in her backyard keeled over, but her family had been hungry, so she had fed them the figs and pork anyway. Now she worried that her entire family might die. Keys confessed that she didn't know if the figs and hogs were contaminated but said the Lord was good and would provide for Powell and her family. Cradling Powell in her arms like an overgrown baby, Keys rocked her back and forth and hummed "We Shall Overcome."

Jerri Forbes, whose wood-paneled home sat adjacent to the factory site, told Keys that nothing grew in her garden anymore. She rolled up her sleeves to reveal the itchy pimples full of yellowish pus that speckled her upper body. When Keys suggested she visit a doctor, Forbes explained she already had and, much to her chagrin, the confused doctor advised her to wash with Dial soap and apply chamomile lotion. Forbes asked Keys if the pine-tar smell emitted by the plant the day it exploded might explain her children's asthma. Keys said she was uncertain but that many neighbors complained about constant wheezing. She offered to pray for Forbes's family, but Forbes said she had more practical plans. Over the next three years, Forbes put herself through nursing school.

Keys listened to churchwomen discuss their multiple miscarriages and lament the alarming number of babies carried to term who suffered from serious birth defects. Then, in 1985, Keys herself experienced a miscarriage that her gynecologist attributed to her weak physical condition. Keys and her husband found the doctor's explanation dubious, insisting she was neither "weak" nor had a "condition." Keys informed the doctor that her parents had taught her the importance of eating healthy from an early age and that smoking and drinking were devilish temptations. She said she seldom took sick days from classes as a child and, as a young adult, stayed fit by competing in track, volleyball, and basketball.

In the late 1980s, Keys and her family mourned the death of her fifty-year-old cousin, Juanita Maxwell, who succumbed to lung cancer. At the funeral, Keys counted off neighbors who had recently died of cancer and worried that the disease was becoming Columbia's own Biblical plague, slowly visiting every family.

■ ∎ ■

Columbia falls near the eighty-five-mile stretch of the Mississippi River from Baton Rouge to New Orleans that was once dubbed the "petrochemical corridor." However, after reports of numerous cases of cancer occurring in small rural communities on both sides of the river, the area is now known as "cancer alley." In 2000, Toxics Release Inventory (TRI) data showed that seven of the ten plants in Louisiana with the largest combined on- and off-site releases were located in cancer alley. Industrial accidents similar to the Reichhold Company explosion occur often in cancer alley; in 1994 Condea Vista, located on Lake Charles, reported thirty-nine chemical accidents that released 129,500 pounds of chemicals.

In the 1980s, during a protest against the siting of a hazardous waste landfill by the state government in a middle of a low-income African American community in Warren County, North Carolina, Reverend Benjamin Chavis Jr. attempted to explain why some communities suffer from environmental poisoning far more frequently than others by coining the term "environmental racism." Today, "environmental racism" refers to the institutional practices that subject low-income and minority neighborhoods to the vast majority of America's polluting industry and causes already impoverished residents to disproportionately suffer from toxic pollution, government indifference, and corporate negligence.

The issue of environmental racism further entered public consciousness after Robert Bullard, director of Clark Atlanta University's

Environmental Justice Resource Center, published damning evidence that low-income minorities live closer than whites to waste facilities across the nation. In 1987 the United Church of Christ released a similarly startling report, *Toxic Wastes and Race in the United States*, which was the first comprehensive attempt to draw an explicit relationship between the location of hazardous waste landfills and their proximity to ethnic minority communities. Pinpointing race rather than poverty as the determining factor for siting new hazardous waste units, the report found that three out of the five largest commercial hazardous waste landfills nationwide—which account for 40 percent of the total estimated US commercial landfill capacity—were located in predominantly black or Hispanic communities.[5] A 1983 study of landfills in the southeast by the General Accounting Office independently corroborated the report, which largely dispelled any remaining doubts about the reality of environmental racism.[6] The Toxics Release Inventory later confirmed a similar racial disparity is true of communities in the vicinity of mammoth chemical plants.[7] Then, in 1992, a *National Law Journal* study concluded that Superfund waste sites in minority communities were subjected to less stringent enforcement of regulations and lower penalties for breaches of conduct than those in white communities.[8]

Companies such as Reichhold may not be deliberately racist, but they do follow the path of least resistance when selecting communities in which to site new factories. All companies are concerned with generating a profit and naturally prefer not to fight expensive legal battles or finance costly cleanup efforts unless they are forced to do so. Communities less empowered to protest the incursion of chemical plants or demand redress after an accident occurs are, for this reason, attractive to them. Given the relationship between class and race in the United States, these communities are largely composed of low-income minorities—communities such as the one in Columbia in which Keys grew up. In an interview with *Chemical Week*, Ryan disputed allegations that racism was a factor in siting the Reichhold plant or delaying cleanup decisions. "We've worked with the community from day one," Ryan told *Chemical Week*. "[We're] a model of how a company should behave." He claims the plant improved the town's economy by providing jobs and training local workforce.[9]

Middle- and low-income minority communities across the nation say that environmental racism—intentional or not—poses challenges similar to the ones that Keys's community faced in Columbia. In Carver

Terrace, a planned community built as a magnet for middle-income African American families in northeast Texas, municipality officials informed residents in the 1980s that their homes sat atop a cesspool of toxic chemical residue from a wood preservatives plant. Long suffering from health ailments resulting from corroded plumbing, residents learned their lawns were soaked with creosote, an oily black accretion that results from incompletely burned wood. Homeowners called on government agencies to redress their grievances but eventually settled for low buyout prices that forced them to relocate to crime-riddled ghettos.[10]

In the late 1980s, around the time Keys learned about her community's skyrocketing health predicaments, the nexus between mainstream environmental concerns about toxic substances and allegations that such substances disproportionately affect low-income, minority communities gave rise to the ecojustice movement. The brainchild of the United Church of Christ—not Greenpeace or the Sierra Club—ecojustice is a prophetic vision of a social order in which both nature and people are treated with respect and care.[11] Environmental justice advocates denounce the fact that environmental burdens are unfairly and unequally distributed across the globe and that people of color and the working poor are more vulnerable to environmental catastrophes, yet less empowered to seek redress for their grievances. In September 1993 Beulah Grove United Methodist Church rallied one hundred ecojustice advocates under expansive magnolia trees on the front lawn of the Pontotoc courthouse to protest plans to build a regional landfill in their community. Later that year, Native Americans similarly protested the toxic waste injection wells cropping up on ancestral lands. In Houma, Louisiana, an ecojustice group called Citizens Against Nuclear Trash sued a nuclear processing plant for alleged environmental racism.

Back in the early 1990s, Keys knew very little about "environmental racism" or the wider ecojustice movement, but she had grown increasingly concerned about her community's failing health. In 1991, while working at the Marion County courthouse, Keys discovered that two businessmen were filing lawsuits against Reichhold Chemical Company for knowingly selling them contaminated land. She was shocked to learn these businessmen were going to receive a $3.5 million settlement, even though they lived several miles out of town and did not suffer from the health ailments plaguing her neighbors. "There's something strange going on, because the little people don't know what to do, but the big people are filing major lawsuits," Keys told her father. "The Lord has moved upon me to start looking into this." Her father nodded and replied, "Whatever the Lord called upon you to do, you do."

In the following months, Keys pieced together what had transpired at the Reichhold plant the day it exploded. Later, in an interview, she insisted God spoke directly to her as she began organizing a local ecojustice movement in Columbia. Accentuating somewhat irreconcilable differences between America's religion-infused ecojustice movement and its secular-leaning environmental movement, Keys's religiosity mobilized congregants of her church, but she experienced considerably less success galvanizing secular environmentalists.

In 1992 Keys began describing herself in the third person as "Evangelist Keys who has been chosen, anointed, and appointed by the Lord to work to help souls be delivered, healed, and set free through his holy plan of salvation." She officially launched Jesus People Against Pollution (JPAP), an ecojustice organization that sought redress for Reichhold's alleged crimes. Incorporating environmental justice into her outreach ministry, Keys preached the good news that God did not want to see the residents of Columbia suffer. Whenever a sickly neighbor voiced despair, Keys reminded her that Christ loved her infinitely and would see her through any difficulties.

"When you study the Bible, you read about how long it took justice to prevail for the children of Israel held in bondage and recognize God delivers, but we have to keep the faith," Keys said. "He's slow, but he does show, and—when he does show—he's never late." Keys continued fasting, studying the Bible, and waiting for God to reveal the next step. She addressed her own moments of crippling doubt by reminding herself that God led the children of Israel through the Red Sea and he would lead the children of Columbia through the toxic smog, too.

Keys convinced passersby to join JPAP by saying that the world would never know their suffering unless they came together to call upon the Lord for help. She structured JPAP around the community's shared Christian belief that love produces action. "If I tell you I love you, I've got to produce some action," Keys explained to *Sojourners* in the early days of JPAP. "With the Lord, his way is love. He came for us to have life . . . it is not for people to think that folks need to go to heaven to enjoy life—you can enjoy abundant living right here, if we know how to treat and help one another."[12]

Keys started each JPAP meeting with a prayer or a song of praise, such as "This Little Light of Mine." She prefaced each community discussion with riveting sermons connecting the plight of Columbia residents to that of dispossessed Israelites in the time of Pharaoh. The meetings soon drew over four hundred Columbia residents and were held in the vicinity of the Superfund site at neighborhood libraries, schools, and Columbia's Duckworth Community Center. After reading a scripture on good stewardship of God's creations, Keys facilitated community discussions and helped draft a list of demands: medical evaluations, free clinics, funding for relocation, reparations for devalued property, and transparent criminal investigations.

As local media started running stories on JPAP, ecojustice activists from across the nation called Keys to share their stories and inform her about their common struggles against environmental racism. After further educating herself about environmental racism, Keys concluded that Reichhold had indeed moved into Columbia because of its demographic, and she began speaking out against the racist and classist "monstrous environmental genocide" experienced by her community. JPAP organized efforts to secure health services, lobbied for more local participation in decisions that affected the Columbia community—from the siting and operating of toxic facilities to the disposal of potentially hazardous waste—and designed plans to relocate the 150 to 200 families near the Reichhold site.

▪ ▪ ▪

In the summer of 2010, I visited Keys in Columbia to learn more about Jesus People Against Pollution. Driving east on MS-44 past towering oil rigs and ubiquitous fast-food chains, I spotted a sign for Keys's hometown that read "City of Charm on the River Pearl." With few attractions beyond greasy-spoon diners and a Seago's Pawn Shop, the town of Columbia is anything but charming, especially in the middle of a scorching hot summer. When Keys arrived at the Subway restaurant where we decided to meet, she embraced me warmly and pecked me on the cheek as if we were childhood chums. For someone who has spent half her life rallying against chemical contamination in her town's water supply, Keys looked like she drank from a fountain of youth. A towering, big-boned woman with wide-set eyes and soft features who wears her short, curly hair parted along the side, Keys appeared considerably younger than her forty-seven years. Wearing a pastel pink blouse hemmed with ruffles, Keys arrived loaded with press clippings and summary reports on the Reichhold plant explosion.

When I ask Keys to describe her transformation from preacher to activist, she explains in a deep, husky voice marked by a revivalist's cadence:

> In December 1990 I prayed the old year out and the new one in. I told the Lord, "Look, I want to be effective with everything you've given me to do. I'm getting up and going to work every day unsatisfied and not help-ing people." On January 2, 1992, I was praying in the courthouse early in the morning before anyone came to work, and the Lord moved up upon me. He said, "I want you to rise up to work and the name of the organiza-tion shall be called 'Jesus People Against Pollution.'" I said, "'Jesus People Against Pollution'? What am I going to do with a name like that?" I said, "I don't know what's going on! What am I to do with this organization?" And the Lord said to me, "I want you to go out into your community and, all around the [chemical] site, I want you to knock on people's doors and I want you to examine the health effect of the people that is sick, and I want you to collect any and all information that the people have about the operation of the plant."[13]

Keys said she never questioned her conversation with the Almighty and brushes off suggestions that her conscience was guiding her rather than the divine. However, she admitted to having experienced extreme anxiety about successfully fulfilling what she regarded as her higher calling: "I was just overwhelmed by the responsibility placed on my shoulders. But I knew God was with me every step of the way so I just needed to listen and follow." Keys said she decided she had no option but to oblige the Lord, since He had chosen her for this special mission to fight on behalf of her community. "I was stunned because I didn't know how my journey would unfold, but if you look at how the all-knowing, all-seeing Lord directed me, he knew all along."

According to Keys, God spelled out the next step with extreme clar-ity: he instructed her to go with pen and clipboard to each trailer parked alongside Chinaberry Street, parallel to the old chemical plant, and ask residents about their health ailments. The first two residents who opened their doors welcomed Keys inside and reported that their youngest children suffered from spina bifida, a developmental birth defect caused by the incomplete closure of the embryonic neural tube. Though spina bifida can be caused by a variety of things—including, but not limited to, diabetes, genetic propensity, obesity, certain medications, or exposure to toxic substances such as lead—Keys regarded it as a divine sign that both families' infants suffered from the same condition and decided she was on the right track.

Keys said she began waking up early in the morning, praying for guidance, and meditating on the Biblical injunction against the idolatry of wealth: *The love of money is the root of all evil things.* According to Keys, God led her back to the abandoned Reichhold plant, where she met a firefighter, Tony Luther, who provided her with a Toxics Release Inventory (TRI) that listed chemicals produced at the Reichhold site. Keys said she then followed God's instructions to visit her old chemistry teacher at Columbia High School. Together, they learned that the buried drums contained over 179 chemicals, many of which were banned during the World War II at the time of the Geneva Convention. Keys also credited God for a phone call she received from an inspector from the Occupational Safety and Health Administration (OSHA), Carl C. McCoy Jr., who complained that Reichhold company officials and politicians had run him out of town for exposing that the plant produced Agent Orange.

Keys had never heard of Agent Orange, so she followed what she said was God's command and read everything she could find on the substance. She soon learned that the United States had sprayed twelve million gallons of the dioxin-laden defoliant during the Vietnam War, which had resulted in half a million Vietnamese children born with birth defects so ghastly that their facial features often ran together like melted wax. Hundreds of thousands of Vietnamese citizens were also left with muscular and skeletal disorders. As a direct result of exposure to Agent Orange, future generations developed a vast variety of cancers in the lungs, larynx, and prostate.[14] *In God's name,* thought Keys, *why would anyone manufacture this diabolic substance in Columbia, Mississippi?*

- ∎ -

Keys ran JPAP out of a bright turquoise-colored trailer plastered with bumper stickers proclaiming "I love clean air" and "Have you received the Holy Ghost since you believe?" The trailer was filled with copies of the Bible as well as other books, such as Rachel Carson's *Silent Spring*, not to mention several filing cabinets brimming with documents relating to the Reichhold case. One day, Keys received an ominous phone call warning her to stop meddling in the Reichhold matter, but she brushed off the call as a prank. Later that evening, she returned to her trailer and discovered her meticulously organized files strewn across the floor, her copy machine stolen, and the trailer's back door broken. "I was spooked," admitted Keys, her eyes growing wide.

After the break-in, Keys says she began looking behind her shoulder more often and informing her parents of her whereabouts each time she left home. The second time Keys received an ominous phone call, she yelled into the receiver, "To die is to gain, and if you remove me from the planet, you're just going to put me closer to where I want to be: the Lord's home!" But she no longer felt safe when she was alone, and she started wondering if her work was making any difference. Keys regained assurance of the righteousness of her cause, though, after word reached her that children playing in the bramble and brier bushes near the abandoned Reichhold site were returning wheezing and dizzy.

Keys and her growing band of supporters spent the next years surveying over two thousand residents of Columbia and its environs affected by chemical dioxins. They slowly built a coalition of 165 community organizations. Guided by Proverbs 29:7, *The righteous care about justice for the poor, but the wicked have no such concern*, members of JPAP spent thousands of hours recording the smallest details of the Reichhold blast and asking residents exactly where they were, what they saw, and how they suffered afterward. Seeing herself as a modern-day prophet crusading against environmental poisoning, Keys declared during our interview, "I am child of God the same way Moses, Joseph, and Esther were children of God. I pray to God to unstop the people's ears and open up their blinded eyes to see what God is doing through our movement and our church."

As health ailments continued to handicap residents of Columbia, the quest for justice seemed more necessary than ever. "I'm done with meetings, greetings, and eatings," declared Keys. "It's time for teaching, preaching, and reaching the Lord!"

Keys frequently reminded her congregants that the "justice" part of ecojustice comes from Proverbs 21:15: *When justice is done, it brings joy to the righteous but terror to evildoers*. She solemnly assured JPAP members, "The wicked will reap what they sow." On another occasion, veering close to a call for divine retribution, Keys declared: "I do know that all who have possession of all this world's stuff and do not share their wealth with the poor, the needy, the underserved communities are going to suffer severely on that Judgment Day when Jesus Christ cracks that sky and comes because they're creating all this hell for people to live [in] . . . people don't have access to the funding they need to create the clean environment that they righteously deserve."[15]

In the following years, JPAP organized letter-writing and call-in campaigns, protested and held public meetings, and even traveled to Washington, DC, to testify to Congress. By preaching against the exploits of the faceless Reichhold Corporation in accessible and impassioned prose, Keys attracted widespread attention from her community and outside funding from the National Library of Medicine, as well as a Robert Wood Johnson Community Health Leader grant.

One day, two local officials from the Marion County courthouse came to Keys's trailer and informed her that she could either keep her job or her organization, but not both. Fired without severance, Keys found herself unemployed for the first time since the age of thirteen. By then, JPAP was growing exponentially and attracting donations from nearby churches that heard of her efforts, so Keys concentrated on her organization full time.[16] She led marches and rallies outside the abandoned Reichhold lot and in front of the courthouse square demanding health care for the community and funds to relocate families. When Reichhold employees attempted to clandestinely relocate drums of chemical waste without explaining their actions to the community, Keys stood in front of their trucks and blocked the road.

In December 1993 Keys shared the stage with Vice President Al Gore at the National Black Church Environmental and Economic Justice Summit and bluntly stated, "I suffer from breathing problems, kidney infections, severe headaches, stomach problems, and I have had a miscarriage myself. My lifespan has been cut in half because of toxic exposure." Keys said Gore later reneged on his promise to visit Columbia, Mississippi. "I was hopeful and prayerful, but he lied just as others do."

When reporters came to Columbia, she told not simply a story of a destitute community, but a cautionary tale of environmental racism. "Columbia, Mississippi, is modern-time slavery," Keys told *E Magainze* in 1994. "The only change is they've upgraded the equipment. We have chemical warfare, a major medical health crisis and legal warfare."

By the late 1990s, Keys had emerged as a national leader in the eco-justice network. She participated in a forum on women leaders in Beijing, China, in 1995; a conference by Amnesty International on Human Rights in 1999; and the World Summit on Sustainable Development in Johannesburg, South Africa, in September 2002. Today Keys's sermons and writings on occasion downplay the contribution of ordinary, low-income people who comprise JPAP. The JPAP press kit is plastered with photos of Keys standing outside the CNN headquarters and alongside public figures such as Johnny Cochran Jr. Inside the press kit are copies of awards that Keys has won and even letters of recommendation from people who have partnered with Keys over the years.

When I mentioned the pioneering work that Professor Robert Bullard carried out on ecojustice, Keys dismissed him, saying her community spearheaded the movement and that "people don't want to give credit where credit is due." At another point, I compared Keys's efforts to those of Erin Brockovich. Keys grew very serious. "The director of that movie came down to speak to me a few years before it was made, and he took all my information, all my work, all my stories, and made this movie that was about me and changed everything." (The film *Erin Brockovich* is the biopic of an environmentalist who currently works for a New York law firm.) Despite Keys's tendency to gasconade, the residents of Columbia clearly appreciate the work she's done to address their plight and raise money for health services. When I asked one elderly resident, Eva Miller, what gives her hope, she pointed at Keys: "Evangelist Keys and the love of Jesus is what gives me hope."

- · -

Today, Keys blames lawyers for what she calls their "get-rich-quick scheme" more than she blames Reichhold. She continues touring the country and speaking at seminaries, Christian colleges, and Mississippi Delta towns where residents are similarly organizing against toxic dumping. Primarily working outside the legal system, JPAP has raised thousands of dollars to relocate families in Columbia to uncontaminated land, hired medical staff to diagnose the ailments of residents, and lobbied state officials to prevent a new chemical company from moving onto the old Reichhold site.

Although Keys herself grew more prominent within the ecojustice movement, the size of JPAP meetings dwindled. Keys said the main impediment JPAP encountered was disillusioned community members who stopped attending meetings once the organization did not achieve immediate results. However, JPAP's bigger problem seems to be its inability to attract widespread interest from larger, secular environmental organizations with established networks of generous donors. JPAP once employed five full-time staff members, but now the organization's funding has dried up. Keys continues her efforts alone off the honorariums she receives from delivering lectures on ecojustice across the country. Keys says JPAP would benefit from the resources of established environmental organizations, but they express only cursory interest in her cause.

Keys's grassroots social movement emerged as a model for communities of faith that are battling environmental racism; however, the impassioned religiosity of JPAP also exposed major rifts in the modern American environmental movement—rifts that seem increasingly difficult to bridge. For years, the nation's most venerable organizations, of which the Sierra Club is the oldest in the United States, have focused their efforts on saving grizzly bears, protecting the Brazilian rainforests, and advocating on behalf of spotted owls. Keys, on the other hand, sees her work as stemming from the Judeo-Christian tradition in which human beings enjoy a superior position in the hierarchy of creation. According to the Biblical account in Genesis, God gave human beings "dominion" over the earth, establishing the stewardship of creation as a sacred trust. At one point Keys told me, "If God wanted us to care more about spotted owls than human beings, God would have given spotted owls dominion of the earth."

Secular environmentalists who devote their life to documenting the damage done to nature by human beings are often uneasy with the claim of religious environmentalists that human species are in a position of inherent superiority in a hierarchy of creation. They see nothing wrong in revering nature for its own sake, whereas religious members of ecojustice organizations instead revere the Creator of nature and focus on how natural disasters affect humans.

Not everyone thinks this fundamental division between religious and secular environmentalists is unbridgeable. Preeminent scientist

E. O. Wilson writes in *The Future of Life*, "I like to think that the environmental values of secular and religious alike arise from the same innate attraction to nature. . . . They express the same compassion for animals, aesthetic response to free-living flowers and birds, and wonders at the mysteries of wild environments."[17]

When I ask Keys about partnering with larger, secular environmental organizations with deeper coffers than JPAP, she immediately says that she would welcome such collaboration. However, in the next breath she says, "They need to focus on God's plan, put him at the center." She ends with a statement that is more riddle than rhyme: "Too much human flesh proves to be the downfall of achieving great success."

When I ask her what she means about putting God at the center, Keys responds, "The two greatest commandments are to love God with all your heart, mind, and strength and to love our neighbor as ourselves—that's what's got to be at the center of our work." I point out that many secular environmentalists may not agree with putting God at the center, and they may find the hell-and-brimstone language in some of her ecojustice sermons off-putting.

Keys pauses and fumbles with the ruffled sleeves of her blouse. "I understand and respect that they may not believe what I believe, and that's fine." Then she narrows her eyes and says very firmly, "But they have *got* to experience what I experience. When you live in a clean, upper-class neighborhood, you don't know what it's like to live in a low-income, minority neighborhood with environmental problems."

Listening to Keys, I suddenly understand that the secular ethos of the environmental movement and the religiosity of ecojustice organizations seem to collide less over questions of faith than questions of class and race.

From the Audubon Club to Greenpeace, the memberships of venerable environmental organizations are made up of predominantly white, upper-class, and secular activists who are largely removed from the hardships experienced by low-income minorities in their own backyards. While secular environmentalists defend humpback whales, ecojustice activists are often religiously inspired minorities protesting the disproportionate impact of hazardous waste, agricultural pesticides, dioxins from incinerators, and air contamination on low-income communities.

Around the time of JPAP's inception in the early 1990s, the Sierra Club's bimonthly publication ran a headline asking, "Are Greens Lily-

White?" A survey conducted by the Environmental Careers Association unequivocally answered that question in the affirmative. The survey found that ten of sixty-one leading environmental groups admit they have no minority members.[18] The racially homogenous and largely secular composition of the nation's leading environmental organizations may explain why they've long overlooked the working-class struggles of minorities.

When the Sierra Club celebrated its golden anniversary in 1992, its departing executive director, Michael Fischer, warned that if it remained "a middle-class group of backpackers, overwhelming white in membership, program and agenda," the club would inevitably "lose influence in an increasingly multicultural country."[19] A year later, the Sierra Club took Fischer's warning seriously and joined Keys for a tour of the Superfund hazardous waste site to witness firsthand the environmental degradation of land, water, and air in her rural community. The brief and somewhat awkward meeting between JPAP and the Sierra Club not only revealed the organizations' divergent approaches to environmentalism, but also suggested how their different economic and racial compositions informed their agendas.

The unusual meeting led Timothy Noah to write an article in 1993 for the *Wall Street Journal* exposing the elitism of established environmental organizations. Noah's article, titled "Sierra Club Takes an Edifying Tour of Black America," noted that the Sierra Club members who surveyed the town inadvertently echoed the doubts expressed by the EPA and out-of-town lawyers: "[They] quietly wonder whether they are witnessing the toxic effect of chemicals . . . or merely the results of extreme poverty."[20] Noah's article highlighted the stark contrast between the Sierra Club members who arrived in their BMWs in the dirt-poor rural town and the JPAP members who lived in rundown trailers, raising doubts about future collaboration between the movements.

— ▪ —

During the eight hours I spent touring Columbia and learning about Keys's efforts, I spoke with half a dozen residents. Lorena Piles, a top-heavy woman with a girlish laugh, told me she would leave her home of fifty-six years in a heartbeat. "I don't want my grandkids growing up here," she said pointing to a cherubic four-year-old girl with five thick braids sprouting in different directions. Jerri Forbes, who is now a full-time nurse and mother of three sick children, told me bluntly, "Reichhold owes us a new life." Eva Miller, a woman in her seventies who sucks air through her teeth when distressed, complained of lesions in her stomach from drinking the tap water. "Anybody that drink that water, they leave early," she said.

As we passed unkempt yards bereft of cars but replete with grocery carts storing recyclable bottles, Keys told me there was one more couple she wanted me to meet. We arrived at a boarded-up motor home surrounded by unruly weeds, and I saw an elderly couple sitting on the porch. The woman wore a dull floral-print dress and looked alarmingly gaunt. The man sat rigidly in his plastic chair wearing an oversized T-shirt caked with dirt, and his eyes seemed fixated on some indiscernible point in the far-off distance. Keys announced, "I've got a journalist here from New York City who is interested in the tragedy." The elderly couple stared blankly at each other. Finally, the man offered a barely audible grunt: "Sure, OK." He asked me what I wanted to know, and I told him I hoped to talk about the tragedy that had occurred a few years ago. "My back gone bust?" he asked. No, I shook my head, not that tragedy. "Can't get no stamps for groceries?" No, I shook my head again, not that one either. "We got no money?" he asked. I was about to clarify that I wanted to know about the Reichhold explosion that occurred over thirty years ago, but then realized he was speaking about a wider tragedy.

10 SHANE CLAIBORNE

The Peaceful Revolution of Downward Mobility

We've become very religious in worshipping greed.
—Senator Bernard "Bernie" Sanders (I-VT)[1]

You cannot serve both God and money.
—Matthew 6:24[2]

On a blustery winter evening in 1995, Shane Claiborne and his friends were lounging in Eastern College's cafeteria and lamenting the subpar quality of college cuisine when they overheard that forty homeless families were facing eviction from an abandoned cathedral in North Philadelphia just twenty miles from their scenic campus.

A native of East Tennessee, twenty-year-old Claiborne, a sociology major, shivered at the thought of braving Philly's bone-chilling winter without a warm sanctuary to call home. The born-again Christian with an aquiline nose and ruddy brown goatee, whose mellifluous drawl betrayed his Southern roots, remembered Matthew 25:40, in which Jesus says, *Whatever you did for one of the least of these brothers and sisters of mine, you did for me.* Claiborne and his friends wolfed down their meals, jumped into their cars, and drove into "the Badlands"—inner-city Philly—to find Saint Edward's Cathedral among the dilapidated buildings.[3]

A year earlier, the Kensington Welfare Rights Union (KWRU) had temporarily helped relocate several homeless families from a rat-infested tent city to Saint Edward's. Although the number of vacant houses surpassed the number of homeless people in North Philly, the abandoned cathedral was the only refuge left for low-income families in an industrial wasteland that provided little opportunity to earn a living wage, let alone afford a house. When Claiborne and his friends located the sprawling cathedral in Kensington, they were greeted with a banner: "How can we worship a homeless man on Sunday and ignore one on Monday?" It took a moment for Claiborne to remember that Jesus, too, was once homeless.

Shortly after knocking on the cathedral's imposing burgundy doors, Claiborne and his friends were embraced by a motley crew of squatters and given a grand tour of the shantytown constructed in the cathedral's parish. Squealing children playfully tossed the visitors' colorful winter hats as solemn adults explained that the Catholic archdiocese planned to evict them in a matter of days. When Claiborne and his friends asked what material goods they should bring to help the homeless families, they were told that their presence was more important than their possessions. The families needed a critical mass of sympathizers to draw attention to their plight so they could remain living in the church instead of freezing on its curbside. The frequently evoked adage "pray as if everything depended on God, but live as if everything depends on your actions" suddenly took on new significance.

Early the next morning, the concerned students plastered their campus with flyers that read: "Jesus is getting kicked out of church in North Philly. Come hear about it. Kea Lounge @ 10 PM tonight." Claiborne expected only a handful of curious students to straggle into the meeting; instead, over a hundred people crammed into the dorm lounge to learn about the looming eviction. The next day, dozens of students poured into the cathedral in solidarity with the families, bringing a unified message: "If they come for you, they'll have to take us too." The homeless shared with Claiborne stories of life on the streets, confiding the embarrassment they felt when passersby shirked from their stench and the fear they experienced when police harassed them for loitering. He listened patiently and, in the following weeks, began ruminating on the special place of the poor in the Gospels. He mentally highlighted over three hundred Biblical verses on the poor, social justice, and God's deep concern for both. Whenever he feared for his friends at Saint Edward's, he reminded himself of Psalms 140:12: *I know that the Lord will maintain the cause of the afflicted, and justice for the poor.* The media picked up the story a week after the students relocated to the poorly insulated parish, which in turn led several prominent city leaders, clergy, and human rights advocates to vocally support the nascent movement.

The students and squatters prepared a "Last Supper" around a rickety table and broke bread together. The homeless families announced to the media that they had spoken to the owner of the building—the Almighty—and were told they were welcome to stay. The students joined Sunday services at the church and sang popular hymns and freedom songs while sharing vinegary apple cider and stale bagels with their new friends. Claiborne said for the first time in his life he experienced true communion.[4]

The charismatic Evangelical knew the police and archdiocese officials would evict the homeless the moment student support waned, so he invested in a cell phone and an air horn. When officials threatened to expel the families, Claiborne received a phone call and immediately sounded the air horn in the middle of the campus. Hearing the warning sign, floods of students headed down to Saint Edward's, belting the lyrics of Tracy Chapman's "Talkin' 'bout a Revolution":

> *Poor people gonna rise up*
> *And get their share*
> *Poor people gonna rise up*
> *And take what's theirs*

Frustrated by the negative press coverage, the archdiocese enlisted the support of a fire marshal to help cool the students' enthusiasm. They planned to diplomatically suggest that the building violated fire and safety standards so evacuation was actually in the best interest of the homeless.

The night before the inspection, two firefighters appeared at the church with a surprising agenda. The rogue firefighters assured Claiborne they supported the right of the homeless to find comfort in God's house; in fact, they felt strongly enough about the issue to jeopardize their own jobs. The firefighters explained that they had clandestinely visited the church after hours to thwart the archdiocese's plan by placing smoke detectors, exit signs, and fire extinguishers throughout the church. The next day, the fire marshal inspected the building and reluctantly admitted it met fire standards.

Shortly after the appearance of the "firefighter angels," Claiborne spotted a comic strip tacked on the church's bulletin board. The comic strip read:

Person 1: I wonder why God allows all this poverty and pain and suffer-
ing in the world.
Person 2: Why don't you ask God?
Person 1: Well, I guess I'm scared.
Person 2: What are you scared of?
Person 1: I guess I'm scared that God will ask me the same question.

Claiborne smiled to himself, the words of Martin Luther King Jr. ringing in his head: "Inhumanity is not only perpetrated by the vitriolic actions of those who are bad, but also perpetrated by the vitiating inaction of those who are good." Away from the rarefied halls of academia and sanctified walls of seminaries, Claiborne reexamined his understanding of his faith. He had long grappled with theodicy, the explanations of why a loving God allows the horrors of poverty, famine, and warfare. Now Claiborne wondered if he, not God, bore the responsibility.

In the following weeks, thanks to a flood of donations from sympathizers across the country, many of the homeless residing in the tatterdemalion cathedral eventually received housing. The student movement at Saint Edward's culminated in the families holding a press conference and marching to the mayor's office with the humble request that he walk in their shoes. To illustrate the point, they discarded their own threadbare shoes outside the mayor's office and extended a standing invitation for him to experience the life of homelessness firsthand.

Nobody answered that invitation more wholeheartedly than Claiborne. Instead of parachuting into the neighborhood with occasional donations and then retreating to suburbia's bubble, Claiborne did the unthinkable. He made the crime-riddled neighborhood his permanent home. He did not tell his neighbors "I'm here to lift you up" but "I'm here to become one with you."

— ▪ —

Claiborne had grown up in the thick of the Bible Belt practicing a Christianity that was safe, comfortable, and trendy. As a self-professed "Jesus freak," he sought out alternatives to what he regarded as blasphemous secular music, such as Guns N' Roses, and only listened to saccharine Christian pop. Claiborne frequently bought Christian bumper stickers with colorful phrases such as "In case of the rapture, this car will be unmanned!" and donned T-shirts plastered with holier-than-thou injunctions like "Repent, You Sinner." The gung-ho proselytizer passed out "Testa-mints" to his classmates—mints wrapped in Scriptural verses—and organized prayer sessions at the flagpole outside his high school. In rural Tennessee, Claiborne's passionate embrace of Christian paraphernalia, coupled with his natural charisma, gained him a group of eager-to-impress disciples who soon elected their outspoken messiah as prom king.

Despite his popularity, Claiborne felt intensely lonely and empty in what seemed like an increasingly claustrophobic world of church socials and small-town gossip. He later confessed to experiencing "spiritual bulimia," gorging himself on all the products of the "Christian industrial complex" and spitting them out with such gusto that he failed to absorb anything nourishing. Although the Bible helped many sinners find redemption, the text only further confounded Claiborne, who noticed with chagrin that the passages featured dying beggars, not prom kings.

As Claiborne studied the Scriptures more closely, he noticed that Jesus preached a message far removed from the one he'd learned in Sunday School. What was so evil about Sodom? According to Ezekiel 16:49, *Now this was the sin of your sister Sodom: she and her daughters were arrogant, overfed, and unconcerned; they didn't help the poor and needy.* When did Jesus ever mention hell? Not often and, when he did, it was a place reserved for those who didn't care for the poor, hungry, homeless, and imprisoned. Why was the Bible full of lepers and sick children? Claiborne found the answer in Luke 4:18–19, which seemed especially sympathetic to their plight: *The Spirit of the Lord is on me, because he has anointed me to proclaim good news to the poor. He has sent me to proclaim freedom for the prisoners and recovery of sight for the blind, to set the oppressed free, to proclaim the year of the Lord's favor.*[5] Living with the homeless at Saint Edward's awakened a sense of the divine in Claiborne, and for the first time the Bible seemed to make sense.

■ ▪ ■

After the initial euphoria of the Saint Edward's campaign fizzled, Claiborne considered brushing off the encounter—or, as the Scriptures say, "conforming to the pattern of the world"—and pursuing a white-collar profession, such as anesthesiology, that would secure him a comfortable upper-class lifestyle. Yet the experience of struggling alongside Philadelphia's poorest residents had awakened a sense of purpose in the young seeker who felt increasingly anxious to find his place in the world.

No longer regarding the Bible as a coffee-table adornment, Claiborne began wondering, *What if Jesus meant all that stuff he said? What if Jesus really expected people to love their enemies, turn the other cheek, and pursue peace? What if the Gospel message really was good news for the poorest of the poor, the homeless at Saint Edward's?* Claiborne knew a lot of people who preached from a pulpit or wrote books on theology, but he didn't know a single person who genuinely tried to live out the Gospel. He decided to embark on a quest for a "true" Christian. Several luminaries came to mind, such as Dietrich Bonhoeffer, who participated in the German resistance movement against Nazism, Martin Luther King Jr., who championed the civil rights movement, and Oscar Romero, who defended the rights of landless peasants in El Salvador.[6] Claiborne realized they were all long dead, mainly because they'd dared to take the Bible too seriously. But then he remembered a petite Albanian nun in the slums of Calcutta—Mother Teresa.

After incessantly badgering Catholic parishes across the country, Claiborne finally tracked down a helpful nun in the Bronx who proffered a phone number for the Missionaries of Charity in Calcutta, India. Shortly thereafter, Claiborne traveled to the slums of the subcontinent and volunteered for ten weeks alongside a woman he affectionately called "Momma T." In the mornings, Claiborne worked in an orphanage called Nabo Jibon, caring for children with physical and mental handicaps, many of whom had been abandoned near train tracks or at government hospitals. In the afternoons, he worked in Khalighat, the Home for the Destitute and Dying, the first hospice Mother Teresa started. Claiborne found others who were similarly shaken out of their complacency by a fresh reading of the Holy Scriptures. For example, a German volunteer named Andy quit his lucrative engineering profession, sold all his possessions, and relocated to the slums of Calcutta. Claiborne knew many fundamentalists back home, but Andy was the first fundamentalist he'd met who literally followed Jesus' command to sell one's worldly possessions and give the money to the poor. Andy told Claiborne he didn't wish to buy his way into heaven by selling his wealth on earth, but instead wanted to emulate Jesus's example in hopes of achieving inner peace.

At a leper's colony in India, Claiborne spent hours sharing stories and jokes with his new friends. Slowly, he came to believe that God dwells not behind the veil in the temple but in the souls of the poor and dying, in the commonplace and the mundane, in things like bread and wine, masala chai and vegetarian cutlets.[7] Claiborne once thought Jesus performed a miracle when he healed a leper, but now he believed the true miracle was that Jesus found compassion to resist social contempt for lepers. Feeling truly alive for the first time in his life, Claiborne decided that leprosy afflicted the shantytowns of Calcutta less than the suburbs of America, where people seemed alarmingly numb to the pain of others. He wondered if the skyrocketing rates of suicide, depression, and loneliness in wealthy, industrialized countries indicated widespread emotional leprosy. While working alongside other volunteers, Claiborne came to agree with the Christian author C. S. Lewis that hell was not a place where God imprisons people but an inner dungeon where one locks God out. He saw himself as a refugee from a land where people compensated for spiritual numbness with expensive electronic gadgetry and reality television shows. Suddenly, the plea in Proverbs 30:8—*Give me neither poverty nor riches! Give me just enough to satisfy my needs*—took on new meaning. Claiborne later credited the lepers for his salvation—a word that he noted comes from "salve" or "to heal"—by delivering him from his spiritual numbness.

As he learned more about Gandhi's mass mobilization against British colonization, Claiborne was struck by the freedom fighter's assessment of Christianity: "I like your Christ, but not your Christians because they're so unlike your Christ." Reevaluating his understanding of his religious commitments, Claiborne wondered if he should spend less time pontificating against the blasphemy of Metallica and more time emulating Christ's example. As his understanding of Christianity evolved from a rigid set of proscriptions to a set of ecumenical values, Claiborne came to understand what Dr. King meant when he wrote in the *Christian Century*: "I believe that in some marvelous way, God worked through Gandhi, and the spirit of Jesus Christ saturated his life. It is ironic, yet inescapably true that the greatest Christian of the modern world was a man who never embraced Christianity."[8]

Viewing Jesus's "third way" as a rejection of both passivity and violence, Claiborne began reading the Bible as a blueprint for creatively protesting injustices. For example, while experiencing poverty firsthand, Claiborne also found new significance in formerly esoteric Biblical passages, such as when Jesus advised impoverished debtors to shame the repo man for his greediness by not only offering the coat on their back but also their underclothes, since nakedness was a taboo. During his stint in Calcutta, he came to agree with the nineteenth-century Danish philosopher Søren Kierkegaard, who once declared, "The Bible is very easy to understand. But we Christians are a bunch of scheming swindlers. We pretend to be unable to understand it because we know very well that the minute we understand, we are obliged to act accordingly." Mother Teresa encouraged Claiborne to contribute to America's struggling communities, to find his "own Calcutta" when he returned home. With the same zeal he once channeled into distributing "Testa-mints," Claiborne began envisioning a new community marked by the interdependence and sacrificial love that characterized the early church: love your neighbor as yourself; nobody has a right to more than she needs when someone has less; if you have two coats, you have stolen one.[9]

— ∎ —

Mapping his own future according to the Christ story, Claiborne decided that Jesus would never sport a "God Bless Rome" T-shirt or recommend that his followers brainstorm ways to run a profit-driven corporation according to Christian ethos. Rather, Claiborne decided, Jesus joined in solidarity with the outcasts and forsaken, spreading his love on the peripheries of society and inviting disciples to join a journey of downward mobility rather than upward aspirations. Claiborne had once considered pursuing a career in politics, but he no longer harbored any illusions of effecting change through existing political institutions. He remembered that Jesus retreated to the desert before starting his public ministry and for forty days was plagued by earthly temptation. One of the temptations he faced was inheriting the kingdoms of the world: *I will give you all their authority and their splendor; it has been given to me, and I can give it to anyone I want to. If you worship me, it will all be yours.* Claiborne decided that Jesus viewed governmental power as the devil's playground so, instead of ascending a throne to establish God's society, he descended into the world as a slave on a donkey. According to Claiborne, Jesus did not want to heal the world through militaries and markets and foreign policies, but through sacrificial love and grace.

Unlike religious conservatives who wish to "reclaim" America for God, Claiborne wished to follow Jesus's recommendation to live as a unique, peculiar, and set-apart people that began with Abraham. [10] After all, thought Claiborne, what good is it to gain the whole world but lose your soul? He decided the great tragedy of rich Christians chasing the so-called American Dream is not that they don't care about the poor, but that they do not know the poor.

Claiborne had previously spent long hours agonizing over his career, especially since his friends and family constantly asked, "What do you want to do when you grow up?" After returning from Calcutta, Claiborne decided that a twenty-year-old Jesus would have responded to that question by saying, "I'm going to comfort beggars, prostitutes, and lepers. I'm going to love my neighbors, not judge them. I'm going to nonviolently oppose unjust social structures."

- ! -

Days after returning from India and still recovering from jet lag, Claiborne walked into the atrium of Willow Creek Community Church in Illinois and entered a food court with a surfeit of dining options. He watched people wantonly discard half their meals in overflowing trash bins and realized how far he had traveled from Calcutta's leper colony. When he tried to explain his discomfort to his friends, they brushed it off as "culture shock." However, Claiborne's shock had far less to do with cultural differences than with global inequality. He wondered why Calcutta's children were forced to eat nothing but unleavened bread while suburban Chicago's children were allowed to waste entire cheeseburgers after eating just one bite. Claiborne decided that God had not made too many people or too little stuff, but that he had made enough for everyone's needs but nobody's greed. Feeling like an outsider in his own homeland, an increasingly introspective Claiborne reflected, "Christians have no problem helping the poor. But question whether our 'blessings' are borne on the backs of the poor and things get messy. The call to 'make poverty history' needs a partner: 'Make affluence history.'"[11]

As an American, Claiborne knew he lived in a disproportionately privileged country. Although less than 5 percent of the world's population lives in the United States, the country consumes over 25 percent of the world's resources and creates roughly 30 percent of its major pollution. After extensively studying the current global economic order vis-à-vis the Bible, Claiborne concluded that the status quo deeply offended God's sensibilities. The study provoked the question, why do an estimated 24,000 people die every single day from hunger-related diseases in a world of plenty? Why are sixty to eighty million people still living in slave-like conditions across the globe? Why does 1 percent of the world's population own 32 percent of the wealth? Why do more than one billion people today live in the slums of the global south? Why does almost a third of the world's population have no access to affordable clean water? How could one billion survive on less than one dollar a day, 162 million of whom live on less than fifty cents a day? How could a God-loving people choose an economic model responsible for a global situation in which less than 25 percent of the world's population uses more than 80 percent of the planet's resources while creating 70 percent of its pollution?[12]

Claiborne didn't have the answers to these questions, but he started to wonder if the American dream starkly contradicted God's dream. He agreed with the renowned author Wendell Berry that one cannot follow God socially if you undermine him economically: "The sense of the holiness of life is not compatible with an exploitative economy. You cannot know that life is holy if you are content to live from economic practices that daily destroy life and diminish its possibility."[13] Claiborne decided that current lifestyles of single-family dwellings, a car per person, and a house full of "my" stuff purchased cheaply from Taiwan went against the teachings of the early church, where members held possessions in common and cared for the least among them. As bleak as the situation was, Claiborne took heart in knowing that Dr. King had already started the gritty work of mobilizing a Poor People's Campaign shortly before his assassination. He was struck by King's pragmatic approach to organizing:

Beginning in the New Year, we will be recruiting three thousand of the poorest citizens from ten different urban and rural areas to initiate and lead a sustained, massive, direct action movement in Washington. Those who choose to join this initial three thousand, this non-violent army, this 'freedom church' of the poor, will work with us for three months to develop non-violent action skills. Then we will move on Washington, determined to stay there until the legislative and executive branches of the government take serious and adequate action on jobs and income. A delegation of poor people can walk into a high official's office with a carefully, collectively prepared list of demands.[14]

Claiborne hoped to follow King's outline for building a Freedom Church of the Poor. Studying the Bible with fresh curiosity, Claiborne began unraveling the arcane Sabbath laws and came to view them as God's system of checks and balances to make sure the Hebrew people did not revert to the exploitative economy of the empire from which they were saved. After learning that Exodus 22 and 23 instructed the Israelites to help the aliens, widows, orphans, and the poor, Claiborne wondered why there were not similar secular laws defending the most vulnerable members of society. He came to believe that God cared about protecting the fragile world that humans were only too happy to exploit. In the ancient world of Exodus, Leviticus, and Deuteronomy, Claiborne found laws for welcoming strangers and for engaging in practices such as gleaning, which allowed the poor to take leftovers from the field. He speculated that God would disapprove of many modern laws, such as those prohibiting Dumpster diving for food. Similarly, Claiborne came to appreciate ancient edicts that aimed to systemically break destructive patterns threatening the community fabric. Such edicts included the Sabbath law of Jubilee, which was applied every seven years and encouraged the Hebrew people to rest from work for a year, reestablish ecological equilibrium, and share all the food grown in their fields with the needy (see Exodus 23:10). Most important, any debt that peasants incurred during the past six years was forgiven. To Claiborne, God seemed to prescribe these laws to ensure the disparity between richest and poorest was minimized and that there be "no poor among you" (Deuteronomy 15:4). The "Jubilee of Jubilee," a giant celebration every forty-ninth year, was the way a benevolent God maintained equilibrium in society through what Claiborne came to call a "regularly scheduled revolution" that leveled the playing the field.

The more Claiborne studied Scripture, the more dissatisfied he grew with the economic and political status quo. By evoking the anti-imperial economic tradition of the Torah, Claiborne decided that God would favor debt cancellation and disapprove of trickle-down economics. He believed the authors of Leviticus channeled God's egalitarian spirit by mandating that, every seven sabbatical cycles, a half century of property sales be reversed, outstanding debts relieved, and all slaves manumitted.[15] Yet, as Claiborne learned, when countries of the global south won independence, the accumulated debts of the colonial powers used to open new markets were transferred to nascent local governments. Today, sub-Saharan Africa—one of the poorest parts of the world—is paying $25,000 every minute to northern creditors. In Africa, in the 1990s, the number of people living on less than one dollar a day rose from 273 million to 328 million—not to mention the fact that the developing world spends thirteen dollars on debt repayment for every one dollar it receives in grants.[16] Claiborne decided that unfairly accumulated debt coupled with neoliberal economic policies prevented already impoverished countries from escaping the manacles of poverty while allowing richer countries to reap more than their fair share, and he found this blasphemous.

Upon reading the ancient injunction against taking financial interest or creating debt, Claiborne wondered if a bank owner in twenty-first-century America was as much a criminal as a bank robber. The young theologian did not desire to reestablish Mosaic Law but did wish to preserve the kernels of wisdom he found in their teachings. Formerly anachronistic Biblical injunctions sprung to life, and Claiborne envisioned updating the purity laws in Leviticus and Deuteronomy to have modern relevance: "Thou shalt not wear clothing marked with a swoosh or any other image that requires the blood of sweatshop children" and "Thou shalt not make virtual friends on Facebook but real friends in soup kitchens" and "Thou shalt not contribute to Middle East wars but, instead, run your automobiles off recycled vegetable oil."

Reading the Gospel message as "good news for the poor," Claiborne connected the Biblical story of David and Goliath to the contemporary struggle of a landless peasant like César Chávez—the devout Catholic labor organizer who successfully resisted an inhumane corporation against all odds. Claiborne tried to imagine what jubilee economics would mean today and decided that turning the entire current system on its head was a good start. He envisioned a new economy in which Third-World debt was forgiven, and the Magnificat of Mary guided the US tax code: *He has filled the hungry with good things, and the rich He has sent empty away.*[17] The more Claiborne studied Holy Scriptures, the more he believed that the Prince of Peace would have wanted taxes to fall on property ownership and not wages, the poor to have sovereignty over the land they tilled, and dispossessed peasants to claim their right to natural resources instead of private corporations seeking to make a profit. Swords should be converted into plowshares.

- ■ -

On July 4, 1845, poet Henry David Thoreau embarked on a two-year experiment in simple living when he retreated to a modest, hand-built house in a second-growth forest around the shores of Walden Pond in Massachusetts. The poet conscientiously disengaged from a society he deemed unjust for condoning slavery and waging war against Mexico to further spread human bondage.[18] Thoreau urged others to demonstrate similar moral opposition to abuse of governmental power and started a proud tradition of conscientious disengagement, a tradition that Claiborne would choose to follow more than a century and a half later.

The more Claiborne and his friends learned about the roots of poverty, the more they, too, wished to withdraw from a society they saw as unjust and exploitative. Yet they based their dissent in Christian theology rather than American transcendentalism. Instead of retreating to Walden Pond, they found a different type of sanctuary—Philadelphia's inner city—from which to practice jubilee economics and build a new society out of the shell of the old. The young Christians saw themselves as a web of subversive friends living on the margins of an empire, setting up an alternative society based on love and the Gospel example. Claiborne saw eerie similarities between the Roman Empire and the American Empire, such as the awe and fear they evoked in the rest of the world, as well as their exorbitant military spending.

In January 1998 Claiborne and five friends moved into a little row house in Kensington, one of Pennsylvania's poorest neighborhoods, just minutes from old Saint Edward's Cathedral.[19] They began an experiment called the Simple Way. Evoking the words of Justin Martyr, an early Christian saint, they ran the Simple Way as a cooperative: "We who formerly treasured money and possessions more than anything else now hand over everything we have to a treasury for all and share it with everyone who needs it."[20] Inspired also by Dorothy Day's House of Hospitality in the slums of New York City and her series of communal farms, they opened their doors to the poorest of the poor, provided the homeless with donated clothes, transformed abandoned lots into community gardens, nonviolently protested police brutality, organized performing arts initiatives for local children, provided homework help to struggling students, and renovated abandoned houses.[21]

The community also found inspiration in Dr. Martin Luther King Jr.'s defense of nonviolent civil disobedience:

> There is nothing wrong with a traffic law which says you have to stop for a red light. But when a fire is raging, the fire truck goes through that red light, and normal traffic had better get out of its way. Or when a man is bleeding . . . the ambulance goes through those red lights at top speed. There is a fire raging . . . for the poor of this society. Disinherited people . . . are bleeding to death from the deep social and economic wounds. They need brigades of ambulance drivers who will have to ignore the red lights of the present system until the emergency is solved.[22]

Members of the Simple Way served jail sentences for protesting laws targeting the homeless and paid fines for distributing free food to the hungry. Building a countercultural village in which power was shared horizontally rather than administered vertically, members hoped to serve as God's hands and feet rather than his bullhorn.

Just as ancient Israel was an alternative to the exploitative economies in Egypt and Canaan, Claiborne says the Simple Way hopes to chart a "third way" in which communities eradicate poverty locally by sharing possessions communally. For example, they started making their own clothes and shoes, growing their own food, and creating a self-sustaining community that aimed to disengage from a global economic system that they deemed environmentally unsustainable and unforgivably exploitative.[23] Members of the Simple Way also wished to disengage from indirectly supporting sweatshops around the world, which they regarded as marked by slave-like labor conditions, nonnegotiable hours, emotional humiliation, physical danger, and human rights violations.

Living in the destitute urban neighborhood changed Claiborne's entire outlook on religion. Sin was no longer just personal—an individual having an affair or committing murder—but also societal. The history of racism, prejudice, and class warfare in this country that left people hungry and homeless was blood on everyone's hands. Sin was the existence of failing schools for the poor and elite academies for the rich. Sin was overcrowded prisons for the poor and cunning lawyers for the rich. Sin was eating out of Dumpsters for the poor and indulging in lavish buffets for the rich. Claiborne had studied sociology at Eastern College with Tony Campolo, the acclaimed founder of a movement called Red Letter Christians, which focuses on Jesus's social teachings. Living among the poor, Claiborne suddenly understood why Campolo lambasted as sinful banks' redlining, real estate speculation taking advantage of racism, and withdrawal of government programs previously earmarked for neighborhood renewal.[24] Sin was the fact that two-thirds of the nation's total income gains from 2002 to 2007 flowed to the top 1 percent of US households, and that top 1 percent held a larger share of income in 2007 than at any time since 1928.[25] Sin was government policy and market forces moving in the same direction—toward increasing inequality.[26] Sin was the reality that, since the late 1970s, the income of the wealthy has soared, while their tax rates have simultaneously fallen more than those of any other group.[27] Sin was billion-dollar bailouts for the richest and understaffed soup kitchens for the poorest.

— ▪ —

When friends asked Claiborne if he was scared of living in the inner city, he promptly replied that he was more frightened by the suburbs. For the young Evangelical, there was no place more dangerous than the safety of wealthy America, detached from the suffering of others and euthanized by creature comforts. When Claiborne and a friend from the neighborhood were beaten by a group of teenagers, they shocked their assailants by refusing to retaliate. Instead, Claiborne locked eyes with the group's ringleader and explained calmly but forcefully, "We are followers of Jesus and we do not fight, but we will love you no matter what you do to us."[28] The rowdy teenagers laughed nervously and eventually dispersed.

In his book *The Irresistible Revolution: Living as an Ordinary Radical*, Claiborne elaborated on the practices and philosophy animating the Simple Way:

> We have always called ourselves a tax-exempt 501c3 *anti*-profit organization. We wrestle to free ourselves from macro-charity and distant acts of charity that serve to legitimize apathetic lifestyles of good intentions

but rob us of the gift of community. We visit rich people and have them visit us. We preach, prophesy, and dream together about how to awaken the church from her violent slumber. Sometimes we speak to change the world; other times we speak to keep the world from changing us. We are about ending poverty, not simply managing it. We give people fish. We teach them to fish. We tear down the walls that have been built up around the fish pond. And we figure out who polluted it. We fight terrorism—the terrorism within each of us, the terrorism of corporate greed, of American consumerism, of war. We are not pacifist hippies but passionate lovers who abhor passivity and violence. We spend our lives actively resisting everything that destroys life, whether that be terrorism or the war on terrorism. We try to make the world safe, knowing that the world will never be safe as long as millions live in poverty so the few can live as they wish.[29]

Shane Walker, the pastor of Andover Baptist Church in Maryland, reviewed the book with a deep skepticism that is pervasive among Claiborne's critics: "His theology is an unbiblical and incoherent synthesis which might be described as popularized Christian anarchism for young, disaffected, middle-class Americans."[30]

Many conservative Evangelicals criticize Claiborne for his alleged disdain of laissez-faire capitalism, his perceived support of socialism, and his radical political views. Living in a country they regard as a meritocracy, his critics worry that Claiborne undermines the American Dream that has inspired countless hardworking individuals to demonstrate an entrepreneurial spirit. His critics ask, if there are certain inequalities in income and wealth that fuel a healthy competitive spirit of entrepreneurship, why not permit them? These critics often scoff at Claiborne's understanding of global economic relations, calling them facile and pointing out that many countries have achieved unprecedented rates of economic growth thanks to foreign direct investment and the export-led growth that followed. They insist that globalization, defined as the integration of economic activities via markets, is improving the world in multifarious ways and lament that Claiborne, who is not an economist, makes a living denouncing the system on the lecture circuit. His critics quote Matthew 22:21—*Give to Caesar what is Caesar's, and to God what is God's*—to support their claim that Christians should obey the state authorities' established economic and political rules.

When his critics accuse him of spouting communist ideology, Claiborne responds that genuinely embracing Christ's call to love our neighbors as ourselves would render capitalism obsolete and communism unnecessary. "Redistribution is only meaningful [inasmuch] as it is rooted in love and relationships," Claiborne told *Faithworks* magazine. "It is not a prescription for community but just a description of what happens when we live our lives alongside people who are hurting. If we really have genuine friendships with the poor then redistribution is inevitable—we see that in the early Church. They ended poverty in the early Church and we believe that we can do that again."[31]

In January 2008 Cedarville University, a conservative Baptist school in southwest Ohio, decided to cancel one of Claiborne's scheduled lectures after a small but vocal number of bloggers deemed his views as a dangerous step toward liberal theology. Ingrid Schlueter, one of the irate bloggers, told *Christianity Today*, "At bottom, what we're concerned about is Biblical truth." She added, "It's a repackaging of liberalism for a postmodern generation."[32] Claiborne responded publicly, "I would love to have a conversation with these folks who disagree with me" and offered to use the honorarium Cedarville promised for the lecture to fly his critics to inner-city Philadelphia so they could have a conversation in the same spirit that Jesus invited tax-collectors to dinner.[33] To date, none of his critics have taken him up on his offer.

— ∙ —

Claiborne, as a student of Gandhi, also believes that embracing homespun creations becomes a small act of resistance to the corporate global economy. He believes it is a revolutionary act to resist the narrow, choking logic of the cult of Mammon and its chorus of naysayers who insist that we must pillage the Democratic Republic of the Congo for its minerals if we want cheap electronics, and we must exploit seasonal tomato pickers if we want to enjoy cheap burritos. The secular equivalent of the cult of Mammon is best captured by a slogan first popularized by Margaret Thatcher: There Is No Alernative (TINA). However, Claiborne believes the Simple Way community is indeed creating an alternative society unplugged from what the book of Revelation calls the maddening whore of an economy that is leeching off the poorest.

Long before Claiborne was born, late-eighteenth-century Quakers encouraged consumers to purchase produce derived only from non-slave labor in an attempt to make slavery economically unfeasible. Similarly, the forgotten grandmother of the Fair Trade Movement, the Free Produce Movement, boycotted goods produced by slave labor. In 1826 the boycott began in earnest when Quaker Benjamin Lundy opened a store in Baltimore, Maryland, selling only goods obtained by labor from free people.[34] The following year, the movement broadened with the formation in Philadelphia of the Free Produce Society, which was founded by Thomas M'Clintock and other radical Quakers.

Over a century later, thanks to the visionary work of a pioneering Mennonite named Edna Ruth Byler, North Americans would learn they were still purchasing goods produced by slave labor abroad. In 1946 Byler was deeply disturbed by the overwhelming poverty and repressive labor conditions she witnessed while visiting Puerto Rico. Six years later, she and her colleague Ruth Lederach brought quality linen needlework from Puerto Rico to a Mennonite world conference in Switzerland, becoming the first people on record to conscientiously trade fairly in the global economy.

For several years, Byler continued to sell the needlework from the trunk of her car and funnel profits to poverty-alleviation efforts. In 1958 she opened her first shop in Akron, Pennsylvania, in hopes of providing sustainable economic opportunities for artisans in developing countries by creating a viable marketplace for their products in North America. Byler toured the nation educating communities about the lives of artisans around the world. The store eventually expanded and changed its name to Ten Thousand Villages, which has grown into a global network of social entrepreneurs working to empower and provide economic opportunities to artisans in developing countries.[35]

Today, "Fair Trade" indicates equitable partnerships across the globe cooperating to protect the human rights of workers and the integrity of the environment during the production of commodities. Although Fair Trade started as a tiny religious movement, proponents now include a growing number of social, religious, and environmental organizations such as Amnesty International, Catholic Relief Services, and Oxfam. The Interfaith Working Group on Trade and Investment, an organization with representatives from a range of faith-based organizations, captures the sentiment of many in the Fair Trade movement: "international trade and investment activities should advance the common good and be evaluated in the light of their impact on the most vulnerable."[36] In 2008 Fair Trade–certified sales amounted to approximately $4.08 billion worldwide, a 22-percent year-to-year increase.

■ ● ■

Claiborne says his steadfast devotion to God has driven his commitment to disrupt the human systems that create poverty and to struggle to create new systems that release debt, set slaves free, prohibit usury, and redistribute property. For Claiborne, Americans need emancipation from both ghettos of poverty and ghettos of opulence because the former deprives the body and the latter the spirit. Mother Teresa once explained to him that the wealthy are afflicted with the most terrible poverty of all—loneliness. The Simple Way, according to Claiborne, seeks to create a community-based alternative that liberates the wealthy from their spiritually malnourished lifestyles and the poor from the yoke of providing the amenities needed to sustain that lifestyle.

Claiborne was deeply influenced by radical Catholic peace activist Dorothy Day's writings on the roots of war, oppression, and poverty. During the Great Depression, Day vowed to house the homeless, feed the hungry, and tend the sick, though her total savings amounted to ninety-seven cents.[37] Often called the American Mother Teresa, Day persisted in her faith and launched the activist newspaper the *Catholic Worker*. For forty years, Day combined orthodox Catholic morality with service to the poor and bold support for peace and justice. She reflected on the Sisyphean struggle for pacifism in the face of the emerging cold war: "Whenever I groan within myself and think how hard it is to keep writing about love in these times of tension and strife which may, at any moment, become for us all a time of terror, I think to myself: What else is the world interested in? What else do we all want, each one of us, except to love and be loved, in our families, in our work, in all our relationships?"[38] Claiborne shared Day's sadness over the amount of money spent on his country's military machinery compared with social programs. Today, cutting global poverty in half would cost $20 billion, less than 4 percent of the US military budget. He began asking himself if allegiance to both "God and country" made sense when the two entities' interests diverged so widely: one said turn the other cheek, and the other said draw your sword; one said the love of money was the root of all evil, and the other elevated corporations to the status of personhood. The riffs on the Beatitudes, such as "blessed are the troops," that Claiborne had often heard in church as a child now sounded more devilish than divine. He believed that the best way to preserve the kingdom of God was to empower the church to resist ruling the world with the sword and resist descending to the level of the beast it wished to destroy.

On the eve of the Iraq Invasion of 2003, Claiborne was one of several peace activists who traveled to Baghdad to stand in solidarity with the Iraqis against warfare. He explained his decision by saying:

> I believe in a safe world, and I know this world will never be safe as long as the masses live in poverty so that a handful of people can live as they wish. Nor will the world be safe as long as we try to use violence to drive out violence. . . . Thousands of soldiers have gone to Iraq willing to kill people they do not know because of a political allegiance. I go willing to die for people I do not know because of a spiritual allegiance.[39]

Claiborne returned from his trip to Iraq and traveled across the country speaking about the suffering he witnessed. Lamenting the horrors of militarized Christianity, Claiborne highlighted the commonalities among Abrahamic religions, saying all three emphasize compassion, humility, and generosity toward one another. This shared fraternal responsibility, he said, should serve as the sacred ground to foster communication.

Some audience members accused him of lacking patriotism while the country waged a war against evil, of devaluing Christianity by granting other religions equal stature, and of undermining the war efforts by traveling into "enemy" territory. Claiborne calmly explained that every major religious tradition encourages alleviating poverty and creating an equitable world, that Iraq was not enemy territory but the cradle of the world's major religions, and that warmongering Christian extremists at home were as dangerous as the worst terrorists abroad. When speaking about George W. Bush, Claiborne reminded his audience of the warning in Galatians 1:7: *Evidently some people are throwing you into confusion and are trying to pervert the gospel of Christ.*

Claiborne received stacks of letters from irate pastors accusing him of anti-American sentiments and a dangerously unpatriotic attitude. He wrote back, explaining that he is a Christian first and an American second. He brushed off outrage from the Christian establishment, reminding himself that Jesus had warned his followers that the world would hate his true followers, drag them before governors and courts, and insult them publicly.[40] Claiborne believes that bearing the cross of Calvary means accepting the results of a moral clash with the powers ruling society, whether those powers are the Biblical Pharisees or the Religious Right.[41]

Attacked from both sides, Claiborne also received letters from secular antiwar Americans who belittled his religious commitments, insisting that Christianity was part of the problem, not the solution. Claiborne recently addressed their concerns in an open letter that he published in *Esquire* magazine:

> I am sorry that so often the biggest obstacle to God has been Christians. Christians who have had so much to say with our mouths and so little to show with our lives. I am sorry that so often we have forgotten the Christ of our Christianity. . . . The more I have read the Bible and studied the life of Jesus, the more I have become convinced that Christianity spreads best not through force but through fascination. . . . I was recently asked by a non-Christian friend if I thought he was going to hell. I said, "I hope not. It will be hard to enjoy heaven without you."[42]

For Claiborne, Christianity is best when it is peculiar, suffering, and peripheral rather than popular, boastful, and powerful.

- ∎ -

Today, thirty-five-year-old Claiborne has emerged as a humorous prophet of his generation, encouraging his tens of thousands of followers to live out their faith by creating a radically better alternative. His piecemeal clothes are recycled from burlap bags and give him the unkempt appearance of a modern-day Saint Francis of Assisi. He depends on the hospitality of strangers when he travels on his lecture circuit and prefers transportation powered by used vegetable oil or homemade biodiesel. He explains that his bus is a political symbol: "It'll be a long time before we fight a war over used veggie oil."[43] At community potlucks, Claiborne labels food as "vegetarian," "vegan," or "rescued" (if it came from a Dumpster). In the Simple Way's garden, old refrigerators serve as compost bins and gutted computers are converted into flowerpots. He joins his friends in making bags out of curtains—using old seatbelts for straps—and shoes out of recycled tires. One of Claiborne's favorite holidays is Buy Nothing Day, which is a protest of the consumer activity that peaks annually after Thanksgiving and before Christmas. The only purchases that he encourages are shares of the crop yield in community-supported agriculture (CSA) to support small farmers whose existence is threatened by agribusinesses. In his books, Claiborne unequivocally encourages soldiers to leave the military. In his lectures, he unapologetically denounces the prison industrial complex as a new form of slavery for African Americans, reminding coreligionists of the Biblical emancipation proclamation: "I have come to set the captives free."

During election years, Claiborne encourages friends not to choose the lesser of two evils (or, as he prefers to say, "the evil of two lessers") but instead partner with undocumented immigrants and channel their views at the voting booth. Personally, he believes any political platform Jesus would endorse today would resonate far less with neoconservative Christians than democratic socialists, but he is of course all too aware that more than 75 percent of Evangelicals voted for George W. Bush in 2004. As he told a crowded Baptist church in Pittsburgh, Pennsylvania, in the summer of 2008: "With the respectability and the power of the church comes the temptation to prostitute our identity for every political agenda."

Claiborne urges his coreligionists to concentrate less on how they vote November 4 than on how they live November 3 and 5. They should live as Good Samaritans and citizen peacemakers.[44] Although his radical critique of economic disparities resonates strongly with Reverend Billy of the Green Party, Claiborne eschews political labels. He says that Christian theology, not political ideology, informs his messages of economic justice, environmental protection, and antimilitarism. A typical call-and-response of his goes:

Claiborne: With governments that kill . . .
Audience: We will not comply!
Claiborne: With the theology of Empire . . .
Audience: We will not comply!
Claiborne: With the business of militarism . . .

Audience: We will not comply!
Claiborne: With the hoarding of riches . . .
Audience: We will not comply!
Claiborne: With the dissemination of fear . . .
Audience: We will not comply![45]

Claiborne is not alone in his use of the phrase "theology of Empire." Describing the rampage of corporate globalization, a third-world Christian theologian named Mary John Mananzan reminds us that global development "has its God: profit and money . . . its high priests: GATT, WTO, IMF-WB . . . its doctrines and dogmas: import liberalization, deregulation . . . its temples: the super megamalls. It has its victims on the altar of sacrifice: the majority of the world—the excluded and marginalized poor."[46]

■ ▪ ■

Religious criticism of the current economic order further penetrated mainstream consciousness in 2009 when documentary director Michael Moore released *Capitalism: A Love Story*. Moore told *Fortune* that capitalism is not only antidemocratic and anti-American, but also anti-Jesus:

> I think religion should be a private matter. But I thought it was important to this discussion. I'm not a proselytizer, but I do have very strong beliefs and these beliefs were formed not in the school of Karl Marx, but in the Catholic Church. Priests and nuns taught me these lessons of how we're to treat each other, how we're to treat the poor, and how we're to divide up the pie.[47]

In Moore's documentary, Father Dick Preston proclaims: "[Capitalism] is contrary to the common good. It is contrary to compassion. It is contrary to all the major religions."[48]

Claiborne found himself emphatically nodding when watching the documentary, asking himself, "When did Jesus become a hard-nosed capitalist?" He says he would have appreciated more examples of how myriad faith traditions are challenging the Church of Corporate Globalization. For Claiborne, the Simple Way resists conforming to the world in order to remain relevant to the homeless and the outcast, the marginalized and the excluded. As he notes, the challenge is not merely "right thinking," but also "right living." When Claiborne speaks about "conversion," he refers to renewing one's mind, expanding one's imagination, and breaking free of the patterns of hedonism, apathy, and passivity that are destroying our world.

Several other radical faith communities have emerged globally since the foundation of Claiborne's Simple Way. They all emulate the third-order Franciscans' unofficial motto: "Live simply so others may simply live." These interconnected communities, sometimes referred to as the New Monasticism Movement, seek to emulate the example of Jesus, to rediscover the spirit of the early Church, and to incarnate the "Kingdom of God"—a way of life standing in stark contrast to the world of militarism and materialism.[49]

EPILOGUE

Interfaith Covenant for Peace and Justice in Modern America

This call for a worldwide fellowship that lifts neighborly concern beyond one's tribe, race, class, and nation is in reality a call for an all-embracing and unconditional love for all mankind. . . . When I speak of love I am not speaking of some sentimental and weak response. I am not speaking of that force which is just emotional bosh. I am speaking of that force which all of the great religions have seen as the supreme unifying principle of life.

—MARTIN LUTHER KING JR.,
"BEYOND VIETNAM: A TIME TO BREAK THE SILENCE"

In 1914 Christians seeking to prevent the outbreak of war in Europe convened an ecumenical meeting in Switzerland. Before the conference ended, however, World War I began and the peacemakers were forced to return to their respective countries. At a railroad station in Germany, two of the participants, Henry Hodgkin, an English Quaker, and Friedrich Sigmund-Schultze, a German Lutheran, promised to find a way to work for peace even though their countries were hell-bent on destroying one another. Thanks to this pledge, religious peace activists gathered in Cambridge, England, in December of that year and created the Fellowship of Reconciliation (FOR). One year later, FOR-USA was founded. With the mission of organizing the "progressive religious community," FOR today has branches and groups in over forty countries and on every continent. The organization has helped rescue political refugees from Nazis, supported Dr. King's Montgomery bus boycott, created the precursor of the ACLU, assisted conscientious objectors during the Vietnam War, circulated the writings of Gandhi and Dorothy Day, led nonviolent educational workshops across the world, violated US economic sanctions against Iraq by distributing medical aid, and organized an interfaith prayer vigil against hate crimes after the murder of Matthew Shepard. Challenging the vogue in progressive America to regard religious affiliations as divisive, an overwhelming multitude of organizations such as FOR envision a beloved community where differences are respected, conflicts are addressed nonviolently, and oppressive structures are dismantled.[1]

Such efforts are not limited to the Judeo-Christian tradition, but extend to Islam as well. Muslims clerics from every major Islamic country are involved in a new initiative called "A Common Word." They hope to foster interreligious amity by focusing on verse 3:64 of the Qur'an: *O People of the Scripture! Come to a common word between us and you.*[2] Similarly, Baha'is are fostering greater international dialogue through education campaigns that teach tolerance; Zoroastrians are demonstrating ecological wisdom through green burial practices; and Hindus are promoting animal rights through free vegetarian cooking classes. As Homer said, "All men need the gods"; social justice activists have realized that the gods also need them.

Interfaith collaboration is important, but so is collaboration between religious and secular Americans who share a common vision. Many of us on the secular left are aware of religious zealots who wave signs declaring "God hates faggots." Yet how many know about a group of Christians who set up a tent at a Gay Pride parade to apologize on behalf of those who wrong the LGBTQ community in the name of their God?[3] The real division is no longer between believers and atheists but political conservatives and progressive visionaries.

This is not to suggest that religion is never at the heart of conflicts or that religious people are never responsible for heinous acts. The world-famous theologian Reinhold Niebuhr noted we must criticize religion for its insularism, oppressiveness, and claims to absolute truth. Religion does often foster moral indignation and self-aggrandizement. However, it is not a Rosetta Stone for understanding the world's myriad problems.

It is worth remembering that people have committed equally horrifying deeds in the name of scientific progress, Marxist ideology, and spreading democracy.

Religiously inspired progressives are the first to cringe when confronted by the Religious Right's tyranny and religious extremists' militancy, but too often they are not given the opportunity to articulate their motivations for embracing a particular creed. Dr. Cornel West explains why he joined the church:

> I vowed then that just when I joined church and accepted Jesus, I'd be faithful unto death, that I would be faithful until the day I die to struggling for the same kinds of conceptions of justice that Martin King and Malcolm [X] and Philip Berrigan and Dorothy Day and Rabbi Abraham Joshua Heschel and others represented and, in my own feeble way, try to enact and embody the kind of ideals that they were putting forward.[4]

Religion is disruptive, but not necessarily destructive. Karl Marx famously wrote, "Religion is the opium of the masses," but religion stirs people awake as often as it lulls them to sleep. If religion is opium, it is also caffeine. Atheists who decry religion as a crutch of the ignorant and frightened do a disservice to people of faith who dedicate their lives to improving the human condition. Those of us who are not religious must have enough humility to admit we don't possess all the answers and enough foresight to partner with religious communities protesting environmental degradation, economic inequalities, and perpetual warfare.

The division of church and state is sacrosanct, but there is a place for a symbiotic relationship between religion and politics that combines personal peacefulness with the pursuit of justice. Scholar Roger S. Gottlieb notes: "Religious passion without political understanding slips all too easily into the errors of historical ignorance and personal narcissism. And political activism without the gifts of religion may well be blind to our own humanity and that of those we wish to reach."[5]

Whether a person draws on Jesus Christ, Eugene Debs, or the Enlightened Buddha to support her positions, she must earn the right to be heard by the quality of her arguments without expectation of favoritism or discrimination. And, sometimes, spiritual insights offer a much-needed additional perspective to the civic religions of mass consumption, hedonism, and passivity. The evolving interpretation of what is or isn't sacrosanct is a gradual process of imagining, creating, and advancing a more utopian society.

A relatively unknown man, Tom Fewel, is among those providing a much-needed alternative narrative by suggesting religious compassion provides emancipation from world-weariness.[6] In 1985, Fewel's eight-year-old daughter was kidnapped and murdered in cold blood. Shortly afterward, a grief-stricken Fewel heard his pastor at Binkley Church in North Carolina share a story about a child afraid to go to bed alone. When her mother said, "You'll be OK because God is with you," the girl exclaimed, "But I want somebody with skin!" Fewel remembered how his entire church came together to help his grieving family in the wake of his daughter's murder. He reflected, "The folks at Binkley Church became the presence of God to us—with skin." He added, "They practiced the essential commandment, to love." More than twenty years later, Fewel still misses his daughter, but he has found a sense of peace through his involvement with Murder Victims' Families for Reconciliation, which advocates abolishing the death penalty. "I believe that human life is sacred, that this sanctity is imparted by God to every individual and cannot be forfeited," notes Fewel.

The spiritual imperative to live one's values—rather than simply assess their political efficacy—affords a sense of humility and integrity often lacking in purely secular political movements.[7] When I mentioned to Fewel that I regretted that I might not have space to include his story in my manuscript, he nodded understandingly and said, "It is important to me that the power of faith lived out in love is included, whether in my story or not."

I hope this book shows that we are all the skin of God. We are the ones with the power to love one another, answer each other's prayers, and create a more heavenly world.

AFTERWORD

Roger S. Gottlieb

The day I received this manuscript, my local newspaper informed me that Islamic clerics were criticizing Pakistan's new antidomestic violence law as a "threat to the family." At the same time, a papal spokesman was decrying public condemnation of the church's handling of abusive priests as somehow similar to anti-Semitic persecution during the Holocaust. On a day like that you could certainly be forgiven for wondering why we should bother with religion at all, especially if our central concerns are to make the world more just, peaceful, and ecologically sensible.

But of course the moral failings of Islamic clerics in thrall to the patriarchy and Catholic spokesmen slavishly protecting their institution are only part of the story. It is the other part that Deena Guzder has chronicled intelligently and engagingly in this fine book.

Contrary to the secular folks who think that "religion just makes things worse," religion actually has an extremely mixed, and often contradictory, relation to a broad range of social justice concerns: democracy, women's rights, racial and ethnic minority rights, gay and lesbian liberation, environmentalism, international peace, disarmament. On the one hand, it is not hard to point to the centuries during which Christian authorities opposed democracy and supported royalty or to the traditional Buddhist view that a monk's dedication to the goal of enlightenment is fundamentally at odds with political action. By contrast, however, some scholars have actually argued that a number of the basic ideas of democracy itself—human rights and equal respect under the law, for example—are in fact derived from basic religious principles (such as the Biblical claim that we are all made in the image of God). And it is not hard to find—if one is looking—many times when religiously motivated people made clear and important contributions to the advancement of social justice. The abolitionist movement in the United States and the antiapartheid movement in South Africa are two obvious examples.

Guzder offers us here a wealth of such examples. Though she references some of the usual suspects, such as religion's inspirational role in the civil rights and antiwar movements, she also highlights Christianity's less-well-known presence in contemporary struggles against the death penalty and globalization and for environmental sanity. While Guzder acknowledges Marx's often true claim that religion is the "opium of the masses," she adds that the reverse is also true: "If religion is opium," she tells us, "it is also caffeine." It can put us to sleep or rouse us to a higher, more politically engaged and socially responsible, consciousness and life.

Thus this book helps us realize, once again, the complexity of both political and religious life. How much easier—and, as this book shows, how inaccurate—it would be to lump all religious people into a single moral category. Believing that "they are all crazy" makes it unnecessary to look at each one carefully. The temptation to make damning generalizations often stems from the familiar human need for self-congratulation and externalization. If "they"—religious fanatics bound to violence, misogyny, and racism—are the problem, then "we"—secular people guided by science and democracy—are not. How comforting—but how untrue. For every religious fanatic who would behead his enemies on video, there is a secular technocrat whose crime is not reasonless faith but the soulless pursuit of power or money. All those religious traditionalists who preach values riddled with superstition and parochialism are matched by all those who seem to believe that morality is purely a matter of convenience or who think that privatizing faith allows us to have a "rational" society. In fact we are often simply exchanging the evils of religion for those of multinational corporations, soul-deadening media spectacle, and an ever-widening range of addictive substances (Prozac, scotch, heroin, nicotine) and activities (surfing the Web, watching 183 cable channels, texting your pals, checking out Facebook).

The simple truth is that the twentieth century had a wide range of secular political movements that were at least as destructive and deranged as Al-Qaeda or the Religious Right. And these movements even included groups that claimed to be on the side of progressive values. The bewildering and depressing implication is that *every* philosophy, political theory, ideology, ethical code, or spiritual teaching has been espoused one time or another by people who are misguided, immoral, selfish, opportunistic, and brutal.

Perhaps, as the old saying goes, religion simply makes good people better and bad ones worse. The good ones find love, compassion, humility, and a burning desire to right wrongs and spread some joy around. The bad ones find rigid moral rules, male power, self-interest for a narrowly defined group, and a savage joy in self-righteousness. Again, this dichotomy is evident in the worlds of secular politics as well. One can look into Marx and find grounds for Stalin but also the socialist side of Martin Luther King Jr. or the progressive policies of Eugene Debs and Michael Harrington.

But goodness is goodness wherever we find it. And perhaps the greatest gift of this fine book is to display fascinating and inspiring examples of human goodness to us. These people listened to God and became better people. Whether or not we hear what they heard, seeing how they lived can make us better people as well. If that is not the core of both religion and secular social justice, I don't know what is.

NOTES

Introduction: The Universe Bends Toward Justice

1. Helder Camara, *The Desert Is Fertile* (Maryknoll, NY: Orbis Books, 1974), 13–14.
2. Kay Mills, *This Little Light of Mine: The Life of Fannie Lou Hamer.* (New York: Dutton, 1993).
3. Christian Peacemaker Teams, www.cpt.org.
4. Muslim Peacemaker Teams, www.mpt-iraq.org.
5. Michelle Goldberg, "Dodging Bombs for Peace," *Salon.com*, April 24, 2003, www.salon.com/news/feature/2003/04/24/activists_return/index.html.
6. Shane Claiborne and Chris Haw, "Appendix 2: Mohammed for President? Pluralism and Uniqueness," *Jesus for President* (website), www.jesusforpresident.org/download/Web_Appendix_2.pdf.
7. For more, see Donald B. Kraybill, Steven M. Nolt, and David L. Weaver-Zercher, *Amish Grace: How Forgiveness Transcended Tragedy* (San Francisco: John Wiley and Sons, 2007).
8. Quoted in David J. Garrow, *Bearing the Cross: Martin Luther King, Jr., and the Southern Christian Leadership Conference* (New York: William Morrow, 1986), 200.
9. Rayner Wickersham Kelsey, *Friends and the Indians, 1655–1917* (Philadelphia: The Associated Executive Committee of Friends on Indian Affairs, 1917), 116.
10. James Bowden, *History of the Society of Friends in America*, vol. 1 (London: Charles Gilpin, 1850), 123–125.
11. W. E. B. Du Bois, *John Brown: A Biography* (New York: M. E. Sharpe, Inc., 1997), 98.
12. Quoted in Rory Dicker, *A History of U.S. Feminisms* (Berkeley, CA: Seal Press, 2008), 28.
13. Howard Zinn, *A People's History of the United States: 1492–Present* (New York: HarperCollins, 2003), 14.
14. John R. McKivigan and Mitchell Snay, eds., *Religion and the Antebellum Debate Over Slavery* (Athens: University of Georgia Press, 1998), 331.
15. Zinn, *A People's History*, 108.
16. http://religions.pewforum.org/reports.
17. John Micklethwait and Adrian Woolridge, *God Is Back: How the Global Revival of Faith Is Changing the World.* (New York: The Penguin Press, 2009).
18. Clive Hamilton, *Growth Fetish* (Sydney, Australia: Allen & Unwin, 2003), 16.
19. Quoted in Roger S. Gottlieb, *Joining Hands: Politics and Religion Together for Social Change* (Cambridge, MA: Westview Press, 2002), 87.

20. Hanna Siegel, "Christians Rip Glenn Beck Over 'Social Justice' Slam," *ABCNews.com*, March 12, 2010, http://abcnews.go.com/WN/ glenn-beck-social-justice-christians-rage-back-nazism/story?id=10085008.

21. Jim Wallis, "What Glenn Beck Doesn't Understand About Biblical Social Justice,"*God's Politics* (blog), *Sojourners*, March 24, 2010, http://blog.sojo.net/ 2010/03/24/what-glenn-beck-doesnt-understand-about-biblical-social-justice/.

1. Jim Zwerg: The Faith Driving the Freedom Riders

1. Quoted in Aldon Morris, "The Black Church in the Civil Rights Movement: The SCLC as the Decentralized Radical Arm of the Black Church," in *Disruptive Religion: The Force of Faith in Social Movement Activism*, ed. Christian Smith (New York: Routledge, 1996), 44.

2. Patrick Allitt, *Religion in America Since 1945: A History* (New York: Columbia University Press, 2003), 103.

3. Taylor Branch, *Parting the Waters: America in the King Years, 1954–63* (New York: Simon & Schuster, 1988), 419.

4. Zinn, *A People's History*, 453.

5. Stokely Carmichael with Ekwueme Michael Thelwell, *Ready for Revolution: The Life and Struggles of Stokely Carmichael (Kwame Ture)* (New York: Scribner, 2003), 178.

6. Quoted in Garrow, *Bearing the Cross*, 156.

7. Raymond Arsenault, *Freedom Riders: 1961 and the Struggle for Racial Justice* (New York: Oxford University Press, 2006), 6.

8. Ibid., 184.

9. This chapter is largely based on two interviews with Jim Zwerg conducted on September 30, 2009, and May 10, 2010.

10. James Baldwin, *The Fire Next Time* (New York: Random House, 1993), 7.

11. Martin Luther King, Jr. *Stride Toward Freedom: The Montgomery Story* (Boston, MA: Beacon Press, 2010), 51.

12. Quoted in Garrow, *Bearing the Cross*, 24.

13. Morris, "The Black Church in the Civil Rights Movement," 32.

14. Quoted in Garrow, *Bearing the Cross*, 57–58.

15. Branch, *Parting the Waters*, 271.

16. Quoted Garrow, *Bearing the Cross*, 129.

17. *The Autobiography of Martin Luther King, Jr.*, ed. Clayborne Carson (New York: Time Warner Co., 1998), 351.

18. Zinn, *A People's History*, 453.

19. Mary King, excerpt from *Freedom Song* in *The Columbia Documentary History of Religion in America Since 1945*, eds. Paul Harvey and Philip Goff (New York: Columbia University Press, 2005), 159.

20. Harvey and Goff, *The Columbia Documentary History*, 155.

21. For more information, see Davis W. Houck and David E. Dixon, eds., *Rhetoric, Religion, and the Civil Rights Movement: 1954–1965* (Waco, Texas: Baylor University Press, 2006), 1.

22. Quoted in Garrow, *Bearing the Cross*, 171.

23. Zinn, *A People's History*, 453.

24. "Interview with Jim Zwerg Civil Rights Activist, United States," in *People's Century*, episode "Skin Deep," PBS, June 17, 1999, www.pbs.org/wgbh/peoplescentury/episodes/skindeep/zwergtranscript.html.

25. Arsenault, *Freedom Riders*, 186.

26. *Freedom Riders*, directed by Stanley Nelson (American Experience, 2010), www.freedomridersfilm.com.

27. Arsenault, *Freedom Riders*, 187.

28. Branch, *Parting the Waters*, 432.

29. Ibid., 440.

30. Arsenault, *Freedom Riders*, 171.

31. This account comes from an interview with Jim Zwerg on Wednesday, September 30, 2009; Arsenault, *Freedom Riders*, 241; and Branch, *Parting the Waters*, 420.

32. Footage from the Freedom Rides, www.pbs.org/wgbh/amex/eyesontheprize/about/pt_103.html.

33. Branch, *Parting the Waters*, 468.

34. Ibid., 474.

35. Ibid., 483.

36. *Freedom Riders*, Nelson.

37. Quoted in David Remnick, *The Bridge: The Life and Rise of Barack Obama* (New York: Random House, 2010), epigraph.

38. Author's interview with Jim Zwerg on Wednesday, September 30, 2009

39. Ann Bausum, "James Zwerg Recalls his Freedom Ride," *Beloit College Magazine*, Winter/Spring 1989, www.beloit.edu/archives/documents/archival_documents/james_zwerg_freedom_ride/.

40. Quoted in Garrow, *Bearing the Cross*, 307.

41. Gottlieb, *Joining Hands*, 124.

2. Daniel Berrigan: The Soul of the Vietnam Antiwar Movement

1. James Farrell, *The Spirit of the Sixties: The Making of Postwar Radicalism*. (New York: Routledge, 1997), 1.

2. Howard Zinn, Mike Konopacki, and Paul Buhle, *A People's History of American Empire: A Graphic Adaptation* (New York: Metropolitan Books, 2008), 163.

3. Ibid.

4. Howard Zinn, "The Impossible Victory," in *Against the Vietnam War: Writings by Activists*, ed. Mary Susannah Robbins (Lanham, MD: Rowman & Littlefield, 2007), 9.

5. Madeleine Albright with Bill Woodward, *The Mighty and the Almighty: Reflections on America, God, and World Affairs* (New York: HarperCollins, 2006), 43.

6. Tom Cornell, "We Are Still Talking" (sermon, May 1, 2002), www.catholicworker.org/roundtable/essaytext.cfm?Number=181.

7. Sharon Erickson Nepstad, *Religion and War Resistance in the Plowshares Movement*. (New York: Cambridge University Press, 2008), 45.

8. Ibid.

9. Nancy Zaroulis and Gerald Sullivan, *Who Spoke Up? American Protest Against the War in Vietnam, 1963–1975* (Garden City, NY: Doubleday, 1984), 3.

10. Ibid., 2.

11. Robert S. McNamara with Brian VanDeMark, *In Retrospect: The Tragedy and Lessons of Vietnam* (New York: Times Books, 1995), 216.

12. Zaroulis and Sullivan, *Who Spoke Up?*, 3.

13. Ibid.

14. Ibid., 4.

15. Daniel Berrigan and Thich Nhat Hanh, *The Raft Is Not the Shore: Conversations Toward a Buddhist Christian Awareness* in *A Lifetime of Peace: Essential Writings By and About Thich Nhat Hanh*, ed. Jennifer Schwamm Willis (New York: Marlowe & Company, 2003), 114.

16. Allitt, *Religion in America*, 71.

17. Quoted in Murray Polner and Jim O'Grady, *Disarmed and Dangerous: The Radical Life and Times of Daniel and Philip Berrigan, Brothers in Religious Faith and Civil Disobedience* (New York: BasicBooks, 1997), 138.

18. Daniel Berrigan, *To Dwell in Peace: An Autobiography* (San Francisco: Harper & Row, 1987).

19. Marian Christy, "Berrigan Shows Courage of Convictions," *Boston Globe*, January 17, 1988, B15.

20. Daniel Berrigan interviewed by the author, New York City, June 11, 2010, 2–3:30 PM.

21. Ibid.

22. Thomas Merton, *The Nonviolent Alternative* (New York: Farrar, Straus and Giroux, 1981), 188.

23. Polner and O'Grady, *Disarmed and Dangerous*, 108.

24. "The Berrigans: Conspiracy and Conscience," *TIME*. January 25, 1971.

25. Daniel Berrigan, *No Bars to Manhood* (Garden City, NY: Doubleday, 1970).

26. Robert S. Ellwood, *The Sixties Spiritual Awakening: American Religion Moving from Modern to Postmodern* (New Brunswick, NJ : Rutgers University Press, 1994), 205.

27. Ronald G. Musto, *The Catholic Peace Tradition* (Maryknoll, NY. Orbis Books, 1986), 255.

28. Polner and O'Grady, *Disarmed and Dangerous*, 144.

29. Berrigan, *To Dwell in Peace: An Autobiography*, 142.

30. Allitt, *Religion in America*, 105.

31. Quoted in Polner and O'Grady, *Disarmed and Dangerous*, 151.

32. Daniel Berrigan, *Night Flight to Hanoi: War Diary with 11 Poems*. (New York: Harper & Row, 1971), 61.

33. Daniel Berrigan, *The Dark Night of Resistance* (Garden City, NY: Doubleday, 1971), 92.

34. Barry Bearak, "Berrigan at 70: Still Protesting," *Los Angeles Times*, April 10, 1993, A1.

35. Polner and O'Grady, *Disarmed and Dangerous*, 173.

36. Quoted in Polner and O'Grady, *Disarmed and Dangerous*, 189.

37. Jeff Kisseloff, *Generation on Fire: Voices of Protest from the 1960s: An Oral History* (Lexington: University Press of Kentucky, 2007), 112.

38. Polner and O'Grady, *Disarmed and Dangerous*, 173.

39. Daniel Lewis, "Philip Berrigan, Former Priest and Peace Advocate in the Vietnam War Era, Dies at 79," *New York Times*, December 8, 2002.

40. David Maraniss, *They Marched into Sunlight: War and Peace, Vietnam and America, October 1967* (New York: Simon & Schuster, 2003), 501.

41. Francine du Plessix Gray, *Divine Disobedience: Profiles in Catholic Radicalism* (New York: Knopf, 1970).

42. Berrigan, *To Dwell in Peace: An Autobiography*, 202–3 and 224.

43. Quoted in Angie O'Gorman, ed., *The Universe Bends Toward Justice: A Reader on Christian Nonviolence in the U.S.* (Philadelphia, PA: New Society Publishers, 1990), 205–206.

44. Zaroulis and Sullivan, *Who Spoke Up?*, 236.

45. Ibid.

46. Howard Zinn, "Peace Pilgrim to Vietnam," in *Apostle of Peace: Essays in Honor of Daniel Berrigan*, ed. John Dear (New York: Orbis Books, 1996), 66.

47. Polner and O'Grady, *Disarmed and Dangerous*, 205.

48. Quoted in Philip Berrigan, *Fighting the Lamb's War: Skirmishes with the American Empire* (Monroe, ME: Common Courage Press, 1996), 105.

49. Daniel Berrigan, *The Trial of the Catonsville Nine* (New York: Fordham University Press, 2004), 101.

50. Ibid., 121; *Investigation of a Flame*, directed by Lynne Sachs (Brooklyn, NY: First Run/Icarus Films, 2001), DVD.

51. Frank Green, "For Berrigan, the Fires are Still Burning," *San Diego Union-Tribune*, February 11, 1985.

52. Quoted in Francine du Plessix Gray, "Notes from the Underground," the Talk of the Town, *The New Yorker*, July 25, 1970, 20.

53. Roger G. Betsworth, *The Radical Movement of the 1960's* [sic] (Metuchen, NJ: Scarecrow Press, 1980), 288.

54. *The Camden 28*, directed by Anthony Giacchino (New York: First Run Features, 2007), www.camden28.org.

55. Cover Story: "The Berrigans: Conspiracy and Conscience," *TIME*. January 25, 1971.

56. Joe Sabia, "The Catholic Fringe," *Cornell Daily Sun*. September 23, 2003.

57. Chris Echegaray, "Berrigan lectures on loss," *Telegram & Gazette* (Worcester, MA), April 12, 2002.

58. For more see Gary Smith, "Peace Warriors," the *Washington Post Magazine*, June 5, 1988.

59. Berrigan, *The Trial of the Catonsville Nine*, 139.

60. Katherine Marsh, "A Jesuit Lion of Protest Turns 80, Unrepentant," *New York Times*, May 13, 2001.

61. Smith, "Peace Warriors."

62. Ibid.

63. Michelle Boorstein, "Activists Pose as Guantanamo Prisoners," *Washington Post*. January 13, 2008, www.washingtonpost.com/wp-dyn/content/article/2008/01/12/AR2008011202615.html.

3. Roy Bourgeois: The Crusade to Close the School of the Americas

1. Phyllis Zagano, *Ita Ford: Missionary Martyr* (Mahwah, NJ: Paulist Press, 1996).

2. The website for the Western Hemisphere Institute for Security Cooperation (formerly known as "School of the Americas") www.benning.army.mil/whinsec/content/aboutInstitute/index.html. Access date December 5, 2010.

3. This account comes from Wayne Ellwood, "Romero Remembered: 25th Anniversary of Martyred Archbishop," *New Internationalist*, April 2005.

4. Quoted in Gottlieb, *Joining Hands*, 56.

5. Zinn, *A People's History*, 590.

6. Quoted in Ellwood, "Romero Remembered."

7. Gottlieb, *Joining Hands*, 56.

8. Zinn, *A People's History*, 590.

9. Ibid.

10. Ibid.

11. Biographical information on Father Roy Bourgeois comes from three separate interviews conducted with Bourgeois over the span of three years: July 2007 in Ferdowsi Hotel in Tehran, Iran; April 2009 at NYU School of Law; and May 2010 at Brooklyn College. I also benefited greatly from the authoritative biography on Roy Bourgeois, James Hodge and Linda Cooper's *Disturbing the Peace: The Story of Father Roy Bourgeois and the Movement to Close the School of the Americas* (Maryknoll, NY: Orbis Books, 2004).

12. Hodge and Cooper, *Disturbing the Peace*, 17.

13. Matt. 19:21.

14. "Gaudium et Spes,"Documents of the II Vatican Council. English version: www.vatican.va/archive/hist_councils/ii_vatican_council/documents/vat-ii_const_19651207_gaudium-et-spes_en.html.

15. Pope Paul VI, *Pastoral Constitution on Church in the Modern World: Gaudium Et Spes* (Boston: Pauline Books & Media, 1965), www.vatican.va/archive/hist_councils/ii_vatican_council/documents/vat-ii_cons_19651207_gaudium-et-spes_en.html.

16. Ibid.

17. Hodge and Cooper, *Disturbing the Peace*, 20.

18. David Nicholson-Lord, "Vietnam Makes Peace with the Rain Forest," *The Independent* (London), July 1, 1990.

19. Tim Weiner, "Robert S. McNamara, Architect of a Futile War, Dies at 93," *New York Times*, July 7, 2009.

20. Saul D. Alinsky, *Rules for Radicals: A Practical Primer for Realistic Radicals* (New York: Vintage Books, 1989).

21. *New York Times,* November 24, 1972.

22. Quoted in Hodge and Cooper, *Disturbing the Peace*, 32.

23. Christian Smith, "Correcting a Curious Neglect, or Bringing Religion Back In," in *Disruptive Religion*, ed. Smith, 9.

24. Joseph Raso, "A Bolivian Butcher Running for President," *New York Times*, May 30, 1997.

25. *New York Times*, "The World; In Summary," December 30, 1973.

26. Hodge and Cooper, *Disturbing the Peace*, 43.

27. Council of Inter-American Security, *A New Inter-American Policy for the Eighties*, ed. Lewis Tambs (Washington, DC: The Council, 1980). Popularly known as "the Santa Fe Document."

28. Renny Golden and Michael McConnell, *Sanctuary: The New Underground Railroad* (Maryknoll, NY: Orbis Books,1986), 87. Also see Penny Lernoux, *Cry of the People: The Struggle for Human Rights in Latin America—The Catholic Church in Conflict with U. S. Policy* (New York: Penguin Books, 1980), 142–145.

29. Paulo Freire, *Pedagogy of the Oppressed* (New York: Continuum, 2000), 49–50.

30. Quoted in Hodge and Cooper, *Disturbing the Peace*, 60.

31. Terry McCarthy, "Old War that Failed to Make a New Order," *The Independent* (London), February 12, 1991.

32. Roy Bourgeois (speech, Augustana Lutheran Church, Portland, OR, September 15, 2008).

33. Hodge and Cooper, *Disturbing the Peace*, 80.

34. William Blum, *Killing Hope: U.S. Military and C.I.A. Interventions Since World War II* (Monroe, ME: Common Courage Press, 2003), 352–369.

35. For details, see Hodge and Cooper, *Disturbing the Peace*, 1–4.

36. Shirley Christian, "1981 Salvadoran Massacre Survivors Resurface," *New York Times*, November 28, 1991; Sean Cronin, "Salvador Army Responsible for 80% of Atrocities: A United Nations Group Damns the U.S. Record in El Salvador," *Irish Times*, March 30, 1993.

37. "Obituaries: J. Robert Elliott," *The Globe and Mail* (Canada), July 1, 2006.

38. Quoted in Hodge and Cooper, *Disturbing the Peace*, 100.

39. Archbishop Romero's prayer is quoted widely, including in Ruth Haley Barton, *Strengthening the Soul of Your Leadership: Seeking God in the Crucible of Ministry* (Downers Grove, IL: IVP Books, 2008), 217.

40. Eduardo Galeano, *Open Veins of Latin America: Five Centuries of the Pillage of a Continent* (New York: Monthly Review Press, 1973), 12.

41. Douglas Waller, "Running a 'School for Dictators'," *Newsweek*, August 9, 1993.

42. Quoted in Hodge and Cooper, *Disturbing the Peace*, 150.

43. Quoted in Vincent A. Gallagher, *The True Cost of Low Prices: The Violence of Globalization* (Maryknoll, NY: Orbis Books, 2006), 66.

44. Lesley Gill, *The School of the Americas: Military Training and Political Violence in the Americas* (Durham, NC: Duke University Press, 2004), 214.

45. More information available in the comprehensive DVD *Shut Down the School of the Americas: A Compilation of Films to Close the SOA/WHINSEC and to Change Oppressive U.S. Foreign Policy*. More information on this DVD is available at School of the Americas Watch, www.soaw.org.

46. Jack Nelson-Pallmeyer, *School of Assassins: Guns, Greed, and Globalization* (Maryknoll, NY: Orbis Books, 2001), 137.

47. "Vatican Threatens to Excommunicate Catholic Priest for Supporting Ordination of Women into Priesthood" *Democracy Now!* November 20, 2008, www.democracynow.org/2008/11/20/vatican_threatens_to_excommunicate_catholic_priest.

48. Dennis Sadowski, "Priest Confirms Excommunication; Will Keep Urging Women's Ordination," Catholic News Service, September 1, 2009, www.catholicreview.org/subpages/storyworldnew-new.aspx?action=6776.

4. Jim Corbett: Convictions of the Hearth in the Sanctuary Movement

1. InterReligious Task Force on Central America, *Central American Refugees: Flight from War Pamphlet* (New York, January 1985).

2. Quoted in Hilary Cunningham, *God and Caesar at the Rio Grande: Sanctuary and the Politics of Religion* (Minneapolis: University of Minnesota Press, 1995), xi.

3. "James Albert Corbett, a provider of sanctuary, died on August 2nd, aged 67," *The Economist*, August 18, 2001.

4. Miriam Davidson, "Appreciation: Corbett Offered Sanctuary to Refugees," *National Catholic Reporter*, September 14, 2001, http://natcath.org/NCR_Online/archives2/2001c/091401/091401j.htm.
5. Cunningham, *God and Caesar at the Rio Grande*, 24.
6. Ibid.
7. Sharon Erickson Nepstad, *Convictions of the Soul: Religion, Culture, and Agency in the Central America Solidarity Movement* (New York: Oxford University Press, 2004), 5.
8. Norman L. Zucker and Naomi Flink Zucker, *Desperate Crossings: Seeking Refuge in America* (Armonk, NY: M. E. Sharpe, Inc., 1996), 89.
9. Gary MacEóin, ed., *Sanctuary: A Resource Guide for Understanding and Participating in the Central American Refugees' Struggle* (San Francisco: Harper & Row, 1985), 17.
10. Cunningham, *God and Caesar at the Rio Grande*, 25.
11. Ibid., 27.
12. Jim Corbett, *The Sanctuary Church* (Lancaster, PA: Pendle Hill Pamphlet 270, 1982), 2.
13. Golden and McConnell, *Sanctuary*, 37.
14. Michael J. McConnell, "Sanctuary Movement: Immigration and Naturalization Service, Chicago Religious Task Force on Central America," www.jrank.org/cultures/pages/4415/Sanctuary-Movement.html.
15. MacEóin, *Sanctuary*, 1.
16. Daniel Santiago, "The Aesthetics of Terror, the Hermeneutics of Death," *America*, March 24, 1990, 293.
17. Nora Hamilton, Jeffrey A. Frieden, Linda Fuller, and Manuel Pastor Jr., eds, "Introduction," in *Crisis in Central America: Regional Dynamics and U.S. Policy in the 1980s* (Boulder, CO: Westview Press, 1988), 6.
18. MacEóin, *Sanctuary*, 1.
19. Kevin Sullivan and Mary Jordan, "In Central America, Reagan Remains a Polarizing Figure," *Washington Post*, June 10, 2004.
20. Quoted in Robert Tomsho, *The American Sanctuary Movement* (Austin: Texas Monthly Press, 1987), 96.
21. Sullivan and Jordan, "Reagan Remains."
22. Quoted in Tomsho, *The American Sanctuary Movement*, 99.
23. Ibid., 103.
24. Ibid., 105–107.
25. MacEóin, *Sanctuary*, 179.
26. Douglas Martin, "James A. Corbett, 67, Is Dead; A Champion of Movement to Safeguard Illegal Refugees," *New York Times*, August 12, 2001.
27. Jim Corbett, *Borders and Crossings*, vols. 1 and 2 (Tucson, AZ: xeroxed pamphlet, 1986), 2.
28. Corbett, *The Sanctuary Church*, 10–11.
29. John M. Fife, "The Sanctuary Movement," *Church and Society*, March–April 1985, 19.
30. Golden and McConnell, *Sanctuary*, 132–133.
31. Dick Simpson and Clinton Stockwell, eds., *The Struggle for—Peace, Justice, Sanctuary* (Chicago : Institute on the Church in Urban-Industrial Society, 1985), 112.
32. Quoted in Dana Wilbanks, *Re-Creating America: The Ethics of U.S. Immigration and Refugee Policy in a Christian Perspective* (Nashville, TN: Abingdon Press, 1996), 93.

33. Rose Marie Berger and Susannah Hunter, "Presente! James A. Corbett, 1933–2001," *Sojourners Magazine*, November/December 2001.
34. Tomsho, *The American Sanctuary Movement*, 5.
35. Simpson and Stockwell, *The Struggle for*, 78.
36. Ibid., 23.
37. Cunningham, *God and Caesar at the Rio Grande*, xvi.
38. Quoted in Tomsho, *The American Sanctuary Movement*, 98.
39. Cunningham, *God and Caesar at the Rio Grande*, xvi.
40. Ibid.
41. Quoted in MacEóin, *Sanctuary*, 190.
42. Ibid., 18.
43. Quoted in Tomsho, *The American Sanctuary Movement*, 108.
44. Corbett, *The Sanctuary Church*, 22.
45. Ibid., 19.
46. Quoted in MacEóin, *Sanctuary*, 191.
47. Corbett, *The Sanctuary Church*, 19–22, 33.
48. Ibid., 22.
49. MacEóin, *Sanctuary*, 178.
50. Cunningham, *God and Caesar at the Rio Grande*, xv.
51. Quoted in Golden and McConnell, *Sanctuary*, vi.
52. Ibid., vi.
53. Ibid., viii.
54. Dick Simpson and Joey Sylvester, "Caravan: A Spiritual Journey," *Bear & Company Magazine*, "Anawim," Volume III, Number 4.
55. Simpson and Stockwell, *The Struggle for*, 71.
56. Quoted in ibid., 112.
57. Miriam Davidson, "Appreciation: Corbett Offered Sanctuary to Refugees," *National Catholic Reporter*, September 14, 2001, www.natcath.org/NCR_Online/archives/091401/091401j.htm.
58. Tomsho, *The American Sanctuary Movement*.
59. Dick Simpson, *The Politics of Compassion and Transformation* (Athens, OH: Swallow Press, 1989), 194.
60. MacEóin, *Sanctuary*, 36.
61. David Van Biema, "A Church Haven for Illegal Aliens," *TIME*, July 19, 2007, www.time.com/time/magazine/article/0,9171,1645169,00.html.
62. Paraphrase of the Book of Exodus.
63. Simpson and Stockwell, *The Struggle for*, 36.
64. Ibid.
65. Sasha Abramsky, "Gimme Shelter," *The Nation*, February 7, 2008, www.thenation.com/article/gimme-shelter.
66. Judith Mc Daniel, *Sanctuary: A Journey* (Ithaca, NY: Firebrand Books, 1987), 145.
67. Simpson and Stockwell, *The Struggle for*, 9.
68. Chicago Religious Task Force on Central America "Public Sanctuary for Salvadoran and Guatemalan Refugees: Organizer Nuts and Bolts." Chicago: CRTFCA, 407 S. Dearborn, Room 370, Chicago, Ill. 60005.
69. Quoted in Cunningham, *God and Caesar at the Rio Grande*, vi.
70. Michael McConnell, "Sanctuary: No Stopping It Now," *The Other Side Magazine*, March 1985.

71. Ibid.
72. Ibid.
73. Ibid.
74. McConnell, "Sanctuary Movement."
75. McConnell, "Sanctuary: No Stopping It Now."
76. Simpson and Sylvester, "Caravan: A Spiritual Journey."
77. Quoted in Tomsho, *The American Sanctuary Movement*, 206.
78. Martin, "Obituary: James A. Corbett, 67, Is Dead."
79. Tomsho, *The American Sanctuary Movement*, 208–9.
80. Corbett, *The Sanctuary Church*, 33.
81. Quoted in ibid.
82. Ibid.
83. Karl Eschbach, Jacqueline Hagan, and Néstor Rodríguez. "Deaths During Undocumented Migration: Trends and Policy Implications in the New Era of Homeland Security" (presented at the 26th Annual National Legal Conference on Immigration and Refugee Policy, Washington, DC, April 2003).
84. Ernesto Portillo Jr., "Corbett's Legacy: Aid to Helpless," *Arizona Daily Star*, August 8, 2001.
85. Associated Press, "Immigration Issue Draws Thousands into Streets," *MSNBC .com*, March 26, 2006, www.msnbc.msn.com/id/11442705/.
86. Cardinal Roger Mahoney, interview by Miles O'Brien, *American Morning*, "Catholic Church Officials Spurn Immigration Reform Plan," CNN, March 29, 2006, http://transcripts.cnn.com/TRANSCRIPTS/0603/29/ltm.05.html.
87. Louis Sahagun, "Giving Shelter from the Storm of Deportation," *Los Angeles Times*, May 9, 2007.
88. Van Biema, "A Church Haven for Illegal Aliens."
89. Donna Schaper, interviewed by the author on April 27, 2009.
90. Ibid.
91. Abramsky, "Gimme Shelter."
92. Ibid.
93. "Humanitarian Aid Is Not a Crime," *Democracy Now!* April 27, 2009, www.democracynow.org/2009/4/27/humanitarian_aid_is_not_a_crime.
94. Ibid.
95. "Humane Borders Water Stations," Humane Borders official website, www.humaneborders.org/about/about_wstations.html. Access date: July 7, 2010.
96. Ibid.
97. David Bacon, "NAFTA's Legacy—Profits and Poverty," *San Francisco Chronicle*, January 14, 2004, http://articles.sfgate.com/2004-01-14/opinion/17408184_1_nafta-s-first-year-mexico-border-job-loss.
98. Sophia Tareen, "Deportation Numbers Increasing," Associated Press, November 9, 2008.
99. Amy Dalton, interviewed by the author on May 1, 2010.
100. Patrik Jonsson and Kristen Chick, "Many Iraqi Refugees in U.S. Now in Dire Straits," *Christian Science Monitor*, June 18, 2009, www.csmonitor.com/USA/Foreign-Policy/2009/0618/p02s15-usfp.html.
101. Randal C. Archibold, "Arizona Enacts Stringent Law on Immigration," *New York Times*, April 23, 2010, www.nytimes.com/2010/04/24/us/politics/24immig.html?_r=1.

102. *Sourjourners*, "Rev. Wallis Says Churches 'Will Not Comply' with New Arizona Law," press release, April 23, 2010, www.commondreams.org/newswire/2010/04/23-5.

5. John Dear: Beating Nuclear Swords into God's Plowshares

1. Heinar Kipphardt, *In the Matter of J. Robert Oppenheimer: A Play Freely Adapted, on the Basis of the Documents* (New York: Macmillan, 1968), 126–7.
2. Isaiah 2:4 (New American Standard Bible).
3. Quoted in Daniel Berrigan, *Testimony: The Word Made Fresh* (Maryknoll, NY: Orbis Books, 2004), 19.
4. Ibid.
5. Arthur J. Laffin and Anne Montgomery, eds., *Swords into Plowshares: Nonviolent Direct Action for Disarmament* (San Francisco: Perennial Library, 1987), 55, 65.
6. Nepstad, *Religion and War Resistance*, 33.
7. Berrigan, *Testimony*, 20.
8. Nepstad, *Religion and War Resistance*, 79.
9. Ibid.
10. Berrigan, *Testimony*, 18.
11. Ed. Jim Wallis, *Peacemakers: Christian Voices from the New Abolitionist Movement* (San Francisco: Harper & Row, 1983), 154.
12. Quoted in Berrigan, *Testimony*, 20.
13. Ibid.
14. John Dear, interviewed by the author on June 30, 2010.
15. John Dear, *Living Peace: A Spirituality of Contemplation and Action* (New York: Doubleday, 2001), 63.
16. John Dear, *A Persistent Peace: One Man's Struggle for a Nonviolent World* (Chicago: Loyola Press, 2008), 15.
17. Ibid., 19.
18. Ibid., 56–57.
19. Quoted in ibid., 64–65.
20. G. Scott Cady, Christopher L. Webber, *A Year with American Saints* (New York: Church Publishing, 2006), 540.
21. Ibid., 67.
22. C.A. Cesaretti and Joseph T. Vitale, eds., *Rumors of War: A Moral and Theological Perspective on the Arms Race* (New York: Seabury Press, 1982), 24.
23. For more information, see the Nevada Desert Experiment Web site at www.nevadadesertexperience.org/history/history.htm.
24. Richard C. Paddock, "Protesting Priest's Path Leads Repeatedly to Jail," *Los Angeles Times*, April 9, 2009, www.latimes.com/news/local/la-me-protest-priest9-2009apr09,0,5696122,full.story.
25. See Exod. 20:3: "You shall have no other gods before me."
26. Elizabeth McAlister, "Idolatry of the Sate," *Catholic Agitator*, June 1986, 2.
27. Gerard A. Vanderhaar, *Christians and Nonviolence in the Nuclear Age: Scripture, the Arms Race, and You* (Mystic, CT: Twenty-Third Publications, 1982), 36.
28. Vanderhaar, *Christians and Nonviolence*, 35.
29. Berrigan, *No Bars to Manhood*, 48–49.
30. Dear, *A Persistent Peace*, 243.

31. Grant Parsons, "The Gospel according to PHILIP Peace activist Philip Berrigan is in jail in Lumberton, steadfast as ever to his convictions," *The News & Observer* (Raleigh, NC), December 20, 1993.

32. John Dear interview.

33. Laurie Goodstein, "N.C. Trial Conjures Up Antiwar Era; DC Priest, 3 Others Admit Damaging Jet," *Washington Post*. February 15, 1994.

34. Ben Stocking, "Protesters Rally for 4 Peace Activists," *News & Observer* (Raleigh, NC), December 11, 1993.

35. Steve Ford, "Swords into Plowshares Fits the Christmas Spirit," *News & Observer* (Raleigh, NC), December 19, 1993.

36. Nepstad, *Religion and War Resistance*, 3.

37. Ibid.

38. Ibid., xxii.

39. Zinn, *A People's History*, 601–2.

40. J. Anthony Lukas, "Holier than Some," review of *Fighting the Lamb's War: Skirmishes with the American Empire: The Autobiography of Philip Berrigan*, by Philip Berrigan with Fred A. Wilcox, and *Disarmed and Dangerous: The Radical Lives and Times of Daniel and Philip Berrigan*, by Murray Polner and Jim O'Grady, *New York Times*, February, 9, 1997, Books section, www.nytimes .com/books/97/02/09/reviews/970209.09lukast.html.

41. Anne Montgomery, "Divine Obedience," in *Swords into Plowshares*, eds. Laffin and Montgomery, 28.

42. Quoted in James Farrell, *The Spirit of the Sixties: The Making of Postwar Radicalism* (New York: Routledge, 1997), 191.

43. John Dear interview.

44. "Carol Gilbert, Jackie Hudson and Ardeth Platte—2003 Nuclear-Free Future Resistance Award," Nuclear-Free News, www.nuclear-free.de/english/nuns.htm.

45. Nepstad, *Religion and War Resistance*, 2.

46. "Carol Gilbert, Jackie Hudson and Ardeth Platte," Nuclear-Free News.

47. Berrigan, *The Trial of the Catonsville Nine*, 137.

48. Evelyn Nieves, "For Three Nuns, A Prairie Protest and a Price to Pay: Sisters Reconciled to Prison for Action at Missile Site," *Washington Post*, May 21, 2003.

49. Jim Spencer, "Locking Up Nuns Makes Sense to None," *Denver Post*, July 17, 2003.

50. Nepstad, *Religion and War Resistance*, 2–4; Robin Andersen, "Then and Now: Notes on the Historical Significance of the Trial of the Catonsville Nine," in Daniel Berrigan, *The Trial of the Catonsville Nine* (New York: Fordham University Press, 2004), 140.

6. Robin Harper: Waging Peace by Resisting War Taxes

1. *Bill Moyers Journal*, "Buying the War," PBS, www.pbs.org/moyers/journal/btw/transcript1.html.

2. This account is based on multiple interviews with Robin Harper over the span of three years.

3. For more detail, please see A. Neave Brayshaw, *The Personality of George Fox*. (London: Allenson & Co., 1933), 17–21.

4. Geoffrey Ashe, *Gandhi: A Study In Revolution* (London: Heineman Ltd., 1968).

5. Frank Moraes, *Jawaharlal Nehru* (Mumbai: Jaico Publishing House, 2007) 165.

6. Dennis Dalton, *Mahatma Gandhi: Nonviolent Power in Action* (New York: Columbia University Press, 1993), 137.

7. Quoted in Dalton, *Mahatma Gandhi*, 221.

8. Horace Alexander, *Quakerism and India* (Wallingford, PA: Pendle Hill Pamphlet 31, 1945); Horace Alexander, *Gandhi through Western Eyes* (New York, Asia Publishing House, 1969); Horace Alexander, *Friends in India and Pakistan* (Oxford : Church Army Press, 1952); Horace Alexander, *Consider India: A Essay in Values* (New York: Asia Publishing House, 1961); Muriel Lester, *Gandhi: World Citizen* (Allahabad: Kitab Mahal, 1945); Muriel Lester, *Entertaining Gandhi* (London: Ivor Nicholson & Watson, 1932).

9. Homer A. Jack, ed., *The Gandhi Reader: A Sourcebook of His Life and Writings* (Bloomington: Indiana University Press, 1956).

10. Zinn, *A People's History*, 407.

11. For more information see Hans A. Schmitt, *Quakers and Nazis: Inner Light in Outer Darkness* (Columbia: University of Missouri Press, 1997).

12. National Priorities Project website, www.nationalpriorities.org.

13. "About the Court," United States Tax Court home page, www.ustaxcourt.gov/about.htm.

14. Schmitt, *Quakers and Nazis*, 18.

15. Schmitt, *Quakers and Nazis*, 190.

16. Ibid. Also see Brenda Bailey, "The Integrity of German Friends During the Twelve Years of Nazi Rule," www.quaker.org/minnfm/peace/integrity_of_german_friends_duri.htm

17. Karl Meyer, in discussion with the author February 10, 2007.

18. Richard Mertens, "A Radical Takes Root," *University of Chicago Magazine*, April 2001, http://magazine.uchicago.edu/0104/features/index.htm.

7. Joseph Land: Living in the Clouds to Save the Redwoods

1. Quoted in Derrick Jensen, *The Problem of Civilization*, vol. 1 of *Endgame* (New York: Seven Stories Press, 2006), 395.

2. *Grizzy Man*, directed by Werner Herzog (Santa Monica, CA: Lionsgate, 2005).

3. Don Oldenburg, "Julia Butterfly Hill, from Treetop to Grass Roots," *Washington Post*, September 22, 2004.

4. Julia Butterfly Hill, *Legacy of Luna: The Story of a Tree, a Woman, and the Struggle to Save the Redwoods* (San Francisco: HarperCollins, 2000), 238.

5. Joel Bourne, "Redwoods: The Super Trees," *National Geographic*, October 2009, http://ngm.nationalgeographic.com/2009/10/redwoods/bourne-text.

6. Ibid.

7. "About the Trees," United States National Park Service, www.nps.gov/redw/naturescience/about-the-trees.htm.

8. Bourne, "Redwoods: The Super Trees."

9. Ibid.

10. Ibid.

11. Jason Margolis, "Pacific Lumber Co. Faces Financial Crisis," *NPR*, January 19, 2006, www.npr.org/templates/story/story.php?storyId=5163390.

12. "Rebirthing the Tree/s of Life: Four Teachings for the Four Worlds of Tu B'Shvat," The Shalom Center, www.theshalomcenter.org/index.

php?q=node/782; Roger S. Gottlieb, *A Greener Faith: Religious Environmentalism and Our Planet's Future* (Oxford: Oxford University Press, 2006), 113.

13. Gottlieb, *A Greener Faith*, 23.
14. Bourne, "Redwoods: The Super Trees."
15. Anne Frank, *The Diary of a Young Girl* (Garden City, NY: Doubleday, 1972), 172.
16. Laurie Goodstein, "Evangelical Leaders Swing Influence Behind Effort to Combat Global Warming," *New York Times*, March 10, 2005.
17. Ann Coulter, "Oil Good; Democrats Bad," Townhall.com column, October 12, 2000, http://townhall.com/columnists/anncoulter/2000/10/12/oil_good;_democrats_bad.
18. Quoted in Andrew Linzey and Tom Regan, eds., *Animals and Christianity: A Book of Readings* (New York: Crossroad Publishing Company, 1989), 63–64.
19. http://news.bbc.co.uk/2/hi/8616877.stm
20. Andrew Buncombe, "The Life and Brutal Death of Sister Dorothy, a Rainforest Martyr," *Independent* (London), February 15, 2005.
21. For more information, see Chris Mooney, *The Republican War on Science* (New York: Basic Books, 2005), 74.
22. This account comes from Bourne, "Redwoods: The Super Trees."
23. Chris Hedges, *I Don't Believe in Atheists: The Dangerous Rise of the Secular Fundamentalist.* (New York: Free Press, 2008), 15.

8. SueZann Bosler: Modern-Day Abolitionists Against the Death Penalty

1. Rachel King, *Don't Kill in Our Names: Families of Murder Victims Speak Out Against the Death Penalty* (New Jersey: Rutgers University Press, 2003), 138.
2. SueZann Bosler, interviewed by the author on November 16, 2009.
3. Bruce Frankel, "Fighting for Life: Death Penalty Foe SueZann Bosler Helps Save Her Father's Killer," *People*, August 18, 1997.
4. Bosler, interview; King, *Don't Kill in Our Names*, 141.
5. Bosler interview.
6. King, *Don't Kill in Our Names*, 146.
7. Quoted in King, *Don't Kill in Our Names*, 147.
8. Lori Olszewski, "Should Cooper Die? Victim's Family Divided," *Gary Post-Tribune*, May 12, 1987.
9. For more information, visit the Murder Victims' Families for Reconciliation website at www.mvfr.org.
10. For more information, see "A Declaration of Life," www.quaker.org/declaration-of-life.html.
11. Quoted in King, *Don't Kill in Our Names*, 103.
12. See Michael L. Westmoreland-White, "Capital Punishment and the Practices of the Church: How Renewal in Church Practices Can Transform the Death Penalty Debate" in *Capital Punishment: A Reader*, ed. Glen H. Stassen (Cleveland, OH: Pilgrim Press, 1998), 219.
13. For more information, see "Death Penalty," Amnesty International, www.amnestyusa.org/death-penalty/page.do?id=1011005.
14. Quoted in James McBride, "Capital Punishment as the Unconstitutional Establishment of Religion: A Giradian Reading of the Death Penalty" in *Capital Punishment*, ed. Stassen, 183.

15. E. Christian Brugger, *Capital Punishment and Roman Catholic Moral Tradition* (Notre Dame, IN: University of Notre Dame Press, 2003), 1.

16. J. Gordon Melton, *The Churches Speak On—: Capital Punishment: Official Statements from Religious Bodies and Ecumenical Organizations* (Detroit: Gale Research, 1989), xxiii.

17. SueZann Bosler, interviewed by the author on November 16, 2009.

18. Helen Prejean, *Dead Man Walking: An Eyewitness Account of the Death Penalty in the United States* (New York: Vintage Books, 1994), 5.

19. Albert Camus, "Reflections on the Guillotine," *Resistance, Rebellion, and Death* (New York: Vintage Books, 1974), 224.

20. Ibid.

21. Prejean, *Dead Man Walking*, 124.

22. Ibid., 123.

23. "Press Clippings: Sr. Helen Prejean's Talk at the Democratic Interfaith Gathering in Denver, CO, in August 2008," Sister Helen Prejean website, Accessed December 6, 2010: www.prejean.org/PressClippings/DemocraticInterfaithGathering2008.html.

24. *Campbell v. Florida*, 571 So.2d 415 419 (Fla. 1990).

25. Quoted in King, *Don't Kill in Our Names*, 150.

26. Quoted in King, *Don't Kill in Our Names*, 151.

27. For more information, see the Journey of Hope website, www.journeyofhope.org/pages/index.htm.

28. David Pallister, "'Spare the life of my loved one's killer': Murder victims' families speak out against US death penalty," *Guardian* (Manchester), October 9, 1999.

29. Bosler, interview; King, *Don't Kill in Our Names*, 157.

30. King, *Don't Kill in Our Names*, 145.

31. Craig Haney, "The Social Context of Capital Murder: Social Histories and the Logic of Mitigation," 35 *Santa Clara Law Review*. 547, 548-59 (1995).

32. Bosler, interview; King, *Don't Kill in Our Names*, 157.

33. King, *Don't Kill in Our Names*.

34. Bosler, interview.

35. King, *Don't Kill in Our Names*, 159.

36. This number is current as of November 16, 2009, the date of the author's interview with Beth Wood, executive director of Murder Victims' Families for Reconciliation.

9. Charlotte Keys: Ecojustice Warriors Against Pollution

1. David Snyder, "Mississippi Community Still Reeling from Chemical Plant Wastes," *Times-Picayune*, July 4, 1992.

2. Marcia Coyle and Claudia MacLachlan, "Getting Victimized by the Legal System," *National Law Journal*, September 21, 1992, S8.

3. Snyder, "Mississippi Community."

4. Peter Fairley, "Shintech Siting Dispute Awakens a Sleeping Giant," *Chemical Week*, October 8, 1997, 45.

5. United Church of Christ, Commission for Racial Justice, *Toxic Wastes and Race in the United States: A National Report on the Racial and Socio-economic Characteristics of Communities with Hazardous Waste Sites* (New York: Public Data Access; Inquiries to the Commission, 1987).

6. Unites States General Accounting Office, *Siting of Hazardous Waste Landfills and Their Correlation with Racial and Economic Status of Surrounding Communities* (Washington, DC: U.S. General Accounting Office, 1983), GAO/RCED-83-168.

7. Fairley, "Shintech Siting Dispute."

8. Marianne Lavelle and Marcia Coyle, "Unequal Protection: The Racial Divide in Environmental Law, A Special Investigation," *National Law Journal*. September 21, 1992, S1.

9. Ronald Begley and Elisabeth Kirschner, "The Demand for Environmental Justice," *Chemical Week*, September 15, 1993, cover story, 27.

10. Mike Ward, "Conference Combats Environmental Racism: Activists Unite to Share Stories, Resources," *Austin American-Statesman,* December 7, 1992.

11. Gottlieb, *A Greener Faith*, 45.

12. This account comes from Elizabeth Palmberg, "A Toxic Battle for Justice," *Sojourners*, March 2009, www.sojo.net/index.cfm?action=magazine .article&issue=soj0903&article=a-toxic-battle-for-justice.

13. Charlotte Keys, interviewed by the author on June 1, 2010, in Columbia, Mississippi.

14. Geoffrey York and Hayley Mick, "'Last ghost' of the Vietnam War," *Globe and Mail* (Toronto), July 12, 2008.

15. Mary Wittenburg, "A Virtual Walking Tour of Columbia, Miss., with Charlotte Keys of Jesus People Against Pollution," *Grist*, February 13, 2006, www.grist.org/ article/wiltenburg1/.

16. Will Nixon, "How Green Is The White House?" *E—The Environmental Magazine*, March/April 1994, 38–41.

17. Edward O. Wilson, *The Future of Life* (New York: Vintage Books, 2003), 160.

18. Quoted in Timothy Noah, "Sierra Club Takes an Edifying Tour of Black America," *Wall Street Journal*, June 24, 1993.

19. Noah, "Sierra Club Takes."

20. Ibid.

10. Shane Claiborne: The Peaceful Revolution of Downward Mobility

1. *Capitalism: A Love Story*, directed by Michael Moore (Beverly Hills, CA: Starz/ Anchor Bay, 2010), DVD.

2. Matthew 6:24, New International Version.

3. Shane Claiborne, *The Irresistible Revolution: Living as an Ordinary Radical* (Grand Rapids, MI: Zondervan, 2006), 55–67.

4. Interview with Shane Claiborne at the Simple Way on December 15, 2009.

5. Luke 4:18–19; see also Isa. 58:6; 61:1–2.

6. Claiborne, *The Irresistible Revolution*, 72.

7. Claiborne, *The Irresistible Revolution*, 80.

8. Quoted in Garrow, *Bearing the Cross*, 200.

9. Interview with Shane Claiborne at the Simple Way on December 15, 2009.

10. Ibid.

11. Shane Claiborne and Chris Haw, *Jesus for President: Politics for Ordinary Radicals* (Grand Rapids, MI: Zondervan, 2008), 189.

12. Clifford W. Cobb and Philippe Diaz, *Why Global Poverty? Think Again* (New York: Robert Schalkenbach Foundation, 2009; companion book for the film *The End of Poverty?* directed by Philippe Diaz, 2009), 60.

13. Wendell Berry, *Sex, Economy, Freedom, and Community: Eight Essays* (New York: Pantheon, 1993), 99.

14. Martin Luther King Jr., *A Testament of Hope: The Essential Writings and Speeches of Martin Luther King, Jr.*, ed. James M. Washington (San Francisco: HarperCollins, 1986), 651.

15. For more, see Steven Stoll, "Agrarian Anxieties," Notebook, *Harper's* magazine, July 2010, 6–9.

16. Cobb and Diaz, *Why Global Poverty? Think Again*, 61; *Global Development Finance 2002: Financing the Poorest Countries* (Washington, DC: The World Bank, 2002), 22.

17. Shane Claiborne, interviewed by the author by phone on June 29, 2010.

18. See Henry David Thoreau, *Civil Disobedience*.

19. Interview with Shane Claiborne at the Simple Way on December 15, 2009.

20. Claiborne, phone interview June 29, 2010.

21. Robert Coles, *Dorothy Day: A Radical Devotion* (Cambridge, MA: Da Capo Press, 1987); Claiborne, *The Irresistible Revolution*, 122.

22. Martin Luther King Jr., *The Trumpet of Conscience* (New York: Harper and Row, 1968).

23. Claiborne, phone interview.

24. Tony Campolo, *Revolution and Renewal: How Churches Are Saving Our Cities*, with stories by Bruce Main (Louisville, KY: Westminster John Knox Press, 2000).

25. Avi Feller and Chad Stone, "Top 1 Percent of Americans Reaped Two-Thirds of Income Gains in Last Economic Expansion," *Center on Budget and Policy Priorities*, September 9, 2009, www.cbpp.org/cms/index.cfm?fa=view&id=2908.

26. David Leonhardt, "In Health Bill, Obama Attacks Wealth Inequality," *New York Times*, March 23, 2010.

27. Ibid.

28. Interview with Shane Claiborne at the Simple Way on December 15, 2009.

29. Claiborne, *The Irresistible Revolution*, 123–124.

30. Shane Walker, review of *The Irresistible Revolution: Living as an Ordinary Radical* by Shane Claiborne, *9Marks*, May/June 2008, www.9marks.org/books/book-review-irresistible-revolution-shane-claiborne.

31. Lucinda van der Hart, "The Simple Way: Talking to Shane Claiborne," *Faithworks* magazine, Autumn 2007, reprinted at www.jesus.org.uk/ja/mag_talkingto_claiborne.shtml.

32. Katelyn Beaty, "Braking for Bloggers," *Christianity Today*, February 11, 2008, www.christianitytoday.com/ct/2008/februaryweb-only/107-22.0.html.

33. Shane Claiborne, "Don't Fear Disagreement," *Sojourners* magazine, GodTalk, February 2, 2008, http://blog.sojo.net/2008/02/08/dont-fear-disagreement-by-shane-claiborne-2/.

34. Peter Hinks and John McKivigan, eds., *Encyclopedia of Antislavery and Abolition*, R. Owen Williams, asst. ed., vol 1: A–I (Westport, CT: Greenwood Press, 2007), 266–268.

35. For more information, see the Ten Thousand Villages website at www.tenthousandvillages.com.

36. "An Interfaith Statement on International Trade and Investment," www.maryknollogc.org/economic/IWG%20statement.pdf.

37. *Entertaining Angels: The Dorothy Day Story*, directed by Michael Ray Rhodes (1996; Burbank, CA: Warner Home Video, 1998), videocassette (VHS).

38. *Dorothy Day: Selected Writings*, ed. Robert Ellsberg (Maryknoll, NY: Orbis Books, 1998), 213.
39. Claiborne, *The Irresistible Revolution*, 366.
40. Interview with Shane Claiborne at the Simple Way on December 15, 2009.
41. John Howard Yoder, *The Politics of Jesus* (Grand Rapids, MI: William B. Eerdmans Publishing Company, 1994), 129.
42. Shane Claiborne, "What If Jesus Meant All That Stuff?" *Esquire*, November 18, 2009, www.esquire.com/features/best-and-brightest-2009/shane-claiborne-1209#ixzz0YBmpBgP4.
43. Eric Marrapodi and Kate Bolduan, "Evangelical Movement Touts 'Jesus for President'," *CNN.com*, June 29, 2008, www.cnn.com/2008/POLITICS/06/29/evangelical.campaign/index.html.
44. Ibid.
45. To watch one of Claiborne's sermons, see the website for the film *The Ordinary Radicals* at http://theordinaryradicals.com.
46. Mary John Mananzan, "Globalization and the Perennial Questions of Justice" in *Liberating Faith: Religious Voices for Justice, Peace, and Ecological Wisdom*, ed, Roger Gottlieb (Lanham, MD: Rowman & Littlefield, 2003), 271.
47. Scott Cendrowski, "Michael Moore: 'Capitalism Is Anti-Jesus'," *Fortune*, September 23, 2009.
48. *Capitalism: A Love Story*.
49. See the Simple Way's Web site: http://thesimpleway.org.

Epilogue: Interfaith Covenant for Peace and Justice in Modern America

1. For more information, see FOR-USA: www.FORUSA.org.
2. For more information see A Common Word: www.acommonword.com.
3. Quoted in Claiborne and Haw, *Jesus for President*, 224.
4. "Dr. Cornel West Releases Long-Awaited Memoir, 'Brother West: Living and Loving Out Loud.'" *Democracy Now!* September 30, 2009, www.democracynow.org/2009/9/30/dr_cornel_west_on_his_new.
5. Gottlieb, *Joining Hands*, 212.
6. Tom Fewel, interviewed by the author on November 19, 2009.
7. Gottlieb, *Joining Hands*, 57.

INDEX